DATE DUE

GAYLORD			PRINTED IN U.S.A.

Richard Ford

Twayne's United States Authors Series

Frank Day, Editor

Clemson University

TUSAS 718

RICHARD FORD
By permission of Kristina Ford.

M

Richard Ford

Elinor Ann Walker

Twayne Publishers
New York

Twayne's United States Authors Series No. 718

Richard Ford
Elinor Ann Walker

Twayne Publishers
1633 Broadway
New York, NY 10019

Library of Congress Cataloging-in-Publication Data

Walker, Elinor Ann.
　　Richard Ford / Elinor Walker Ann.
　　　　p. cm—(Twayne's United States authors series ; TUSAS 718)
　　Includes bibliographical references and index.
　　ISBN 0-8057-1679-3 (alk. paper)
　　1. Ford, Richard, 1944—Criticism and interpretation. I. Title. II. Series.

　PS3556.O713 Z85 2000
　813'.54—dc21　　00-030269

This paper meets the requirements of ANSI/NISO Z3948-1992 (Permanence of Paper).

10 9 8 7 6 5 4 3 2 1

Printed in the United States of America

For Walker

Contents

Acknowledgments   ix
Chronology   xi

Chapter One
Richard Ford: Itinerant yet Located   1

Chapter Two
Uncharted Territory in *A Piece of My Heart*   25

Chapter Three
"As if Located Was the Illusion":
A Modern Predicament in *The Ultimate Good Luck*   47

Chapter Four
Truth Versus Fiction in *The Sportswriter*   63

Chapter Five
Redeemed by Telling in "Great Falls" and *Wildlife*   100

Chapter Six
Infinite Remoteness in *Rock Springs*   118

Chapter Seven
Locution, Location, and Existence:
From Seeming to Being in *Independence Day*   133

Chapter Eight
Crossing the Divide in *Women with Men*   177

Chapter Nine
Richard Ford's Odyssey   201

Notes and References   209
Selected Bibliography   215
Index   223

Acknowledgments

I am eternally indebted to my husband Will Phillips, whose love, sense of humor, and devotion to our son ensured the completion of this book; and to my parents, Barbara and George Walker, exemplary in every way, and for whom my gratitude is too profound for words.

I thank my extended family, Jayne and Mel Phillips, April and Robb Phillips, and Alice and Chuck Phillips, for their support and accommodation of my work.

For making possible several productive conversations with Richard Ford, I thank the English departments at the University of North Carolina–Chapel Hill and the University of the South, as well as the organizers of the Morgan Family Writers-in-Residence Program and the Sewanee Writers' Conference, especially Wyatt Prunty and Cheri Peters.

Thanks also to Fred Hobson and Linda Wagner-Martin for the provisions of their work; to Frank Day for his careful eye; to Bob Benson and Bill Clarkson for their encouragement over many years.

I am grateful to all of my far-flung correspondents whose experiences have broadened my own and especially to those friends who have endured my musings on this subject and ventured opinions in return: John F. Clark IV, Huey Guagliardo, Hilary Holladay, Rick McConnell, and Kathryn B. McKee.

I also wish to thank Richard Ford for his supreme cooperation and graciousness during the research and writing of this book and for permission to quote from his works.

Permission to use the following material protected by copyright has been granted by the publisher: Elinor Ann Walker, "Redeeming Loneliness in Richard Ford's 'Great Falls' and *Wildlife*," in *Perspectives on Richard Ford,* ed. Huey Guagliardo (Jackson: University Press of Mississippi, 2000).

Chronology

1944   Richard Ford is born February 16 to Parker Carrol Ford and Edna Akin Ford in Jackson, Mississippi, the only child of his parents.

1950   Begins public school at Jefferson Davis School in Jackson, Mississippi.

1960   Ford's father dies from second and fatal heart attack on February 20.

1962   Graduates from Murrah High School in Jackson, Mississippi.

1966   Earns B.A. in English from Michigan State University in East Lansing, Michigan. Later teaches English and coaches baseball at Whittier Junior High School in Flint, Michigan.

1967   Attends Washington University Law School in St. Louis, Missouri, for one semester.

1968   Marries Kristina Hensley. Moves to New York and works as an assistant science editor for *American Druggist.*

1970   Earns M.F.A. from the University of California at Irvine, where he studies with E. L. Doctorow and Oakley Hall. Moves to Chicago, Illinois.

1971   Elected to the Society of Fellows at the University of Michigan, Ann Arbor, and receives stipend from 1971–1974 that allows him to devote time to writing his first novel, *A Piece of My Heart.*

1975   Teaches at the University of Michigan for one year as an assistant professor.

1976   Publishes his first novel, *A Piece of My Heart,* with Harper & Row. Moves to Princeton, New Jersey.

1977   Receives a fellowship from the Guggenheim Foundation. Publishes "Walker Percy: Not Just Whistling Dixie" in *National Review,* the first of many nonfiction essays he will publish in various journals and magazines.

1979   Receives a fellowship from the National Endowment for the Arts. Teaches at Williams College for one year as an assistant professor.

1980   Teaches at Princeton University for one year as lecturer and the George Perkins Fellow in the Humanities.

1981   Publishes *The Ultimate Good Luck.* Moves back to New York to pursue career in sportswriting at *Inside Sports,* but the magazine folds. Ford's mother dies following a long battle with breast cancer.

1982   Begins work on novel that will become *The Sportswriter.*

1983   Ford's stories are included in three major anthologies: *Matters of Life and Death,* ed. Tobias Wolff (Tendril Press); *Dirty Realism: Writing from America,* ed. Bill Buford (Granta/Penguin); and *Fifty Great Years of Esquire Fiction,* ed. L. Rust Hills (Viking/Penguin). Ford's play, *American Tropical,* is produced by the Actors Theatre of Louisville in November. It is later published in *Antaeus* 66 (Spring 1991).

1985   *A Piece of My Heart* reprinted by Vintage Books.

1986   Publishes *The Sportswriter.* Receives fellowship from the National Endowment for the Arts; is awarded the Best American Short Stories Prize and the Pushcart Prize.

1987   Receives citation for PEN/Faulkner Award for Fiction as well as the Mississippi Academy of Arts and Letters Award for Literature. Publishes *Rock Springs,* his first collection of short fiction.

1988   Receives New York Public Library "Literary Lion" Award and Northwest Booksellers Award for Fiction.

1989   Receives the American Academy of Arts and Letters Award in Literature.

1990   Publishes *Wildlife. The Best American Short Stories* (Houghton Mifflin), which Ford edited, is also published.

1991   Receives Echoing Green Foundation Award for Literature. Film based on Ford's screenplay, *Bright Angel* (Hemdale Productions, 1990), is released.

1992   Serves as the Avery Hopwood Memorial Lecturer at the University of Michigan. Acts as one of the founding directors of the William Faulkner Foundation, University of Rennes, Paris, France. *The Granta Book of the American Short Story,* which Ford edited, is published.

1993   Wins Mississippi Governor's Award for Artistic Achievement as well as the Lyndhurst Prize; is awarded a Fulbright Fellowship (Sweden).

1994   Teaches at Harvard University as a lecturer. Receives an honorary doctorate, *Docteur Honoris Causa,* from the University of Rennes.

1995   Wins the Rea Award for the Short Story. Publishes *Independence Day.*

1996   Wins the Pulitzer Prize for Fiction and the PEN/ Faulkner Award for Fiction for *Independence Day;* is awarded the Honorary Doctorate of Humane Letters from Loyola University; named *Officier, L'Ordre Des Arts Des Lettres,* by the Republic of France; is a finalist for the National Book Critics Circle Award; edits fall issue of *Ploughshares.*

1997   Teaches at Northwestern University, Evanston, Illinois, as visiting professor until 1999. Wins Humanist of the Year Award from the Louisiana Endowment for the Humanities and the Award of Merit in the Novel from the American Academy of Arts and Letters. Publishes *Women with Men.*

1998   Awarded Honorary Doctorate of Humane Letters from the University of Michigan and elected as a member of the American Academy of Arts and Letters. *The Essential Tales of Chekhov* (Ecco Press), *Eudora Welty: The Complete Novels* (Library of America), and *Eudora Welty: Stories, Essays, and Memoir* (Library of America) which Ford edited, are published. Ford edited the Welty collections with Michael Kreyling.

Chapter One
Richard Ford: Itinerant yet Located

Richard Ford likes places, so much so that he has moved many times and has owned residences in Louisiana, Montana, and Mississippi. Such affection for geographical locations seems in keeping with Ford's own southern heritage, though Ford's peripatetic nature and disavowal of the "southern tradition" make categorizing his fiction a complicated endeavor. Like William Faulkner and Eudora Welty, Ford is a native Mississippian, and scholars and readers of southern literature have long asserted that southerners, and southern writers in particular, find solace and story material in "postage stamps of soil," as Sherwood Anderson once called Faulkner's fictional Yoknapatawpha County. Any reader of Faulkner and Welty knows that community and setting provide the foundation for character and voice in works by these two writers. In fact, an entire generation of southern literary scholars created criteria by which southern literature could be identified, and a reverence for place and an awareness of the tragic history associated finally with a land-based economy are among such definitive characteristics.[1] Unquestionably, Ford departs from this tradition; only his first novel *A Piece of My Heart* (1976) is set in the South.

In his acceptance speech for the Nobel Prize in 1950, Faulkner himself uttered a litany of words once closely yoked with the South: the writer's duty is to depict "courage and honor and hope and pride and compassion and pity and sacrifice which have been the glory of his past."[2] To contemporary readers of southern literature, these words have moved beyond their original connotations, largely due to both historical and literary research that suggests that "honor" and "pride," no matter their evocations of virtue and tradition, may also mask a grimmer reality. But place and gentility are bound inextricably together in southern history, even if the link between them is faulty beneath the surface. After all, the landowners' leisure and decorum depended upon slave labor. For some years, the South's own "burden of history," as historian C. Vann Woodward puts it,[3] produced writers whose characters, or in some cases their autobiographical personae, acted in part out of shame and guilt, apologizing for the South even as they were unable to escape

1

from its presence in their lives. This context provides a strange cradle for
Richard Ford's work and characters. Richard Ford likes places, but
unlike his literary antecedents and even many of his contemporaries, he
does not call one place home. His self-imposed itinerancy, combined
with his resistance against southern literary prescriptions, make Richard
Ford's place in the southern canon difficult to determine. Indeed, Ford
considers himself more of an American writer and not so much a "southern" one.

Going: The "Motif of Things"

The fact remains that Ford was born in Jackson, Mississippi, in 1944,
and thus is a southerner by birth. He was the only child of Parker Carrol
Ford (1904–1960) and Edna Akin Ford (1910–1981). Edna was born
in Benton County, Arkansas, and before she married his father, Edna
herself moved around frequently, in part due to her stepfather's work on
the railroad and accompanying travel. Ford's maternal grandmother left
her first husband for Ben Shelley, then a "boxer and a roundabout" as
Ford later characterizes him.[4] "Kid Richard" was Shelley's boxing ring
name, and Ford is in fact his namesake. Since Ford's grandmother was
older than Ben Shelley when she married him, she sought to arrange her
life so that those eight years between them weren't so pronounced.
Accordingly, she sent Ford's mother Edna off to school, the Convent
School of St. Ann's in Fort Smith, Arkansas, while she and Bennie Shelley moved around to places such as El Reno and even Tucumcari, New
Mexico. Shelley paid Edna's tuition for a time and then just as suddenly
ceased to support her education, and that was all of the schooling that
Edna Akin received. According to Ford, her convent school experience
made Edna a "secret Catholic. A forgiver. A respecter of rituals and pro-
tocols" ("Mother," 45).

After Edna rejoined her family, they continued to move, accommo-
dating Ben's work. Shelley had quit boxing by this point and had begun
working in dining-car service on the railroad. This food service experience served him well, when he later left the railroad to cater for the
Arlington Hotel in Hot Springs, Arkansas. Ford's mother worked in the
cigar shop, where no doubt she met other itinerant and traveling people,
and perhaps Ford's father was among them. Ford suspects their
courtship took place in Little Rock around 1927 when his father was
working as a produce stocker for a grocery. Unlike Edna, who had traveled and received some education, Ford's father was a country boy

whose last schooling occurred in the seventh grade. The child of a father who had committed suicide, Parker was the youngest of three children raised only by their mother. In 1928, in Morriltown, Arkansas, Edna and Parker were married by a justice of the peace. Parker was 24 years old ("Mother," 45 – 46).

In 1932, Parker was fired from his job as a grocer in Little Rock, and he went to work as a starch salesman for a Kansas City company called, strangely, the Faultless Company. The job required travel, and Edna traveled with him, living in hotels, spending off-time in Little Rock. The couple lived this kind of life, traveling, drinking, having fun, until 1944, the end of World War II and the year of Ford's birth on February 16. They moved to Jackson, Mississippi, the center of Parker's traveling territory, where Edna would settle. Life was good until Ford was 16, in 1960, when his father suffered a second, and fatal, heart attack on February 20. Until that time, Ford remembers traveling with his parents whenever they all could go, to Louisiana, Arkansas, Florida, Tennessee. As Ford writes, "We *went.* That was the motif of things" ("Mother," 49).

During his father's earlier illness and after his father's death, Ford spent summers in Little Rock with his grandparents, who by this time were running a large hotel named the Marion, and Edna began work at what would become a series of jobs, first at a company that took school pictures, then as a rental agent at an apartment complex, then as a night cashier in a hotel, and finally, many years later, as an admitting clerk in the emergency room at the University of Mississippi Hospital. Throughout his teenage years, Ford remembers feeling both distant from and close to his mother—distant because each was working out his or her own grief and loneliness over Parker's death and because Edna worked so hard, close because neither had anyone else to whom to talk. And talk they did, about all sorts of things, even Ford's early sexual experiences and fears that he may have gotten a girl pregnant ("Mother," 52).

At 17, Ford left home to work, first as a fireman and then as a switchman for the Missouri Pacific Railroad, living away from his mother for a time in Little Rock, Arkansas, then in Memphis, Tennessee, at the William Lenn Hotel, as well as in other towns in Arkansas and Missouri. Certainly these early itinerant experiences and his father's death when Ford was only 16 have informed Ford's perspective as a writer. Many of his works, including quite a few stories in the collection *Rock Springs* (1987), the novel *Wildlife* (1990), and, most recently, "Jealous," published first in the *New Yorker* and then as part of the collection *Women with Men* (1997), deal with sons on the brink of adulthood, facing some loss or absence of a parent, whether that loss be literal or figurative. Ford admits, too, that he still travels seeking new locales and new stories and that being in different places yields something to a writer that living and staying in one place can never provide. For Ford, traveling remains the "motif of things."

Ford's Independent Act

On his own brink of adulthood and with ambitions to become a hotel manager like his grandfather, Ford had no desire to go to college in the South. Instead, he sought institutions that could prepare him for what he believed would be his chosen field. In 1962, Ford and his mother rode the trains from Mississippi to Michigan, where Ford matriculated at Michigan State University, which had a well-respected hotel science school. But Ford soon abandoned his aspirations to become a hotel manager and switched his major to English, an unlikely choice for a child who was dyslexic. Ford maintains, however, that it was his dyslexia that first prompted him to pay close attention to words, and reading slowly, he believes, is crucial to his own sense of the language. "Being a slow reader admitted me to books at a very basic level—word by word. That doesn't seem like bad preparation to me, if writers are people who essentially live in sentences," Ford has told one interviewer.[5] A member of Sigma Chi, Ford apparently wrote his first story in the Sigma Chi House for a class with the late Carl Hartman, a professor who later suggested that he could get into graduate school in creative writing if he wanted to. It was also at the Sigma Chi House that Ford met Kristina Hensley, Sigma Chi Sweetheart, who would become his wife.[6] In 1966, Ford graduated from Michigan State with a B.A. in English.

Finding a job was another matter entirely. Although Ford had joined the ROTC program at Michigan State, first joining the Air Force but then switching to the Marines, a bout of hepatitis caused him to be medically discharged from the Marine Corps in late 1965 and thus ended any thought of a military career. He applied for a number of jobs upon his graduation, including one with the Arkansas State Police, who, Ford would later joke, didn't want to hire anyone with a college degree who could quote Dostoyevsky.[7] Still seeking a "career," Ford taught junior high school and coached baseball in Flint, Michigan, moved to New York and worked as an assistant science editor for *American Druggist,* and, in 1967, even went to law school at Washington University in

St. Louis, Missouri. After one semester, however, he moved back to Arkansas and occasionally served as a substitute teacher at a high school while he tried to get a job as a sportswriter for the *Arkansas Gazette* and applied to the CIA. He actually got an offer from the latter, but he turned the position down. He flew to New York and proposed to Kristina, the daughter of an Air Force test pilot, and by the age of 23 he was married but without a profession per se.

At some point, Ford told his mother that he had decided to become a writer, and thus he embarked upon what would become a distinguished career. As Ford confesses, "deciding to try to be a writer was something I did purely on instinct and whimsy. It was a gesture against the practical life of going on with law studies. It may have been—other than loving Kristina—my first important independent act" (Lee, 228). He decided to go to the University of California at Irvine, not because he knew of a specific teacher there who might be a good mentor for him but because, simply put, "they admitted me" (Lee, 228), and he began the program in 1968. Irvine did have distinguished writers on its faculty, including Oakley Hall and E. L. Doctorow, whose instruction Ford still appreciates. Ford finished the M.F.A. program in 1970, but he found himself still unable to get anything published. In 1971, he was elected into the prestigious Society of Fellows at the University of Michigan, a scholarly honorary group modeled upon the society at Harvard University that gives young scholars three years of free academic life. As a Fellow between the years 1971 and 1974, Ford attended classes, particularly those taught by Don Hall, and devoted his time to writing. In 1975–1976, Ford himself became an assistant professor at the University of Michigan.

In "First Things First: One More Writer's Beginnings," Ford tells of the frustration and paralysis that resulted from researching "appropriate" places to submit his work, keeping stories circulating in the mail, and still finding rejection after rejection in the mailbox day after day. Ford concluded that he needed to become a better writer, and he set out to do something that would give him the time to improve without the constant presence of rejection: writing a novel,[8] an act he accomplished in part because of the freedom and support provided by the Society of Fellows at the University of Michigan. Eventually an excerpt from this novel, *A Piece of My Heart,* was accepted for publication in the *Paris Review,* though it was not until 1976 that the book in its entirety was published by Harper and Row.

Neo-Faulknerian?

Some reviews of Ford's first novel were less than kind, despite the fact that the book was nominated for the Ernest Hemingway Award for Best First Novel. *A Piece of My Heart* takes place on an island between Arkansas and Mississippi, and its characters include a drifter, Robard Hewes, in love with another man's wife; a law student, Sam Newell, trying to figure out his life; and an older couple whose home is the site of these characters' intersecting paths. The couple, Mr. and Mrs. Lamb, are grotesque, physically and otherwise, though it is Mrs. Lamb's strength that becomes most evident over the novel's course. In any case, the novel has evoked comparisons to fiction by both William Faulkner and Flannery O'Connor, namely through its effective rendering of place, the randomness of violence, and the grotesqueries suggested literally and metaphorically through characterization. Although Ford did not intend these similarities to overshadow the novel in its own right, reading the novel without noting its seemingly southern heritage proved impossible to some critics, including Larry McMurtry in his article in the *New York Times Book Review.* McMurtry writes,

> It is the men who are forced to carry the narrative [Robard Hewes and Sam Newell] who invariably discover that they are also carrying the burden of Southern history. In this case, as in so many others, it squashes them into a mulch of pronouns and pulpy adjectives, of which "imponderable" is the one I personally have come to dislike most. . . . One would hope that, in Mr. Ford's case, these vices won't prove incurable. His minor characters are vividly drawn, and his ear is first-rate. If he can weed his garden of some of the weeds and cockleburrs of his tradition, it might prove very fertile.[9]

In the cadence of Ford's writing, McMurtry located signatures of Faulkner's style: unclear pronoun references, a narrative more focused on the past than the present, an overreliance on rhetoric. Unable to categorize Ford's work in any other way, McMurtry labeled *this* novel, at least, "neo-Faulknerian" and furthermore concluded that it "reads like the worst, rather than the best, of Faulkner. It reminds us of the Faulkner whose passion for rhetoric so often swamped his instinct for syntax" (McMurtry, 16).

Turning Away from the South, Still Writing

Ford was, of course, disappointed with this assessment of his work, but this period marked a turning point in his literary career. He claims he has always wanted his books to be read as something more than southern texts, and after these kinds of reviews of *A Piece of My Heart,* he resolved never to set another book in the South again. Ford says, "I'm a southerner, obviously; I like the South, I still live some in the South, but the South is just not a subject on which I have any interesting things to say, and probably having made that decision back in the middle 70's, my southern experience is even thinner now."[10] Ford's readers now find that the settings for his fiction include such disparate places as New Jersey, Montana, Paris, and Mexico.

Mexico is in fact the setting for his second novel, *The Ultimate Good Luck* (Houghton Mifflin, 1981), which tells the story of a Vietnam veteran, Harry Quinn, and his attempts to free his former girlfriend Rae's brother Sonny from prison, where he has been incarcerated on counts of drug trafficking. Sparer in style than his preceding book, this novel is more apt to remind a reader of Hemingway than of Faulkner. Having sold fewer than 12,000 copies combined (Lee, 229), Ford's first two novels did not strike him as particularly successful with a reading public, despite the generally favorable reception by reviewers. Ford's wife Kristina was teaching at New York University during this time; with her Ph.D. in city planning, she would be consistently employable regardless of where she and Ford lived. Having always resolved to stop writing should he run out of anything significant to say, Ford wrestled again with his decision to forgo "real" work for fiction.

Several colleges and universities were glad to have Ford on their writing faculties, and Ford taught part-time during this period at such prestigious institutions as Williams College (assistant professor, 1979–1980) and Princeton University (lecturer and the George Perkins Fellow in the Humanities, 1980–1981). But Ford did not aspire to be a full-time professor. He also received a Guggenheim Fellowship in 1977 and a National Endowment for the Arts Fellowship in 1979. Despite these successes and because his second novel sold relatively few copies, Ford quit writing fiction to pursue a career in sportswriting at *Inside Sports,* a magazine based in New York. For this publication, Ford covered baseball and college football, and he maintains that he would have made a career out of sportswriting had *Inside Sports* not folded in 1981. Once again, Ford had time on his hands and no job to demand his attention, and between 1981 and 1982, he spent time back and forth between Montana and the Delta, in Mississippi. Meanwhile, he also published stories and essays in magazines, literary journals, and quarterlies. To borrow Ford's earlier characterization of his nomadic existence, the "motif of things" during the late seventies and early eighties was this: Ford was writing, whether the words formed fiction or not. This period produced a variety of personal essays, from a thoughtful assessment of Walker Percy's fiction,[11] to a confession of appreciation for Hemingway, Faulkner, and Fitzgerald,[12] to a poignant recollection of his mother Edna's centrality in his life ("My Mother, In Memory"). And, even as he published other pieces, Ford worked out of his home in Princeton, New Jersey, putting together a novel that would be markedly different from his other work.

Frank Bascombe and a Shift in Style

This new novel became *The Sportswriter,* published by Knopf and released as a paperback original by Vintage Books in 1986. In this novel Ford introduces Frank Bascombe, who also narrates Ford's *Independence Day* (1995). A first-person account, *The Sportswriter* invites the reader into the mind of Bascombe, newly divorced and recently bereaved by the death of his son from Reye's syndrome. The book opens in a cemetery, where Bascombe meets with his former wife, called "X" in the novel because Ford could not think of a name for her. Ford used the letter to refer to her in the manuscript, somewhat appropriately, as it would turn out, because she is Frank's ex-wife after all, and his longing for that former intimacy is almost nameless. The two have arrived predawn on Good Friday morning to commemorate their dead son Ralph's birthday. Shortly thereafter Frank leaves for Detroit with his current girlfriend, Vicki Arcenault, on a business trip. His sportswriting job requires that he interview a crippled professional football player for an "inspirational" story, but his journey turns out to be anything but uplifting. Upon returning to his home in Haddam, Frank encounters his friend and fellow member of the Divorced Men's Club, Walter Luckett, in a bar, where Walter confesses that, several nights prior to this one, he had allowed another man to pick him up and, eventually, to sleep with him. Quietly distraught, Walter clearly feels awkward about his confession, not wanting Frank to think of it as such. And Frank, rather self-ishly, thinks little of this scene until later, when Walter commits suicide. Meanwhile, Frank spends the weekend imagining X's life even as he plans to go to Vicki's family home for Easter dinner. By novel's end, Frank has embarked on another relationship with the younger Catherine Flaherty; this one, too, is just a passing fling, as Frank recounts in the book's last chapter, though he remains in close touch with Catherine, he tells us. He also tells the reader that he has gone to Florida, where he strives to live his life fully and in the moment, undistracted by former musings and mourning. The novel's plot is not at all complicated, but Ford creates texture beneath its surface with his characterization of Bas-combe, whose thoughts, finally, supersede the plot in importance.

More intellectual than Ford's earlier protagonists, Bascombe muses philosophically over loss and love in what some readers have called the tradition of the overly cerebral southern narrator, a narrator that critic Fred Hobson defines in *The Southern Writer in the Postmodern World*.[13] Ford holds true to his resolution, however, not to set another work in the South; the novel takes place mostly in New Jersey in a fictional suburb called Haddam. Of interest, though, is the fact that Bascombe is from the South, and one could argue that in Bascombe's characterization Ford is clearly indebted to Walker Percy, whose male characters question the universe, fall down on golf courses, and take sudden journeys out West. Ford would assert, however, that southerners cannot corner the market on this kind of thoughtful narrator, citing John Updike and Joseph Heller as two writers who also create intellectual male characters who question their choices and their decisions (Walker, 132). This "tradi-tion," Ford says, is a Western one and not a southern one. Percy's land-scapes do verge on the possibility of becoming less southern and more generic—marked by motels, infected by the rhetoric of advertising, and more conducive to individual anonymity. But Ford departs from Percy's fictional terrain in other ways as well. Unlike Percy, Ford insists upon a secular world, even in *The Sportswriter,* despite the fact that the book's action takes place during Easter Weekend. Although Ford acknowl-edges in an interview that the "Easter myth is . . . compelling," he also says that he "certainly would hate for the book to be read as a book just about Christian redemption, because it's not a Christian book. The kind of redemption that goes on in [*The Sportswriter*] is entirely unreligious."[14] By novel's end, what Bascombe has embraced in religion's stead is "this glistening one moment,"[15] a transient yet intense state of contentment in the face of uncertainty.

Defining "Locatedness"

This "moment" has its counterpart in Ford's earlier novel *The Ultimate Good Luck,* despite the stylistic differences that characterize the two books; it is in the earlier novel that Ford first uses the term "locatedness" in his fiction. As I explore in the longer chapter on *The Ultimate Good Luck,* the book is, to some extent, a modernist novel. That is, one of its themes concerns the alien and external world in which we are all isolated, despite our best attempts to communicate and establish relationships with other human beings. In *The Ultimate Good Luck,* Ford uses the idea of being "located" to denote an experience of individual centeredness, an experience that can, at times, be illusory. Harry Quinn, the novel's central character, defines this moment as "the high density sensation . . . [that] made you feel out of time and out of real space and located closer to yourself, as if located was the illusion, the thing he'd missed since he'd come back [from Vietnam], the ultimate good luck."[16] In this novel, Quinn also refers to love as a "place."

By transforming the abstract into the concrete and vice versa, Ford provides new connotations for a number of words. For example, in Ford's fictional universe, "location" may have nothing to do with one's surroundings and everything to do with one's ability to recognize crucial moments in one's life. Underlying the principle of "locatedness" is in fact its transience; the moment cannot be sustained over time but finally possesses the power to transform those who experience it. Like Bascombe's "glistening one moment," "locatedness" entails one kind of spiritual reckoning, capable of redeeming self or other. By redefining language such as this, Ford sidesteps categories once again, and as I suggest in the chapter on *The Ultimate Good Luck,* Ford—verging on the postmodern—exceeds the boundaries set by the novel's modernist themes and the usual associations with "place."

Home: A Variable Concept

In his nonfiction, Ford also uses the concept of "locatedness" and theorizes about the distinctions among the terms "place," "home," and "location." He acknowledges that place is "supposed" to be important to southerners, but he suggests that many places become devoid of meaning for their inhabitants. It is not geography or landmarks, Ford contends, that make a person feel at home. Even home itself, Ford claims, is "a variable concept."[17] His attitude springs at least in part from his childhood experience of living periodically in his grandfather's hotel in Little Rock, Arkansas. The hotel was a nice one, with a "curving marble fish pond in the lobby; a tranquil, bannistered mezzanine with escritoires and soft lights; a jet marble front desk; long, green leather couches, green carpets, bellboys with green twill uniforms and short memories" ("Accommodations," 38). But it was, no doubt, a strange place to call home, especially for a boy whose father was ill and for whose grandfather the hotel was absolutely crucial to his livelihood. As the manager, and not the owner, Ford's grandfather Ben Shelley did have to think about his job security; Ford remembers knowing "how fast we could be 'put on the street' " (43). Ford surely felt a few of his own insecurities at this time, realizing that he was partaking of an odd existence, even apt to be perceived an eccentric one by southern visitors who were, as Ford rightly notes, eager to find and label eccentricity outside of their own lives. Ford acknowledges, "To live in a hotel as a boy knowing nothing was to see what adults did to each other and themselves when only adults were present" (38). Perhaps this statement reveals a penchant for eavesdropping, for voyeurism, on the young Ford's part, but readers of his work are also beckoned to take this partially concealed stance. Ford's young male protagonists, in particular, often witness what they should not have to see, as I attest in later chapters on *Rock Springs* (1987), *Wildlife* (1990), and *Women with Men* (1997). But as part of a memoir Ford's statement also suggests a poignancy that comes from grappling with adult issues at a relatively young age, knowing some real consequences of failure, adjusting to the early death of a parent. Ford's recollections, though, also hint at the strength he acquired by living in the present despite the unpredictability of any given day:

> In the hotel there was no center to things, nor was I one. It was a floating life, days erasing other days almost completely, as it should be. The place was a hollow place, like any home, in which things went on, a setting where situations developed and ended. And I simply stood alongside that for a while in my young life—neither behind the scenes nor in front. What I saw then—and I saw more than I can say . . . —matters less than what I thought about it. And what I thought about it was this: this is the actual life now, not a stopover, a diversion, or an oddment in time, but the permanent life, the one that will provide history, memory, the one I'll be responsible for in the long run. ("Accommodations," 43)

If Ford's life continues to "float," it does so by design. The ephemeral placelessness of the hotel, where lives come together and apart and people come and go, nonetheless provided "history" and "memory" for Ford.

"History" and "memory," two words forever yoked with southern fiction, mean different things to Ford than they did to William Faulkner, for instance, who was born in the late nineteenth century and whose works deal mostly with the post–Civil War South. Furthermore, Ford cannot blame his characters' failures to connect with one another on some large and abstract entity called "the South." Ford's characters either take responsibility for their actions or failures to act, or they deny responsibility, but, either way, the story comes down to specific situations, and Ford's fictional material, more often than not, is drawn from the present and not the past. As Ford states eloquently, his experience at his grandfather's hotel was real—not an oddment but a permanent piece of his existence for which he will always be responsible.

Ford has said many times that too much has been made of his penchant for relocation, despite the fact that by 1992 he had moved "twenty times, probably in twenty years."[18] By 1997, Ford's comment is that such considerations are, finally, "dull" (Walker, 130); he admits, "I keep trying to come up with interesting answers, but I even get tired of my own interesting answers. I mean, if you live some place and stay there, do you want to talk about that all the time? My sense of locatedness is actually just a matter of where I work, and the contact I keep with the people I love. That's as much location as I feel is absolutely essential" (Walker, 130). Ford comes back again and again to the importance of what he calls the "lived life,"[19] sustaining Ralph Waldo Emerson's conviction that the "lived life" is "its own evidence." For Ford, as his interview response suggests, the work is critical. Wherever the work can be done, Ford feels located, as long as he is not also deprived of contact with those whom he loves.

Despite Ford's insistence that the topic is boring, the notion of relocation appears in his work in many guises. He writes with humor, for example, about why writers give in to some strange all-consuming desire to live in the country, as if by traversing the land writers can tap into the same creative reservoirs that quenched William Wordsworth or Samuel Taylor Coleridge, two nineteenth-century British poets whose walks became somewhat legendary. Or perhaps, as Ford muses, writers seek the country to follow in the footsteps of the nineteenth-century American writer Henry David Thoreau, whose experience of living deliberately and undistractedly is immortalized in *Walden*. As Ford questions, clearly tongue-in-cheek, "In all those forced walks over acreage, down those leafy corduroys and stone walls, in all those ostentatious root cellars and truck cabs and woodsheds, what are they putting in a claim for? Why do they want to convince me they need this? Can the cardinal points really be more locatable out there? Is the country, so stocked with silence and primitive sound, more conducive to words?" ("Country Matters," 82). Ford's answer, of course, is "no." He believes that place "is wherever we do good work" (84); otherwise "place" is a meaningless abstraction, open only to whatever we bring to it. Ford argues, "*Place* cannot be extolled, except in the abstract or in the most purely private sense. And this is especially true for writers, for whom place is said to be important" (84).

Place in Southern Fiction

Ford clearly resists the claim that many readers and critics of southern literature espouse: for southern writers, place is always and under every circumstance important; the land in and of itself embodies a tragic history of slavery, occupation, and defeat, the likes of which the United States as a whole has never known, except perhaps in Vietnam. (But even that situation is different, some may contend, since that battle was fought in another country.) At any rate, this kind of history arguably produced a different kind of writer, a writer for whom regional concerns and memories necessitated at first a defensiveness and then a self-consciousness; this writer's past was fraught with moral failure and man's inhumanity to man. At the same time, place became associated with all that was potentially good in humanity: self-reliance and sustenance, the simple life, the embracing of certain kinds of values not dependent on industry. All of this is to say that the concept of "place" is a complicated one in the South, and implicit in Ford's rejection of "place" as an integral factor in writing is a rejection of the label "southern writer."

Richard Ford and Frank Bascombe: Unburdened Southerners?

Ironically, Ford's creation of Frank Bascombe in *The Sportswriter* inspired Fred Hobson to call Bascombe the "unburdened Southerner" (Hobson 1991, 48). Hobson goes on to explain, "the more Frank protests he is not interested in the past, in family, in place, and in the South, the more we are convinced that he is. . . . Frank's great interest in the *absence* of past, of historical burden, of family heritage, of fixed place, of community suggests a southern mind that is fascinated by these things" (Hobson 1991, 49). Like Faulkner's famous Quentin Compson who says from Harvard, "I dont hate the South. I dont. I dont,"[20] perhaps Frank Bascombe protests too much (Hobson 1991, 50). So it would seem that the simple act of setting a book in New Jersey is not enough to get Ford off the hook of critics seeking evidence of southern writing in his work.

Ford believes that criteria generated by critics to qualify writing often end up excluding other good writers. As he tells Elizabeth Farnsworth in an interview on PBS's *The News Hour with Jim Lehrer,* the southern tradition could be "easily debunked"; furthermore, Ford says that "conventional wisdom about the South, which is that people are always sitting around on porches admiring their family members and drinking mint juleps and telling stories . . . turns out to be a conventional wisdom that just concerns white people and finds a way to exclude blacks from the notion of what Southern tradition is, and when you begin to include African Americans into that formula, it becomes somewhat less easy to hold."[21] For these reasons, among others, Ford finds the critic's penchant for categorizing distasteful and limiting: "those kinds of distinctions are just not native to me. I think that at a young age critics and scholars and reviewers begin to have their minds narrowed in behalf of some spurious precision" (Walker, 135). Ford does have a point; unrelenting comparisons to the southern literary greats, of whom Faulkner looms over all, have caused critics and scholars of southern literature to lament that southern writers of the present generation—both black and white—lack what critics call a "tragic scope." What this lament may overlook is that what was tragic to Faulkner will not be tragic to more contemporary minds.

A Turning Point

But critics and reviewers liked *The Sportswriter. Time* magazine named it one of the five best books of the year, and it was also a PEN/Faulkner finalist. More important, though, and certainly to Ford, is the fact that readers liked the book, too; it sold well—more than 60,000 copies—and it has since been reissued in hardback by Knopf. Readers responded well to Frank's struggles to maintain his relationship with his secretary Vicki (originally from Texas) as he mourns the stability once embodied by his marriage to "X"; his paralyzing grief over his son's death; his despair reflected uncannily back at him by his friend Walter Luckett's suicide. These situations are real, and Frank's musings and attendant crises are rendered evenhandedly and with humor by Ford. He admits in an interview that his wife Kristina had something to do with Bascombe's creation: "she thought I'd find a wider audience if I stopped writing about dark souls and dark fates. In retrospect, I'd say she was right. I know it's much more of a challenge—for me in particular—to find language for people essaying to be better and happier, than for people wrestling with murder and mayhem" (Lee, 230). *The Sportswriter* could, in fact, be a grim novel, but it is not, namely because of Ford's deft handling of sensitive subjects with a good deal of self-conscious wryness.

Rock Springs and *Wildlife:* West to Montana

Ford did not abandon darker themes entirely, however. In 1987, shortly after the publication of *The Sportswriter,* Ford's collection of short fiction, *Rock Springs,* was published; in it were gathered stories previously published in magazines and literary journals such as *Esquire,* the *New Yorker, Antaeus,* and *Tri-Quarterly,* among others. Set primarily around Great Falls, Montana, *Rock Springs* includes stories told predominantly in the first-person voices of men, both young and old, who are divorced, parentless, criminal, or all of the above. Several of the stories are classic coming-of-age tales told in retrospect, descriptions of a time when a teenage boy confronted the considerable failings of his parents and thereby the distance that separated him from them. For example, in puzzling over the choices his parents have made and the many questions attendant upon their decisions, the narrator of "Great Falls" concludes, "Though possibly it—the answer—is simple: it is just low-life, some coldness in us all, some helplessness that causes us to misunderstand life when it is pure and plain, makes our existence seem like the border between two nothings, and makes us no more or less than animals who meet on the road—watchful, unforgiving, without patience or desire."[22] The stories deal with all kinds of relationships, but the dominant threads of bereavement, disappointment, and isolation weave the stories into a coherent collection. Not all of the stories are quite as bleak as the citation above would imply, but abandonment and the fragility of the family are recurrent themes, themes, in fact, that Ford will pick up in *Wildlife.*

Wildlife (1990), Ford's favorite of his own novels (Walker, 140), deals with a young boy's witnessing of his parents' dissolving relationship. After Joe's father loses his job as a golf instructor, he leaves the family in

Great Falls to get work putting out fires; Ford uses the literal smoldering of these fires to symbolize the nonextinguishable problems in Jerry
and Jeanette's marriage as well as the bond that won't let them quite
escape each other. Alternately, Joe is confidant for each parent, but as
such he is doomed to witness their imperfections first-hand: his mother's
drunken and then deliberate dalliance with Warren Miller and his
father's volatile response to that upon his return, his attempt to burn
down Miller's domicile. Like Faulkner's Sarty in the face of too many
barn burnings, who is still able to cry of his father, "He was brave!" Joe
will respond to his father's statement, "I wouldn't even blame you if you
hated me, right now," with the thoughts, "I didn't hate him. Not at
all. . . . he was my father. Nothing had changed as far as that was concerned. I loved him in spite of it all."[23] Despite such loyalty to his father
and his consistent love for his mother, Joe must acknowledge, like his
fictional counterpart in Ford's earlier "Great Falls," that he can never
know all of the answers. Finally, in spite of his uncomfortable closeness
to each parent, each remains ultimately unknowable; as Joe acknowledges, "there is still much to [his parent's breakup and reunion] that I
myself, their only son, cannot fully claim to understand" (177). This is
the lesson that Joe learns: life is wild and unpredictable, and people fail
each other because of their frailties and desires.

Frank Bascombe Revisited

Wildlife was published in 1990, and 1991 found Ford thinking once
again about Frank Bascombe. Ford claims to Elizabeth Farnsworth that
he never intended to write a sequel, but as early as 1989, he apparently
mentioned the possibility to an interviewer that he might (Lee, 232). In
any case, Frank's voice continued to assert itself in Ford's notebooks, in
which Ford keeps notes and writes in longhand well before he's ready to
put a novel together. Writing a novel is hard work, as Ford has often
acknowledged; he does his own research, writes out drafts in longhand,
and then types the manuscripts himself, revising as he goes. He admits
that as he was thinking about another novel after *Wildlife*'s publication,
he found that all of his notes and his thoughts for a new book were in
"Frank's voice" (Farnsworth).

So with the publication of *Independence Day* in 1995, Ford moves back
to the sophisticated musings of the addled Frank Bascombe, toward the
crowded, suburban East and away from the vast and violent landscapes
of the West. *Independence Day* met with enthusiastic reviews and won

both the Pulitzer Prize for fiction in 1996 and the PEN/Faulkner Award, marking the first time a book has ever won both prestigious awards. In this novel, the "sequel" to *The Sportswriter*, Ford's prior themes culminate. He deals with a father/son relationship and a love story, of sorts, and, as in *The Sportswriter*, a holiday weekend again determines the time frame of the book. In *Independence Day*, as the book's title implies, the holiday is July 4, the epitome of American fervor and zeal for independence, loud noises, parades, picnics, baseball, road trips, and, possibly, unforeseen accidents related to any one of these activities. Location, in all its meanings, is paramount, since Frank Bascombe is now a real estate agent. In fact, Ford evokes a pun with the novel's emphasis on and Bascombe's obsession with real estate; for Bascombe, some very "real" things are "at stake"—his relationships with his son, his former wife, and his girlfriend. He embarks on a journey with his son, a visit to the basketball and baseball Halls of Fame, but his journey, of course, is also a figurative endeavor to find himself, and some meaning in life. Ironically, there is no longer a real estate; instead, land is now divided up, packaged and marketed and sold almost as a reflection of the individual who purchases it. As Bascombe observes, "you don't sell a house to someone, you sell a life."[24] Bascombe views selling real estate as the perfect occupation for someone who, as he professes to be, is in his "Existence Period," which Frank describes as

> the high wire act of normalcy, the part that comes *after* the big struggle that led to the big blow-up, the time in life when whatever was going to affect us "later" actually affects us, a period when we go along more or less self-directed and happy, though we might not choose to mention or even remember it later were we to tell the story of our lives, so steeped is such a time in the small dramas and minor adjustments of spending quality time simply with ourselves. (*ID*, 94–95)

Frank's narrative voice here differs from those of Ford's other fictional storytellers, and I address the ramifications of these and other stylistic differences in the chapter on the novel. The economy of place, the selling of an idea of one's self, and the changing face of the American landscape are notions that I further explore through references to some of Ford's nonfiction essays published in *Harper's* magazine, particularly "Country Matters," "Accommodations," and "Heartbreak Motels."

In the chapter on *Independence Day* I also assess Ford's mining of an American idiom by which to tell a story, making some connections between his literal reconstructions of voice and sounds, such as "Boom-

Haddam, boom-Haddam, boom-boom-ba-boom" (*ID,* 3) and resonances
in the poetry of Wallace Stevens, who, like Ford's father and several of his
fictional characters, was a salesman. Stevens uses word play and sounds,
such as "tink and tank and tunk-a-tunk-tunk" in "A High-Toned Old
Christian Woman," for example. Furthermore, Ford's characterization of
Bascombe recalls Stevens's own "thin men of Haddam" ("Thirteen Ways of
Looking at a Blackbird"), who are prey to letting their imaginative musings about blackbirds obscure the things-in-themselves. Perhaps not so
coincidentally, Ford's Frank Bascombe is a Haddam resident, though of
New Jersey and not of Stevens's Connecticut. Nonetheless, like a Percy
character and Stevens's thin men, Bascombe is prone to get lost in thought
and miss the most amazingly obvious signs.

Ford's Recent Accomplishments

In the 1990s, Ford taught fiction writing at Harvard University and
Northwestern University. He also was named the Morgan Family Writer
in Residence at the University of North Carolina–Chapel Hill, directed
the William Faulkner Foundation at the University of Rennes in Paris,
France, and was named general editor for the two-volume American
Library Eudora Welty Project. His readers may not know that he is the
literary executor for the estate of Raymond Carver; he also is a close
friend and literary advisor of Eudora Welty. In these roles, he believes
that he honors two writers whom he admires and loves, and he takes
these responsibilities very seriously. In addition, he is one of the principal
financial supporters of an organization called Literacy Partners in New
York City. He has received several honorary degrees, including a *Docteur
Honoris Causa* from the University of Rennes (1994) and Doctor of
Humane Letters degrees from Loyola University (1996) and the University of Michigan (1998). In 1998, he was elected to the American Academy of Arts and Letters. He remains married to Kristina Hensley, who
directs the New Orleans City Planning Commission, and although he
and Kristina live apart much of the time, Ford cites her frequently in his
interviews and dedicates every book simply, with "Kristina" centered on
the dedication page. Ford's reason for living apart from his wife (the two
have no children) and, indeed, from almost everybody else, is that writing is solitary work that requires a certain amount of obsession and com-
pulsion. He often retreats to Montana to work on his fiction, but almost
every six months will find him in a different place. He continues to insist
that it's "ridiculous the big deal people make of it . . . Because no matter

how much I move around I still write books and I'm still married to the same girl, and all the rest is just filigree."[25]

Ford's Newest Fiction

Women with Men (Knopf, 1997) is a collection of three long stories—"The Womanizer" (originally published in *Granta,* Summer 1992), "Jealous" (*New Yorker,* November 30, 1992), and "Occidentals"—each of which deals with the various ways that men and women, though confronted by the same or a similar predicament, succumb to different desires, ultimately failing, at times, to connect even in the midst of confusion or pain. Misunderstandings, misprisions, and mistakes abound in these stories. As one character puts it as he wanders around Paris, "It could get to be addictive, he believed, not understanding what people were saying. Time spent in another country would probably always be spent misunderstanding a great deal, which might in the end turn out to be a blessing and the only way you could ever feel normal."[26] Each story functions as a vignette, capturing a short but critical time in the characters' lives and presenting unflinching portraits of humanity at its best or worst. Told from a male character's point of view, each narrative nonetheless depends upon its female characters to illumine the shortcomings or strengths of its males and thus locate the reader in settings as diverse as hotels and flats in Paris and train stations in the American West.

In "The Womanizer," Martin Austin embarks on an affair with a French woman that changes his life. Most of the time, Martin seems to live a mundane existence in and around Chicago. Fifteen years in service to the same company, one that makes treated paper designed for foreign textbook companies, Martin is a salesman, and in that capacity he travels frequently. He leaves behind his wife, Barbara, with whom he has no children. On one such trip, he becomes immediately and obsessively enamored of Joséphine Belliard, an editor at a publishing house. He meets her at a cocktail party, later sees her at the publishing house, and asks her out to dinner; then, fascinated by her exotic fragility, he kisses her in the car before she drops him off at his hotel. Although Joséphine does not physically resist his advances, she whispers "non" over and over again as Martin kisses her, a sound that fascinates him so much that he hears the word incessantly in his head even after he has gone back to Chicago. Back in the States, he and Barbara suffer through tense moments of noncommunication, though Martin has no reason to believe that she suspects him of having an affair. Finally, in a restaurant, Barbara calls him a womanizer and walks away, leaving him alone. Freed from any responsibility for this rupture, or so he believes, Martin takes advantage of the breakup to go back to Paris, where he eventually gets back in touch with Joséphine. From this point in the story's plot, its crux depends upon Martin's agreement to watch Léo, Joséphine's son, while she meets with her lawyer to sign papers to divorce her husband.

Without Joséphine's knowledge or her permission, Martin takes Léo to the park. While musing upon his failed marriage and his attraction to Joséphine, who had mysteriously refused to kiss him earlier that day, Martin neglects to pay attention to the boy, who wanders off. Martin solicits the help of the police, but it is he who finds Léo, naked and crying, sitting on the dirt in the undergrowth. It turns out that Léo has been molested, a fact for which Joséphine, as a mother who loves her son, cannot forgive Martin. His liaison is thus terminated, leaving Martin bewildered and unwitting, questioning attachments and misunderstandings at story's end, acknowledging that he'll have to sleep on the subject "many, many nights."[27]

"Jealous," the middle story in the collection, is possibly the most optimistic of the three. Centered around the journey of its central character, Larry, to visit his mother in Seattle, the story also sensitively depicts the strength of Larry's relationship with his father, who lives in Montana. As Larry comes to terms with the shortcomings of the adults in his life, he also witnesses a violent episode in a train station bar. Forced to be a kind of voyeur, rather like the young Ford in his grandfather's hotel, Larry sees the kinds of things that adults do to one another. His ostensible chaperone for the trip, his Aunt Doris, proves less mature than Larry himself, and as Larry witnesses that violence and sex prove only temporary explosions of human interaction, he happens upon the truth about intimacy. Like "The Womanizer," this story closes with the main character's pursuit of rest and repose in less than ideal circumstances, but Larry, unlike Martin, has achieved an inner calm that complements his literal descent into sleep.

The final vignette, called "Occidentals," relates the story of Charley Matthews and Helen Carmichael and their trip to Paris. The two conceive of the trip as a celebration of Charley's good fortune; he is to meet with the French editor who has recently expressed an interest in a novel Charley had published in the States to little critical acclaim. A former academic, Charley has written the novel based on his marriage's dissolution; some years after its publication, a French publisher decides that the book would be worthy of a French translation and edition. A series of disappointments ensue, including his editor's cancellation of the appointment, and the Paris that Charley has imagined all but fails him. Somewhat oblivious to his companion's pain, Charley gives in to solipsism while Helen suffers from cancer and its attendant despair, finally committing suicide in their hotel room while Charley is out taking a long walk. Ironically, it is upon this walk that Charley believes he has finally *seen* Paris.

Schools of Realism, Minimalism, Dirty Realism

Women with Men chronicles characters who are not nearly as self-aware as Frank Bascombe, and Ford's tone here is likewise not as forgiving. In fact, the prose offers little in the way of judgment—positive or negative—for its readers. Ford's characterizations are unflinching, reminiscent of his style in the *Rock Springs* collection published 10 years earlier. In *Women with Men,* the reader still finds attention to detail that preserves the verisimilitude to ordinary life, psychological verity in characterization, and the author's detached narrative stance—all traits that have earned Ford the title of "realist." This attempt to categorize his work is not as slippery an endeavor as calling his writing "southern," and, in fact, after *A Piece of My Heart*'s publication (1976), the presence of rhetorical flourishes that might encourage a reader to identify Ford with Faulkner is conspicuously absent. Instead, the reader finds prose that targets its subject without excess verbiage, a style, that, among other things, requires the *reader* to determine the character's likability, moral failure, self-consumedness, or virtue. These spare renditions of character and situation have prompted further comparisons of Ford with his late friend Raymond Carver, whose minimalist stories, though stark on the page, nonetheless conjure layers of meaning, again for the reader to determine or identify. Not surprisingly, readers have also cited Ernest Hemingway, whose tough prose seemed fitting given Hemingway's own public persona, as a clear literary antecedent of Ford.

In 1983, *Granta* magazine, which has regularly published Ford's work and for which Ford has edited a special issue, coined the term "dirty realism" to describe Ford's fiction. The adjective "dirty" simply suggests Ford's ability to capture all that simmers beneath the surface and then erupts, often in the form of violence, cheap sex, or other extremes of behavior. For instance, Ford's characters may be former cons on the run, murderers, petty thieves, or drifters; his plots, though simple, may chart rehabilitation or further descent into poverty, loneliness, or despair and may take place in the vast expanses of the American West or the tight hustle and bustle of northeast suburbia. With his own penchant for hunting and living in Montana, Ford is not afraid to get his hands callused and bloody, a fact that is belied by his graciousness, eloquence, and slight southern drawl.

Ford's fiction does differ from earlier kinds of American literary realism, the nascence of which has become associated with nineteenth-century writer William Dean Howells's work. In his fiction, Howells focuses on the rising middle classes, and in some instances Howells comments upon the moral decay that he believed was attendant upon society's obsession with material culture and industrialization. Ford's fiction, by contrast, rarely addresses the moral problems inherent in society directly, nor does he offer any utopian ideals as solutions. But like Howells, he writes at the end of a century, and Howells's European predecessors (Flaubert, Tolstoy, Hardy, Dostoyevsky) might also be said to have influenced Ford. In fact, Ford's standard reply when pushed to identify a southern literary heritage is to insist that he is writing out of a Western tradition. When pressed to identify the ghost of a writer who may be looking over his shoulder, Ford says, "I dunno. Everybody. There's a zillion of them; I've got a shoulder full of them" (Walker, 135).

A few of Ford's contemporaries in the dirty realism enterprise are also known for their liberal sprinkling of popular culture icons in their works, a method by which a writer may establish a familiar setting and situate a reader in a specific time and place. For example, Kentucky fiction writer Bobbie Ann Mason has created characters who watch *M*A*S*H* on television and listen to Bruce Springsteen. Although Ford is also a Springsteen fan[28] and even was inspired to entitle his novel "Independence Day" after one of Springsteen's songs (Walker, 128), he nonetheless resists the impulse to cite references to popular culture in his fiction. He reasons:

> if I stuck a Springsteen lyric into a line of mine or a scene in the story, I would always be afraid that I'd never be able to reauthorize the scene, that the lyric would just suck all my particular authority out of the scene. . . . In fact, there's a scene in *The Sportswriter* that takes place pretty close to the Jersey shore in which Frank is in a phone booth, where he actually gets hit by a car, and a girl comes over from a root beer stand. A carhop. And when I got her over to where he was, I write that she was wearing a sweatshirt, and I really wanted to . . . put "Springsteen Tour 1985" or

something like that [on it]. But I thought, no, no, no, you keep that out
of there, because it'll just gobble up your scene. (Walker, 129)

Instead, Ford creates his own names for stores and locations and bands,
so Frank finds himself near the "Ground Zero Burg" when the telephone
booth from which he calls a former lover is hit by a grocery cart, itself
flung across the "Acme lot" by a car. The young woman who comes to
his aid is wearing a T-shirt stenciled with the name of a rock group,
"The Blood Counts." In Bascombe's voice, Ford writes, "I squint at the
orange awnings of the Ground Zero, fluttering like pennants in the
breeze, and feel weak. The girl, the broken phone booth, the bent shop-
ping cart suddenly seem a far distance from where I am. Inexplicably
far. A gull shouts in the high white sky, and I have to stand against my
car fender for balance" (*SW,* 306). Rather than utilize recognizable references to pop culture that might "gobble up" his scenes, Ford relies upon
his ability to reproduce minute details that communicate an imaginable
literary landscape.

Clearly, Ford's readers have attempted more than once to characterize
his fiction, allying him with this literary school or that one. No doubt
this effort will continue, as Ford's work is taught increasingly in high
school and college classrooms and written about in respected literary
journals and books. It is safe to say that Ford, as well as many other
writers whose work has been termed regional, resists such easy classification; to restrict his subject matter in such a way might also restrict his
readership. Every writer writes to be read, as Ford has insisted in his personal essays, and Ford himself pays just as much attention, possibly even
more, to responses elicited from a wider community of readers than
from learned academics and influential reviewers. This is not to suggest
that Ford is anti-intellectual. On the contrary, he talks with ease about
fishing and fighting and about Ralph Waldo Emerson and Fyodor Dostoyevsky. Well-read and with a vast vocabulary, Ford cannot help but
earn the respect of the literati as well as the lay-reader. Close readings of
his fiction will remind his audience of other writers, as this volume will
show, but, finally, Ford's place in American literary history will take a
long time to determine. However, it's unlikely that his eligibility for
such consideration will ever be questioned; Ford *is* located in the American literary canon.

In the subsequent chapters, each targeting a specific work or phase in
Ford's career thus far, I further examine points introduced here and

make a specific argument about each individual text. In so doing, I comment upon Ford's stylistic choices and his creation of a kind of fictional terminology ("locatedness," for example) as well as connections between Ford and writers in other literary traditions. By offering critical readings of Ford's fiction and explications of what have become his dominant themes, I suggest that Ford is indebted to, yet departs from, established trends in American and southern literature, and, in so doing, achieves a truly contemporary voice.

Chapter Two
Uncharted Territory in
A Piece of My Heart

The action in *A Piece of My Heart* (1976) occurs primarily on a little island between Arkansas and Mississippi that does not appear on any map. Despite this evocation of placelessness, Richard Ford's first novel caused some readers and reviewers to identify it as another novel in the southern tradition, "neo-Faulknerian" in substance and in style.[1] Any book by a southern-born writer that is set in the South becomes a contender for the title of "southern novel." Ford, however, is after more than an exploration of southern themes; in fact, *A Piece of My Heart* becomes more of a parody of a southern novel than a southern novel itself. A collage of several genres and literary types, Ford's first novel blurs clear boundaries between the gothic, literary film noir, local color, and southwest humor, traditions that Faulkner also mined but that, with the exception of film noir, preceded his work, making Faulkner no less derivative than Ford. Alternately tragic and comic, *A Piece of My Heart* explores the convergence of several lives in its rather claustrophobic setting, evoking imagery of suffocation, entrapment, and drowning to underscore its close confines. Metaphorical signs become literal ones in this fictional world and vice versa. Robard Hewes and Sam Newel, whose alternating narratives govern the novel's structure, are the island's outsiders, temporarily located there in order to find out something important about their lives. For Robard, this quest means exploring fully his long-repressed attraction for his cousin Beuna, who lives across the river in Arkansas. For Newel, the search entails remembering parts of his childhood and attempting to piece together fragments of his life. Their hosts, Mark and Fidelia Lamb, provide comic relief and counterpoint the emptiness embodied by Robard and Sam. Ford in fact uses the proprietors of the uncharted island, two physically grotesque characters, as foils for the emotionally hollow men who have come there seeking "salvation." Similarly, the wild and uncharted island exists both in direct opposition to and as an appropriate setting for the closed worlds that finally engulf Robard Hewes and Sam Newel.

Divided into seven sections, each with its own shorter chapter breaks, in addition to a brief prologue and epilogue, the book is narrated in the third person from the points of view of Hewes and Newel, respectively, with one more section devoted to Hewes's perspective than to Newel's. Newel's sections also include intermittent italicized flashbacks to childhood memories. He was the son of a traveling starch salesman, a fictional detail that finds its source, no doubt, in Ford's own biography. Despite stark differences in social class and career aspirations, Hewes and Newel are both sons of dead fathers, and the recollection of each father's death figures prominently in both narratives. Ford intends for the two men to embody opposing sensibilities: Hewes as a down-to-earth, task-oriented, tough guy and Newel as a world-weary, physically inept intellectual. Like many of Ford's male characters, these two drift from place to place, from desire to desire, until place and desire align, drawing them both to the island.

Hewes arrives at the island more by chance than by design. His journey has taken him all the way from California, where he has left his wife Jackie, toward his destination in Helena, Arkansas, where his cousin Beuna now lives with her husband W. W., a baseball player. Beuna has carried on a torrid correspondence with Hewes, and Hewes's departure from California signifies his decision to give in to his desire, to succumb to Beuna's secret words of illicit love and the gardenia scent that clings even to her letters. But to do so will require continued stealth and secrecy, since W. W. is the kind of man who would sooner shoot a man who is sleeping with his wife than blink. Hewes can also handle a shotgun, and his experience as a hunting guide serves him well when he learns of a position on an island in Mississippi, a job that requires guarding the place against poachers for only one week. For Hewes, this job is the perfect cover: he can get paid, have a place to live and a legitimate reason for being in the area, be based *away* from Helena so that he will arouse as little suspicion as possible, and be unrecognizable in the Helena community. Furthermore, he will park his truck in Elaine, Arkansas, where the boat camp is located, not Helena. To get the job, he first speaks with Gaspareau, the old man who runs the boat camp and ferries visitors across the lake from Elaine. Once Hewes gets to the island, Mark Lamb hires him on the spot.

Newel ends up on the island more intentionally: Mark Lamb is his girlfriend Beebe's grandfather, and Beebe has encouraged Newel to go to Mississippi so that he can sort out his life. On the brink of graduation from law school in Chicago, Newel feels lost, ill-defined; Beebe accuses him of having a "poor tolerance for ambiguity," an inability to "continue what you're doing when nothing is very clearly defined."[2] The island is a good place to "compose yourself," Beebe says; "It's Mississippi in its most baronial and ridiculous" (84). Before Newel quite knows it, Beebe has left on her next trip as an airline attendant, and he is headed to the island, where Beebe's "Popo," Mr. Lamb, will have much less tolerance for Newel than Beebe does.

"Mississippi in Its Most Baronial and Ridiculous"

Beebe's words prove more accurate than Newel has imagined. The island does resemble a barony, at least in its way of governance. Mr. Lamb oversees the place, repairs the buildings, guides hunting parties, and partakes of the island's bounty himself. For 50 years, he and Mrs. Lamb have lived on the premises, ever since Mr. Lamb gave it to Mrs. Lamb for a combined birthday and wedding present. Chicago Pulp and Paper Company, however, still owns the deed and periodically must renew the lease, and the lease is up for renewal as Hewes and Newel converge on the island. Mr. Lamb tells Newel that he "supposes" the lease will be renewed, but he hates the "greasy dagos coming down here in their sorry-ass airplane, making me haul them around like I was a bus driver. It's demeaning" (169). Although the island is not really a barony, Mr. Lamb does live and work on the land like a feudal tenant, feeling proprietary but lacking real ownership. Shouting that it's an "in-dignity to suffer [the Chicago Pulp and Paper representatives'] presence on this island" (170), Mr. Lamb assures Newel that he could not possibly understand the outrage that Lamb feels as he swallows his pride, treats his northern visitors like guests, and hopes once again that his lease will be renewed.

In keeping with this *de facto* hierarchy, Lamb treats his paid assistant, T. V. A. Landrieu, more like a house servant than an equal, though some strange fondness seems to exist between them. As a black man working for a white man in Mississippi in the early seventies, Landrieu is far from liberated from a patriarchal attitude. Upon their arrival at the Lamb house, Newel and Hewes are presented with a curious tableau: "A small turkey-necked old man wearing duck trousers and a yellow pajama top was standing hands on his sides beside a Negro in overalls, who was bent on all fours over a thick iron pipe protruding several inches out of the ground. . . . The colored man had an enormous black pipe wrench he was applying to the pipe at ground level, taking it off each time he turned it half a rotation, refitting it, twisting it again, while the old man stood supervising the whole operation" (109). It turns out that the septic tank has infected the Lambs' well, and fittingly it is Mr. Lamb who sticks his head in the hole to ascertain this truth while the "Negro backed away . . . and gave the goings-on a grave look" (110). In addition to his facility with a pipe wrench, Landrieu also cooks for the Lambs and is apt to hear Mark shouting from the dining room, "What the hell, T. V. A. Have you took up your residence in our dinner?" to which he will quickly retort, "I can't cook it no faster than the stove" (122). Despite his inferior position in the household, Landrieu often responds to situations in more reasonable ways than his employer does. By the novel's end, Mrs. Lamb will have put Landrieu in charge of some very important details concerning her welfare and the island's, even though it is clear on many levels that neither she nor Mr. Lamb (or Hewes or Newel, for that matter) regards Landrieu as anything other than a person standing by to be at one's beck and call.

Upon his arrival on the island, Newel spends some energy assessing Landrieu's various facial expressions, as if by divining Landrieu's attitude he will achieve some insight into his present circumstances: "The colored man . . . gave him an anguished look that suggested that if he looked again he didn't want to see anybody still there. He flicked his eyes at Mr. Lamb, then back at the house, then fixed him with a purely baleful look" (110). But despite these readings of Landrieu's face, Newel will not learn the source of Landrieu's discomfort, though the reader may speculate that it arises from the dread of dealing with Lamb's sometimes unpredictable reactions toward visitors. Lamb alternately shouts, grunts, bellows and exclaims; for example, in the instance with the well water, he yells, "Goddamn it. . . . There's shit in my well water, by God. Mrs. Lamb knows what she's talking about" (110). In a relationship that verges on the comic, Landrieu becomes the straight man for all of Lamb's outrageous pronouncements, just as Newel will later literally find himself the steadying body in a boat prone to capsize because of Lamb's exaggerated gesticulations.

The Island Gothic

At odds with the ridiculous on the island are sinister episodes that foreshadow the rather grim ending of Hewes's story and contribute to the island's own air of unfathomable mystery. Two towheaded boys who give the men directions to Gaspareau's boat camp tell them that "the old scoundrel's mean as ptomaine" (61), referring to Lamb. Gaspareau himself has had a tracheotomy, so that he wears a "thin chain around his neck fastened to a silver disk with a hole in the middle which was buried inside a plug in his throat" (97) and croaks his words rather than speaks them. One of his many deerhounds lies dead in the road where he was hit a month ago, and when Newel asks him if he isn't going to get the dog out of the road, Gaspareau replies in the negative, explaining that if he were to try, the dog would just "come to pieces" (99). Furthermore, Gaspareau tells Hewes and Newel that the larger of the two boys who have given them directions has killed a man, a prison escapee from a road gang that he shot cleanly and without hesitation with a .22-caliber rifle. With the rasping voice of Gaspareau for company, the two men get in the boat and head toward the island, leaving behind the stench of decaying dog and other tales of death.

When a deer that has been swimming purposefully across the lake suddenly disappears, the journey across the water yields its own gothic moment. One minute clearly visible, the next nowhere to be seen, the deer's presence and absence disorient Newel, who tries to figure out where in relation to the boat and the bank the deer has been, half expecting the creature to bob up out of the water, gasping, eluding the clutches of whatever has seized it from below: "But there was nothing, and as he scanned the water he began to feel uncertain where the deer had been in relation to the dock, which was now downlake and only a stitch against the bank" (103). Gaspareau and Hewes betray no emotion, and Newel finds their stoicism strange. When they pull the boat to shore, Gaspareau goads him, "What happened to that deer? . . . That was somethin, wasn't it?" When Newel says eagerly, "What did happen?" Gaspareau smiles, glad to tell him. "Gar . . . Alligator gar come along and sucked him" (104). Newel is incredulous: "He didn't get him in his mouth, did he?" "Not *in* his mouth, *with* his mouth!" (104), Gaspareau tells him gleefully. Newel cannot imagine a fish large enough to pull down a 150-pound buck, and the scene confirms his alienation here in the swampy and wild South, a place far more feral than the streets of Chicago.

Furthering this sense of unbelonging, Gaspareau can't get Newel's name right, calling him "Newman" (104), speaking derisively to him about his unlikely welcome on the island, and telling him that the old man is particular about who sets foot on the place. Still reeling over and unbelieving about the deer's sudden doom, Newel becomes more and more defensive, finally cursing Gaspareau as Gaspareau leaves them at the shore. Robard Hewes, whose silence has by now grown customary to the reader, tells Sam Newel that a man like Gaspareau is not a good one to have mad at you: "he'll kill you," he warns Sam (105). Sam protests that Gaspareau was treating him like a "parvenu," or someone who has risen from a lower class to a slightly better one, only to remain reviled by those in his "new" class. Robard doesn't know what the word means and admits it, repeating his warning that if he were Sam, he'd get somewhere else when the shooting started. In addition to cementing a few of the differences between the two men, the scene is finally ironic, for it is Robard Hewes who will die from a shotgun wound in the middle of the lake, not Sam Newel.

The island's conspicuous absence from maps of the area also contributes to its mythic and gothic nature. Somewhere but nowhere, the place is guarded at one end by its own Charon, Gaspareau the ferryman, and at the other by Lamb, deaf in one ear and equipped with pearly false teeth, and his wife, Fidelia, who has a glass eye. Lamb prides himself on finagling the island's convenient disappearance on paper. Having caught the army engineers who were surveying the place poaching, Lamb makes a deal. With his own knowledge of the island, he is able to sneak up on the men and catch them red-handed:

> I come roaring over the hill with my deer rifle, got them both for tres-passing, hunting deer from a boat, hunting deer with an unauthorized gun, hunting without a license, shooting illegal deer, . . . and hunting out of season. . . . So I lawed the bastards. I told them they was on their way to jail, and the shitasses turned white as paste and started looking at one another like they was trying to figure some way to appease me, and one of them said was there anything they could do to get me to let them loose without turning them over to the sheriff? (*PMH*, 129)

It just so happens that the men were on the island ostensibly for the purpose of drawing a new map for the Army Corps of Engineers, and Lamb requests that they leave the island off the map altogether to make it hard for anyone else to find the place, a proposition they eagerly accept. Like another literary island controlled by its own Prospero, Lamb's place becomes a maze of forest and mire, difficult to navigate without a guide.

Although these elements lack the gothic resonance of details from Edgar Allan Poe's "The Fall of the House of Usher," for instance, in which a main character buries his sibling alive, the setting does contribute to the novel's shifting tone between that which is random, unpredictable, ugly, and terrifying and that which is darkly comic. It is this interplay among the violent, the tender, the humorous, and the torrid that makes this novel sometimes difficult to analyze.

Lust and Vacancy

Robard Hewes's narrative provides the torrid element in the novel. His lust for Beuna has intensified over time, in part because of Beuna's steady stream of correspondence charting her whereabouts and indicating her desire for him. Beuna has moved around with W. W., a baseball pitcher who has traveled in order to further his athletic career. In time, Beuna grows impatient to get back home, and through a series of manipulations, which include leaving W. W. and making him decide between his career and his wife, she does get her wish to live again in Helena, Arkansas. After she returns to Arkansas, the frequency of her letters increases, so that once a week Robard receives a missive that chronicles Beuna's love for him and her pleas for him to come and see her. Each letter is written on rose onionback paper and scented with Beuna's signature fragrance, a heady, sweet gardenia, so "thick and rank" that Robard's "neck prickled when he smelled it" (10).

Every encounter between Robard and Beuna is brimming with pent-up and forbidden sexuality. Once, while W. W. still pitched in Tulare, Robard made a trip to see Beuna, who sat next to him in the baseball stands and wore a red sunsuit with a halter top that "pinch[ed] her breasts up so that he doubted if she could swallow all the way down" (10). Just sitting with their thighs touching is enough to excite Beuna, who declares her love for Robard. He says merely, "All right" (11), a response meaningful enough to Beuna to inspire her confession that she is "*so* wet" (11). Robard seems to be rendered motionless by her attention and her repeated efforts to put her hand in his pants and grab him painfully. Repulsed and enthralled at the same time, Robard finds himself incapable of resisting her.

Oddly, these moments of heated groping and stilted confession provide ostensibly little satisfaction for both characters, neither of whom can identify what is missing in his or her life. It is during the visit to Tulare that Robard remembers that Beuna "had fixed on him with her pale flat eyes like a specimen she was studying, and there had been again the same forlorn miscalculation he had always seen, just as though it marked a vacancy she was beside herself wondering how to fill" (13). He considers that his words, "All right," in response to her "I love you" may have somehow disappointed her. But the vacancy that characterizes Beuna also characterizes Robard, and both try to fill this emptiness with each other, ignoring the fact that love is profoundly absent between them. Robard accepts his own moments of vacancy as "time separating whatever had gone before from whatever was just beginning" (8) and acknowledges that such moments simply require getting used to. He perceives, however, that his own life stands at the brink of a beginning that he makes synonymous with his journey to reunite with Beuna, despite, or perhaps because of, the fact that he leaves his other life with Jackie behind. Prey to his own miscalculation, Robard underestimates the cost of his liaison with Beuna.

Foreshadowing of Robard's fate occurs again during an earlier episode of Robard's journey. On this final trip to see Beuna, Robard picks up a woman who has car trouble, and the two make their way in the heat of the day to a garage, where the woman hopes to find help for her car, where they rent a hot and stifling room, and where each half-heartedly seduces the other. It is on this trip that Robard witnesses two actual signs and one metaphorical one. On the side of a truck covered in grease and dust, Robard sees two phrases in large writing: "WHACK MY OLD DOODLE, and below that, TAKE ANOTHER LITTLE PIECE OF MY HEART, as though one line followed the other and made good sense" (30). For Robard, the two phrases do get all mixed up together, and sex leads to a greater loss than he can imagine. He sees another less literal sign while he waits for the day to cool and to resume his journey; he watches the young girl whose family runs the garage feed caged animals, the largest of which is a lame bobcat. In that cage, she has placed a jackrabbit that huddles paralyzed and wide-eyed at the far end of the pen, against the gate, where it must wait until the bobcat makes its move. At the sight of the rabbit Robard shows more emotion than he does anywhere else in the novel, acknowledging a "tiny vein of panic" (29) and finally "an awful anguish" (41) when the rabbit succumbs. When the reader compares Robard's reaction to the rabbit to his reaction to the gar-devoured deer, his sympathy for the rabbit becomes significant if only by its singularity. Perhaps it is too easy for Robard to imagine the rabbit's plight; caught like the jackrabbit in the bobcat's gaze, Robard himself is subject to Beuna's pale stare, similarly paralyzed, similarly doomed, while Beuna seems as trapped and restless as the lame cat.

Beuna as Femme Fatale

Robard's story plays out very much in the tradition of film noir, complete with violence, treachery, moral ambivalence, and Beuna as the femme fatale. Despite all of the precautions that Robard takes and his apparently safe proximity to Beuna on the island, Robard finds himself double-crossed and, finally, dead, mainly because of Beuna's manipulation. From the very beginning, Beuna flaunts their relationship like the provocative clothing that she wears, keeping Robard scrambling to maintain a low profile. For example, in an early rendezvous arranged so that Robard will pick Beuna up in his truck at night, he catches sight of her in the dark:

> she was wearing tiny terry-cloth shorts that had shrunk up in her crotch and made her thighs look bigger than they could be and made him feel strangled, bound up, as if he wanted to be both in the truck and out of it someplace way away all at the same time. She had worried her hair up in little pencil curls that haloed her head and gave her face a round shape. She turned slightly in the light and smiled at him or toward wherever she thought he was in the truck, and rounded her eyes and unbuttoned her little sleeveless blouse until it sagged open and a big quarter of her breast nosed through the parting. (*PMH*, 148–49)

In passages describing Beuna's physical attributes, her body parts seem to take on a strange animalistic existence of their own (her breast "nosing" open her shirt, for example), a fact that makes it easy for the reader and Robard to objectify her. Such physicality jars with the image of her being illumined, Madonna-like, in the truck's headlights. Furthermore, almost every time Robard sees Beuna or physically touches her, the narrator describes Robard's experience in terms of some crushing weight or pressure, either by a "whirling gyro . . . being turned against him" (10), or shortness of breath, or, as depicted above, a sensation of being "strangled, bound up" somehow by the sight of Beuna's restrictive terry-cloth shorts. Ford's language suggests that Beuna's sexuality threatens Robard even as he is drawn to her. With her curls "haloing" her head, Beuna becomes simultaneously angelic and bestial, and like an actor on stage, she's waiting for the light to find her.

For Beuna, each encounter prompts her to turn her body into a show, an act that the reader must also watch. Such voyeurism occurs when Robard turns on his truck lights and catches a glimpse of Beuna's face "twisted in a mean way" (149) and her breasts breaking free of her blouse as she pulls her arm up to shield her eyes. As she blocks her own sight, she stands, exposed, for all the world to see, and any virginal glow is dispersed by such stark, glaring sexuality. She shouts at Robard; he turns off the lights, and the two of them end up making more commotion than they should. Robard is angry at Beuna for standing around and waiting for him in such a brazen way; she is angry at him for startling her. But their anger diminishes as Beuna confesses that she wants Robard to take her, to "tear [her] up. . . . in the back of the truck in the dirt and the rocks and the filthiness" (150).

For all of Beuna's ravenous appetite for sex, images of her repeatedly convey emptiness, either in her "flat" eyes (150), or her expression as she watches a hawk wing away above them: "Beuna looked up, as though she were hung on the fine edge of disappearing" (156). Only through aggressive sex and dirty talk does Beuna seem to experience her self and her body as something real, worth occupying. The imagery surrounding her sexuality heightens the split between something corporeal and incorporeal, carnal and spiritual. Her attempts at forging a relationship with Robard are savage and desperate, as if only the fiercely carnal can pull her vacant, orbiting self down to earth.

Clearly Robard is fascinated by Beuna's sexual assertiveness, even as his reactions suggest his discomfort in the face of her desire. Because these episodes are told from Robard's point of view, the reader should remember that it is possible that Robard is projecting some of his own emptiness onto Beuna, seeing reflected in her eyes what she may very well also see in his. Either way, the narrative makes it clear that this relationship is a perilous undertaking and will be unlikely to yield any real satisfaction to either party. Stronger in many ways than the men in her life, Beuna simply tries to get what she wants and what she needs, sexually and otherwise. For Robard, there proves to be a logical relation between the signs he's seen on the side of the truck: he loses more than just a piece of his heart. Both he and Beuna remain trapped in desire that is finally self-consuming.

Robard and Beuna's conflicting desires and expectations peak at their last encounter. Robard again is to pick Beuna up on the street, where she stands, "one foot on the curb and one square in the mouth of the gutter, looking like a white peony blossom" (279). But this sweet floral simile quickly gives way to something wilder: "Beuna was got up in a white gauze dress with a sateen boat top that looped down on top of her breasts. . . . She had on a pair of red shoes and a wide red belt that almost matched, and that was cinched so he wondered if she could breathe" (279). Beuna has dressed up because she believes that Robard is taking her to the Peabody Hotel in Memphis, the penultimate site of her sexual fantasies, where she and Robard will engage in the kinkiest sex act that Beuna can imagine. Beuna's last note to Robard, which he carries in his shoe, reads in part, "*Robard. I have me a plastic bag and a way to use it once I see you in the flesh*" (43), and Beuna believes that the two will use the bag at the Peabody. Robard, however, feels outrage at Beuna's posture and clothing; once again Beuna's flagrant appearance undercuts Robard's need to be inconspicuous. Angrily, he tells her she looks like a "harlot" (280), and the two end up at a cheap motel, where Robard has stayed briefly after leaving the island. They exchange more insults as Beuna realizes that Robard is not taking her to the Peabody, but, finally chagrined, she says she forgives him and beckons him into the bathroom. There amid the steam created by hot running water, Beuna starts disrobing Robard, who watches her as if he were mesmerized, her "legs shift[ing] and twitch[ing] behind the gauze dress . . . everything floating" (284); he starts to feel his ears "whir," and in the mirror catches a glimpse of himself with "sweat sprouting on his forehead, his eyes pale and unfocused" (284). He even grows faint in the steamy heat. Seemingly as helpless as the jackrabbit, Robard is transfixed here, practically naked, his paralysis reflected uncannily back to him in the mirror, while the whole scene reads like a spectacle that one grows increasingly reluctant to watch yet can't help watching. It is then that Beuna describes putting the little bag in her mouth and having Robard "go" (285), at which point in confusion and disgust Robard backs out of the humid bathroom until he can feel cooler air on his naked torso, while Beuna screams, "Yes, yes, yes. . . . You have to!" (285). Later, as the two dress, Beuna admits to Robard that she's told W. W. that Robard is in Elaine, and at this moment Robard knows that he needs to get Beuna home and himself as far away as possible.

Robard has decided prior to this last escapade that he's experienced enough of Beuna; he's already put a postcard in the mail to Jackie, promising that he will be home. His story's conclusion, however, obstructs Robard's best intentions, holding him accountable instead for his poor judgment. Eager to get out of town and get back to California, Robard only just comprehends that, even before he failed to meet Beuna's sexual expectations, Beuna had heightened the danger of their relationship by telling her husband that Robard was in town. In a swift and ironic ending, Robard barely manages to elude W. W. by heading back toward the boat camp in Elaine and taking a boat back to the island, where in Mr. Lamb's absence, the larger towheaded boy who has killed a man is now guarding the banks. Helpless in the boat, rather like the proverbial sitting duck, Robard realizes long before the boy raises his gun to his shoulder that in all likelihood he will be shot. In a desperate attempt to reveal his identity, he maneuvers the boat and brings it broadside. He "spread his arms so the boy could see him clearly in the prism of his scope, see his face, and recognize him as the old man's employee heading across to attend to business" (294–95), but the boy shoots and drops him into the water.

In scene after scene, then, Robard appears caught in a freeze-frame, rendered motionless by circumstance or his own obtuse reasoning, captivated senselessly by his own lust. He has literally gotten himself into a situation from which there is no way out. As Ford himself has said about *A Piece of My Heart,* "The end of the line for sex is at some point absurdity."[3] Whether caught in Beuna's strange, pale gaze, a steamy bathroom mirror, or the scope of a rifle, Robard becomes literally and metaphorically fixed as still as "a specimen [Beuna] was studying" (*PMH,* 13), his extinction self-determined, his lesson the vacancy of lust. And just as the reader is invited to watch Beuna's spectacle, at times her literal striptease, so the reader also spectates at the sight of Robard with arms spread, rather like an insect pinned by its wings, as exposed as Beuna ever has been.

Water: Death's Setting

Robard lives out a legacy of suggested infidelity; his father drowned in the company of another woman. Robard dreams about the incident while sleeping at the garage en route to Arkansas, and Ford uses another image of entrapment as he creates Robard's dream-memory. Robard begins to doze and imagine that it's raining so hard that the animals are floating away in the cages and that he must hang on to the bed or be swept away in the water. The scene shifts then, and he sees his mother in the yard talking to two men. His mother is angry, and the two men are "trying to avoid her eyes and get the story told and get gone" (37). The story turns out to be a chronicle of his father's death. Apparently headed to church for a service with a woman who survives to tell the tale, his father tried to ford a creek in his car in the middle of a rain, but the car stopped running in the creek bed's middle. The woman got out and waited out the rain under a bush, while his father stayed in the car, hunkered over the dashboard. While his father worked, the creek began to swell, until a wall of water swept against the car, trapping his father inside. The woman said that they looked at each other for a time, his father making gestures and mouthing words, until another wave washed over the car, which vanished beneath the dirty swollen water. In Robard's dream, he begins to feel the sensations that his father must have felt, providing another instance in which Robard seems trapped, like his father, behind the car windows, doomed only to gesticulate helplessly as the tide overwhelms him: "Robard felt himself to suffer the long breathless suspension, suspended between the moment of purchase and the moment when whatever it was had knocked him [his father] unconscious and made it feasible for him to drown in the floor of his own car, so that he felt that at any moment at all he could expect the impact and the long slow daze that ended by dying" (39). These images of suffocation occur apart from Robard's encounters with Beuna but immediately following his empty liaison with the woman whom Robard has picked up in his truck; they suggest that something about Robard's existence, perhaps his very impulse toward unfaithfulness, also renders him figuratively suspended between his father's indiscretions and his own. The pattern of imagery also occurs upon Robard's own death. After he hits the water, felled by the gunshot, "it hurt and felt cold all at one time, and the surface of the water seemed like a line bobbing in front of his eyes up and sideways and down again, like a lariat being snaked and twirled over the top of itself. And he could hear a loud and tremendous roaring and himself saying 'Oh, Oh,' and tried to see above the water and beyond the rocking boat nearby, but couldn't" (295). Here, the water as twirling lariat tightens around him, and he hears a roaring in his ears not unlike the whirring in his head that struck him in the steamy bathroom with Beuna. The ending to Robard's story, then, seems to ratify the reader's impression of him as one who fails to control his life, letting slip the relationship that he realizes is valuable, his marriage to Jackie, and plummeting instead into the bottomless pool of death.

In the novel, water recurs as the location of near-death or death experiences. The elder Hewes drowns a senseless death. Robard falls into the water when he is shot, and Newel almost drowns while taking a ritualistic swim in the river. Mark Lamb also dies on a boat in the middle of a lake. Both Hewes and Newel struggle to come to terms with their fathers' rather grim demises, and Lamb himself becomes a curious father figure, head of the island household that newly claims Robard and Sam as its members. Water as death's locale, then, unifies these disparate

plots, and the deaths of their fathers and Robard and Sam's memories of
those occurrences shape each son's identity and bridge their two narratives.

More Images of Enclosure and Drowning

Like Robard's father, Newel's father dies confined in a car. Driving to
New Orleans, his father got behind a flat-haul truck from which a load
of corrugated iron steel pipe fell directly into the front seat with such
force that it decapitated him. Newel's father sold starch to wholesalers
and traveled five days a week for 26 years, an existence that Newel finds
tragic. He tells Beebe that his father spent maybe "two-sevenths" (81)
of that time with his mother, whom he loved and with whom he was
even friends. The rest of the time he traveled "one hundred and fifty
miles a day, seven states" (80). Newel can only imagine the boredom of
spending night after night in a different motel room, but he remembers
his father acting like his job was fun, that he was glad to do it. Newel,
who is so paralyzed by his own minor physical afflictions that he can't
even complete an article for his law review, remains prey to his memories
of traveling with his father, puzzling and disconcerting memories that
appear for the reader in italics in Newel's narrative sections. Unlike
Robard, whose obsessions are physical in nature, Newel must come to
terms with some interior world that is, nonetheless, equally suffocating.

Several memories that Newel recollects deal in fact with literal
moments of feeling asphyxiated that occurred while Newel and his
mother traveled with his father. For example, while Newel and his
mother waited in the car, observing his father dealing with a wholesale
warehouse, he remembers a paucity of air even though his mother had
opened the car windows. As they waited, *"his mother drew a pencil diagram
of where the gears were on the steering column, and there, while they were suffocating, he learned to drive"* (86). Another time, he remembers his mother
hugging him *"so tight in the hot sun that he thought he would stop breathing"*
(232). Newel seems to find his own parents' lives so stultifying that he
fears his future will make him like them. His hypochondria and his
depression both seem extensions of his emotional reckoning with his
father's existence.

Significantly, Newel's journey to the island requires at least one trial
by water, a ritualistic swim that Newel takes as he recalls riding with his
father over and around the river but never once having felt the river
itself.[4] As he rejects the mechanistic (symbolized by his father's endless

days in the car) for the pastoral (symbolized by the water and the island), Newel faces death himself. He acknowledges as he waits poised above the water that many people who were really in suicidal throes probably "thought simply that they were taking an innocent swim in the river or the bay" (87). He plunges in to a feeling of breathlessness and cold: "Simultaneously he was confronted with two very unsettling facts. One was that in the time it had taken to get righted and regain a minimum amount of breath, he had moved a surprising distance from his clothes, which he could just see strewn in a circle twenty-five yards upstream. The other fact was that his shorts were now gone and he was floating with his privates adangle in the cold current, prey to any browsing fish" (88). The humor created by his naked exposure to nibbling fish becomes quickly overshadowed by Newel's other concern: the current's strength and rapidity. After extended moments of panic, sensations of static in his ears, numbness from the cold and general humiliation, Newel is rescued by some men who lasso him and pull him to shore, where he finds himself with rope burns and without sympathy from the men, who are amazed at his girth and his stupidity. As he gathers up his clothes, he becomes somewhat of a local spectacle. One little girl even hops out of a car to take his picture. But Newel offers no meditation upon this experience, no clue for the reader about its significance in his life or what, if anything, he has learned from it.

Newel's Open-ended Memories

Rather than have his narrator intrude with explication, in Newel's sections Ford uses the italicized vignettes to gloss many of Newel's present circumstances. Sometimes the connections are clearer than others, with some object providing the narrative link (the hotel towel in the case below), but often these vignettes raise more questions than they answer. For example, as Newel dries off from his river swim with a greasy towel from the Peabody Hotel, he drifts into memory again, a montage of scenes, first of his father and mother drunk and of his wandering off from the Chief Chisca Hotel to the Peabody, and then of his father telling about the ducks that march every day at the same time to the pond in the lobby and about the time that one of them was poisoned and how that made the rest of the ducks distrust their keeper until he dressed in a different-colored coat. Then, after a while, "*his father told him, sitting looking out the window of the Chief Chisca down on Union Avenue, the man went back to wearing his white jacket and the ducks could not remember they had thought he had betrayed them*" (94–95).[5] The anecdote might suggest that a betrayal, such as his parents' drunkenness, often recedes in significance over time, but as a resolution to Newel's anxiety, the story provides little relief. Such recollections are typical of Newel's italicized sections, which evoke Newel's past feelings of helplessness and his father's attempt to make narratives out of uncomfortable situations: stories that, finally, resist interpretation and provide no closure or comfort, but which have made powerful impressions upon Newel just the same.

One such section even closes the novel. The Epilogue is another of Newel's hotel memories, this time of the Roosevelt Hotel in New Orleans. As he and his father walked past an open hall door where a crowd was gathered, his father pushed his way in so that both he and Newel got a glimpse of "*a young man in his thirties with short blond hair and a square meaty face, lying face down half on his bed and half off, with his feet sticking straight up into the air like flagpoles, holding a pistol*" (296). His father told him to listen and "*you can hear the rattle in his throat*" (296). The photographer who has been taking pictures of the scene moved the man, and "*there was a faint sound from somewhere, like someone in the room had caught a fly in his throat and tried to cough it up without making any noise, and his father said, 'See? See? Did you hear it?' And he wasn't ever sure if he had heard it or not*" (296–97). Presumably referring to some death rattle, his father again tells Newel what to hear, but this time Newel expresses doubt that the story turned out the way his father told it: "*he wasn't ever sure if he had heard it or not*" (297). Such doubt suggests that Newel is finally distancing himself from his father's stories and the literal story of his father's life. Caught in a small space and subject to onlookers, the unknown man is not unlike the novel's other characters who find themselves trapped and watched mercilessly. The reader may even be reminded of Newel himself, half-naked in the little girl's camera viewfinder. Furthermore, as the novel's concluding section, Newel's open-ended memory leaves the novel open-ended as well. The reader may very well question what, if anything, redeems the novel from its emphasis on death and violence.

Vestiges of Local Color and Southwest Humor

The novel's comedy finds its origins in local color and southwest humor, both American literary traditions. William Byrd is often credited with the nascence of southwest humor in the eighteenth century. He wrote about the pastoral and the rural with an eye toward capturing the comic, which was almost always associated with depicting the poor white lower classes, capturing their dialect, and satirizing them for their incompetence. Local color as a style characterized much fiction written in the South immediately after the Civil War and refers to a way of dealing specifically with a region through characterization, setting, and voice. In its inception, local color writing usually offered little criticism of the region it described, evoking instead a sentimental or nostalgic view of the past often by characterizing blacks as happy and willing slaves whose lives were filled with singing and storytelling. Ford draws upon some of these strategies in *A Piece of My Heart:* he juxtaposes Newel's more educated speech with the sometimes crude utterances of Mr. Lamb and Beuna, yet he also pokes fun at Newel for his size and his ineffectualness; he satirizes the insular communities of Mississippi and Arkansas, where gun-toting boys regularly commit murder and the river ferryman has a hole in his neck; he even creates in Landrieu a kind of "feckless darky" who rolls his eyes but goes along with the antics of the white folks. But Ford seems to praise the pastoral even as he cautions against its potential for close-mindedness. On the one hand, Ford parodies the Old South associations that are conjured up through the Lambs' agrarian existence and their eternal patronizing of Landrieu. On the other hand, however, Ford uses the Lambs, who, despite their grotesqueries, have constructed their marriage with care and trust, to satirize Robard Hewes and Sam Newel for their failures to connect meaningfully with another person.

Most certainly working class, the Lambs suffer afflictions engendered by their circumstances. Mark lost his hearing in one ear during a cyclone and had all his rotten teeth pulled in Memphis; Fidelia lost her eye while working as a child in a broom factory before child labor laws. Now Mark has false teeth that sometimes "idl[e] uselessly at the bottom of his tea glass" (132), and Fidelia wears a prosthetic eye that is the "same yellowish hazel color" as her other one but is not a "working eye in the ordinary sense and own[s] a slightly mesmerized cast" (163). These, along with their other peculiarities, make Mark and Fidelia Lamb potentially comic figures. Their rather isolated lives make them even more curious. Every night, Fidelia hovers over a radio that Mark has given her, trying to tune in the police scanner, and Mark gets angry because some hunters have failed to show up, even though he has not thought it necessary to confirm their itinerary since last year's trip. The Lambs live by their own rules and succeed remarkably well despite their incapacities.

Their relationship with Landrieu is curious, at best. Like a paid slave, Landrieu follows their orders and often exists as the object of Mark's unrelenting ridicule. He addresses Lamb as Mr. Mark and generally subsists on Lamb's rather patriarchal generosity, having on the one hand the freedom to talk back to Lamb that his enslaved predecessors would not have had but on the other hand finding himself equally subservient and objectified. For example, Lamb tells Newel the story of Landrieu's fishing techniques, a story that ends with Landrieu getting a hook stuck in his face, his flat-out refusal to let Mark pull it out, and his insistence upon emergency room treatment instead. Fascinated by Landrieu but clearly considering himself superior, Lamb tells Newel,

> "Landroo's a comical old coon. When he comes out here [fishing], he won't go right to where them jugs are at. He'll rig him up a cane pole and take a bunch of whatever he likes that day, worms or roaches or whatever's he got in his 'farm,' and start down there in them dead falls and nigger all the way up to here." The old man grinned at him in amazement as if Landrieu were a living mystery to match all mysteries, never divining Landrieu might take some considerable pleasure in the leisurely divertissement of fishing. (*PMH*, 246)

Lamb's colloquial speech, his penchant for the stereotype and derogatory terminology ("coon," and the use of "nigger" as a verb, for example), contrasts sharply in this passage with the narrative from Newel's point of view (the use of the subjunctive "as if Landrieu *were* a living mystery" [italics mine], the phrasing and vocabulary of the "leisurely divertissement of fishing"). Such juxtaposition allows Ford to emphasize the rhetorical failure of language; the reader recognizes Lamb as a type himself, one so mired in certain assumptions about race that he will never see his way clear, no matter how obvious the explanation for Landrieu's preferred fishing method. But the reader also finds in Newel a sensibility that verges on the affected; he may be able to articulate the circumstances more cleanly and less offensively than Lamb, but finally he remains just as narrow in his way of seeing. Using Lamb as the Old South voice and Newel as the equally problematic New South voice, Ford sneaks in a bit of southwest humor here, making clear the class differences and regional traits that lend themselves easily to comedy and satire.

Lamb himself champions humor at every opportunity, often telling jokes and poking fun at Newel for his lawyerly attitude. For example, he says, "there's these two old farmers sittin side by side in the privy, and one old farmer stands up and starts to grab his braces and all his change falls out down the hole. And right quick he reaches down in his pocket, pulls out his wallet, and throws a twenty-dollar bill right in there after it. And the other old farmer says, 'Why, Walter, what in the world did you do that for?' And the first old farmer says, 'Wilbur, if you think I'm going down in that hole for thirty-five cents, you're crazy as hell.' Haw haw haw haw haw." (*PMH*, 116)

Although Robard laughs at this joke, Newel can only bring himself to smile, causing Lamb to speculate that he needs a laxative: " 'You look like you could use a good reamin,' " he says (116). These passages illustrate Ford's use of the vernacular in Lamb's speech and the way that Lamb becomes both spokesman for humor and the target of the reader's amusement. Lamb's main problem is that he fails to distinguish between jokes that are funny and those that are derogatory, in one instance telling Hewes and Newel about a "nigger caught stealing ax handles" (132). Neither Robard nor Sam laughs, though Landrieu giggles, inspiring Lamb's tirade:

"You bastards lack one necessary. . . . A sense of humor. Every god-damned one of you young people don't know what in the fuck's funny and what ain't. I asked some little asshole in Helena last week, just to be a-talking to him, without nothing to gain on it, just bein friendly, I said, 'Where the hell do all you kids come from?' And the bastard looked at me like I was a pail of shit and said, 'You tell me. You're the ones been having us the last thirty years.' " The old man glowered flatly and stumped away into the other room. (*PMH*, 132–33)

The irony is that Lamb is right: to some extent both Hewes and Newel lack a sense of humor, especially about themselves. Landrieu's reaction—"T. V. A. started giggling" (132)—remains uninterpreted for the reader. One reading could account for his "giggle": so long used to Lamb's ways, Landrieu perpetually masks himself for the sake of household harmony, and, in some implicit recognition of societal hierarchy, he acts as the shuffling minstrel figure. Or perhaps Ford offers a parodic nod to local color here, creating a black character whose patience with white folks seems sentimental rather than realistic.

In keeping with literary realism, however, Ford offers no explicit judgment of Lamb or any of the other characters; the reader constructs an interpretation based on his or her own associations. One not offended by the word "nigger," for example, or the implicit stereotyping of black

people as apt to steal, would probably also find Lamb's joke funny.
Given the time of the book's action, the early seventies, it is consistent
with Lamb's attitude and background that he would think nothing of
telling such a joke. Unconcerned with "political correctness," Ford
allows the reader to draw his or her own conclusions. Using all three of
these characters—Lamb, Hewes, Newel—as objects of humor, however,
Ford gives the reader permission to find them absurd at times and even
deserving of their fates, and thus Ford succeeds in satirizing them for
their failures.

Lamb, for instance, dies a comic death precipitated by his own impatience. He insists that Newel accompany him on a fishing trip whereby
he will "telephone" the fish rather than catch them with the usual line
and lure. Toward that end, he hauls along a "little black metal box with a
smooth wood-handled crank and two long half-stripped copper leads fastened to gold thumbscrews at either end" (236). The reader may realize
before Newel does that the old man plans to stun the fish using an electric charge. The first attempt is dramatic: "in a loud stage whisper that
made the one nervous turtle dive for the bottom [Mr. Lamb] said, 'I'm
just going to make a local call.' The old man's eyes squeezed together as
if he could barely keep back the heaves, and he promptly jammed both
wire ends over the side and into the water like an old picador administer-
ing the pic" (247–48). But the end result is that nothing happens. Such
disappointment instigates Mr. Lamb's more vigorous cranking of the
box, his "increasing gyrations" (248) enough to make the boat rock and
sway so fiercely that Newel fears they will capsize. Mr. Lamb cranks until
his face turns red and sweat darkens his shirt. Giving Newel a "defiant
look" (248), he grabs quickly and carelessly for the wires, touches both
ends at once, and unwittingly electrocutes himself: "'Oops,' the old man
said in an obvious surprise, and threw up both his hands, dropping the
cords into the water and pitching straight over backward into the middle
of the boat, making a loud whumping sound on the chinky curvature of
his spine, his eyes wide open as if he were about to instigate another imitation of Landrieu but had somehow gotten sidetracked" (249). Newel
determines that Lamb is dead, then clumsily maneuvers the boat to
shore, gets Lamb into the jeep, and drives him back to the house, where
Landrieu will break the news to Mrs. Lamb. Though Mark's death is
clearly ridiculous on some level, Mrs. Lamb responds with poise and controlled grief, telling Robard and Sam that just that morning Mark had
confessed to a feeling that his heart was going to stop and that she had
been preparing herself all day for the inevitable.

Fidelia as Foil

Transforming the absurd into the preordained, Fidelia preserves her own dignity and Mark's in the face of Newel and Hewes's less focused existences. Her constancy to Mark, the fidelity that her name denotes, exists in stark contrast to the scattered emotions of the two men who find themselves in her company yet unable to chart their own lives on any constructive course. As Newel prepares to go off to Chicago and Hewes prepares for one last visit to Beuna, Newel scoffs at Hewes's lack of discretion, calling him "goddamned stupid" to be "dicking around" after another man's wife (271). Soon after, of course, Hewes will find himself pitching into the lake, and the novel will close with Newel's memory of the dead man on the anonymous hotel bed. Neither Robard nor Sam achieves the intimacy epitomized by the Lambs' relationship.

Fidelia has acted as Mark's ballast, a stabilizing influence, and together she and her husband plot their lives according to their own beliefs and the natural rhythms of the island. Earlier in the novel, Mark becomes flustered, belligerent, and rude. Fidelia calmly tells him to "sit down" and to "wipe [his] mouth" (167). Able to deal sympathetically with her husband even in the midst of one of his many tirades, Fidelia emerges as the voice of reason amid the ridiculous. Both she and Mark protect their family interests above all else, at one time harboring Fidelia's cousin even though he was accused of murder, simply because he was family. Fidelia also questions Sam about his intentions toward Beebe, her granddaughter. Living by their own codes rather than society's, the Lambs seem more than a little anachronistic. Mrs. Lamb tells Newel that they're "very much tied to the river stages . . . more than to the clock and the calendar" (179). What seems absurd and uncontrollable to Robard and Sam—the uncharted mystery of the island—is comforting to Mrs. Lamb, who presides as an ordering maternal force in the midst of male anger, impatience, and lust. Fidelia's attitude makes her husband's absurdity, Newel's indecisiveness, and Hewes's lasciviousness seem constricting and narrow-minded approaches to life. Like the island itself, which is to some extent unknowable, Fidelia will persist in the face of death.

Mysterious Territory

A Piece of My Heart defies easy classification; the novel floats between several traditions of literature and film, belonging finally on no one map. Its very structure—the alternating narratives and the italicized vignettes—keeps the reader on shifting ground. Ford's characterizations make possible the frequent collapsing of the violent and the comic, one undercutting the other, dragging one layer of story aside to reveal its antithesis. Via its many dichotomies, Ford's first novel sustains its open-endedness, resisting thematically and structurally any literary claustrophobia.

Chapter Three

"As if Located Was the Illusion": A Modern Predicament in *The Ultimate Good Luck*

The Ultimate Good Luck (1981), Richard Ford's second novel, departs in theme and style from his first book, *A Piece of My Heart,* and from his more well-known later novels, *The Sportswriter* and *Independence Day.* As its title suggests, *The Ultimate Good Luck* is to some extent about forces—luck, fate, love—that defy a human being's control. In its emphasis on the unpredictable and at times dizzying and disconcerting external world, this book is modernist in its theme: the world is an alien place and we are isolated in it, doomed to desire connection with others but often thwarted in that attempt. As a native Mississippian who resists the category of "southern writer" and who lives much of the year in Paris and Montana, Ford himself seems a bit of an expatriate. A self-confessed admirer of Hemingway and Faulkner, Ford manipulates setting and "location," a word he uses deliberately to refer to something decidedly other than place in this novel. Despite a modernist framework and a main character whose circumstances and attitude make him kindred to such fictional voices as Ernest Hemingway's Jake Barnes, here Ford slips deftly out of the shadow of both a southern legacy and a modernist one.

American Literary Modernism: A Review

Modernism as a literary movement had its origins in Europe in the late nineteenth century; for purposes of brevity and relevance, however, I'll focus here on American literary figures writing in the early-to-mid twentieth century, providing a very brief and general explanation of the meaning of "modernism." The term refers to an artistic response to social and cultural stimuli at the century's turn and following, including the advent of mass communications (electricity, telegraph, telephone), the invention of the automobile, World War I, the eighteenth amendment mandating the prohibition of alcohol, increased freedom for women, more relaxed sexual standards, and scientific, psychological, and cultural theories that undermined old assumptions about universal order and selfhood (Einstein's theory of relativity, Freud's notions of the "unconscious," Marx's focus on economics and social division along class lines, to name only a few).[1] Such radical changes in culture and society prompted a general reaction of disillusionment, uncertainty, and isolation, especially among artists and writers, many of whom left the United States for Europe, or expatriated, spending years in Paris or other foreign cities, where they could paint or write unencumbered by local ties.

Uncertainties about self, other, and society made "meaning" become a relative term. Rather than creating works that provided an easily discernible message, writers began experimenting with forms that would reflect the fragmentation that they observed all around them. Poets and critics such as Ezra Pound and William Carlos Williams advocated "making it new," casting off what they considered worn-out prescriptions for poetry and replacing them with vivid images, details, and lines that did not necessarily depend upon iambic pentameter for their rhythm. Poet Wallace Stevens rejected religion, embracing art in its stead. Because the external world no longer exemplified security or order, art, in form and theme, signified disorder as well, requiring the reader or observer to let go of certain assumptions and grapple with the text or painting without much help from the writer or artist. At the same time, however, art became the source of spiritual enlightenment, the one reliable force worth belief and dedication.

In modernist fiction, less reliable first-person or even multiple narrators, plots that were nonlinear rather than chronological, and open endings replaced the authoritative narrative voice that provided exposition and neatly explained plot and character in the long eighteenth- and nineteenth-century novel. Published in 1926, Ernest Hemingway's *The Sun Also Rises* has often been heralded as an exemplar of modernism. Its narrator, the impotent Jake Barnes, laconically details his experiences with a group of fellow expatriates in France and Spain post–World War I. Jake's physical war wound symbolizes his emotional impotence, his failure to connect with his true love, Lady Brett Ashley, his ironic distancing from anyone about whom he cares. Similarly, Hemingway's spare, tough prose mirrors Jake's suspicion of language and his failure to make words bridge the isolation between one person and another. The novel vividly captures post-world-war despair, lethargy, and empty decadence, and Jake's line to Brett—"Isn't it pretty to think so?"—has become the ironic rejoinder to modernist hopes for redeeming love.

Southern Responses to Postwar Despair

Published in 1930, the agrarian manifesto *I'll Take My Stand,* a collection of essays authored by John Crowe Ransom, Allen Tate, Andrew Lytle, Robert Penn Warren, and Donald Davidson, among others, provided arguments for the sustenance of southern culture in the face of corporate consumerism, increased industrialization, and other effects of the societal changes mentioned above. Due to its response in part to the Scopes Trial in Tennessee in 1925, the infamous debate over the teaching of evolution in Tennessee public schools, and in part to its implicit acceptance of a world made possible largely through slave labor, the volume has always been controversial and subject to much criticism. H. L. Mencken's scathing satire of the South as the "Sahara of the Bozart," the figurative desert of the *beaux arts* or finer manifestations of culture, quickly made the South defensive as a region, at once centering its energies while struggling to define itself aesthetically. Davidson, Ransom, Tate, et al., set out to promote agrarianism over industrialization, to state common beliefs about ways to consider man and his surroundings, to privilege life lived closely to and in accordance with land- and family-based ideals. The essayists suggested that paramount to man's fidelity to religion and to his fellow man was his reverence for nature. Such a reverence would make possible a better way of life, one conducive to spiritual and artistic pursuits. In theory perhaps an attractive idea, agrarianism was nonetheless problematic, if not least because it ignored those whose labor was required to ensure such a leisurely life of the mind for the white male, its audience and its biggest proponent. Nonetheless, the volume depicted human beings as isolated, trapped in a fragmented culture, unmoored from place, and finally subject to a loss of identity, all notions in keeping with the modernist predicament. Although the Scopes Trial and the publication of *I'll Take My Stand* both focused negative attention on the South (ironically, in the case of the latter, since Donald Davidson was attempting to protest what he considered the dismissal of southern intellectualism), they also opened the door for the voluminous discussions and debates among writers, sociologists, literary critics, and journalists that ensued.[2] Even as the intellectual promise of the South was questioned, writers such as William Faulkner and Thomas Wolfe inaugurated what would be known as the Southern

Renascence in the 1920s and 1930s. To some extent, then, the South's response to the forces that instigated modernism also may have sparked the region and its writers' hallowing of physical place.

Without Country, Without Place

Departing from the gothic southern terrain of *A Piece of My Heart,* Richard Ford's second novel supplants place with displacement, recognizable ground with that which is violence-torn, concrete physical sources of comfort with ineffable, perhaps even spiritual, spots of being. Ford's Harry Quinn is a war veteran, in this case of Vietnam, who finds himself expatriate-like in Mexico, where he has gone to free his old girlfriend's brother Sonny, who is jailed on drug charges. Told from Quinn's point of view, *The Ultimate Good Luck* is also the love story of Quinn and Rae, who comes to Mexico bringing the money that Quinn will need to orchestrate Sonny's release. Caught in the middle of complex political maneuvering on the part of their Mexican lawyer named Bernhardt, Quinn and Rae try again to forge their relationship.

However, it is only by becoming "located" that Quinn may escape his self-imposed isolation and reconnect with Rae. But by "location," Quinn means something utterly different from physical place. In stark contrast to the alienation that Quinn feels in Mexico and has felt since his return from Vietnam, for Quinn being "located" signifies a moment of pure being, an intense awareness of self and, perhaps, an other. Setting remains crucial in this novel—as sultry and perspiration-inspiring as any part of Faulkner's Yoknapatawpha County—but Ford's redefinitions undercut the conventional southern reverence for and centrality of physical place. Underlying the potential redemption of each notion—whether luck, location or love—is its predetermined, and perhaps necessary, transience. "Location," then, departs significantly in meaning from its southern counterpart, "place," which usually connotes rootedness, stability, some constant that may bring comfort to a wanderer through memory.

Setting: Reincarnations of Modernist Landscapes

Oaxaca, Mexico, where Sonny is imprisoned, is crowded, patrolled by soldiers, governed in part by rich, corrupt officials, subject to terrorist bombings, and inhabited by those protected by the government and those marginalized by poverty or other marks of class distinction. As such, *The Ultimate Good Luck's* setting contains elements of danger, greed, and instability, an environment in which a Vietnam veteran such as Harry Quinn might spring into action. Money here is the key to power, and the city runs on the same kind of faceless commercialism that earlier twentieth-century thinkers resisted and lamented. One of the most vivid images of modern culture, in fact, is that of the sterile wasteland in dire need of rain or authentic fertility in the wake of mechanistic, automated, and abortive attempts at procreation and creation.[3] Set at least 40 years after the heyday of modernism, with the years between bringing the stock market crash, World War II, the Holocaust, the Korean War, and the Vietnam War, Ford's second novel certainly evokes a state of crisis and the perils—both emotional and physical—associated with such a state. Not a "southern" novel in any traditional sense of that word, *The Ultimate Good Luck* also subverts or undermines several associations with the modernist world it recreates so well, down to the spare Hemingwayesque prose that Ford adopts.

But like his modernist predecessors, Ford uses images and symbols in this novel to suggest meaning, or nuances of meaning, beyond the literal landscapes in which the characters find themselves. The landscape itself in fact becomes crucial to the novel's evocation of character and mood, shifting from lush to cold to bare as it reflects Quinn's, and sometimes Rae's, preoccupations. (Rae is actually a landscape painter.) Ford often inserts an image into these descriptive passages that defies the literalness of its surroundings, that jars, either by trick of color or light, with the rest of the landscape's palette. It is the intrusion of the metaphysical into the world of the physical that makes this novel's landscapes slightly surreal.

Ironically, contemplation of a landscape may permit some escape from place and as such be the first step toward achieving what Quinn calls "locatedness." For example, in Vietnam Quinn has experienced a kind of self-transcendence by studying patterns of light and by seeing things in a certain way. As Quinn's thoughts reveal,

> the right distribution of eastern grey and composite green on the surface of an empty paddy and a line of coconut palms could give you a loop, and for a special celestial moment you wouldn't be there at all, but be out of it, in an evening's haze of beach on Lake Michigan with teals like flecks of grey space skittering down the flyway toward Indiana, and the entire day would back up sweetly against a heavy wash of night air. And you could put it away then, ease your eyes, and wander outside another

moment and join the world before the landscape began to function again as a war zone. (*UGL*, 24)

The "celestial moment," the "loop," the possibility of wandering "outside of another moment" all involve exceeding the boundaries of the present, a warping of time. Here, as in other instances in the novel when a character zooms in on a landscape, the interplay of color and light also proves instrumental; the "right distribution of eastern grey and composite green" allows one place to blur into another. Thus, a verdant, wet landscape and bird-filled sky replace a war zone, if only temporarily, and several times over the novel's course, violence, or the threat of danger, prefigures an image at odds with present circumstance, a vision and revision of reality.

In Mexico, virtually another war zone, Quinn and Rae witness the bombing of a Baskin Robbins in the plaza of the Centro district of Oaxaca, an unpredictable explosion that sends glass and body parts flying. At first Quinn tries to help salvage bodies and look for survivors, particularly an American family whom he and Rae have observed moments before the blast. He soon realizes, however, that he should not draw attention to himself and returns to Rae, who has crumpled to the ground, paralyzed by fear and shock. Urging her to get up, Quinn kneels with her and then stands, suddenly lightheaded. Rae protests that "there's no place to go" (119), a line that succinctly encapsulates their predicament, the fact that they themselves are dislocated in the midst of such danger, or, at least, should be. No longer recognizable as the place they have been inhabiting easily just minutes before, the plaza erupts in confusion, gunfire, and death. Presiding over all is a green parrot that Quinn sees, inexplicably motionless in the midst of chaos, standing "out on the hot pavement perfectly still, its red target eye blinking at the sunlight" (119). Ford closes this chapter with this image and with Quinn's taking of Rae's hand. The exotic bird becomes even more strange in the unexpected aftermath of the bombing, its very colors suggestive of life (green) and blood (red), its eye targeting its surroundings like the bead on a gun. A jarring image, the parrot is not the first strange creature to preside over a landscape in this novel.

Soon after Rae has left Quinn for the first time, Quinn goes to Chicago to see a woman whom he has met. As he dozes on the train in Indiana, he sees a snowman that has been built in the "center of the eastbound main line to Detroit" (86). Certainly out of place in this location, the snowman and its odd accouterments are a peculiar sight: "Its lineaments were crisp, and there were heavy prints flattening a circle around the base. The snowman was tricked out with gravel features, a blue and gold watch cap, and a half broomstick, and stood between the shining frozen rails, smiling perfectly into the face of its own hot doom" (86). In a winter landscape, the brightness of the "shining rails," the snowman's blue and gold cap, and its "crisp lineaments" make the snowman seemingly defiant in the face of its imminent destruction, coldly impervious to its "hot doom." What's particularly interesting about this sight, however, is that Quinn yokes it with his own misfortune later in the day: an altercation with a strung-out driver over Quinn's honking at his car. The crazy man confronts Quinn on the street, ultimately striking him with a sharp object that rips Quinn's coat and leaves a sizable, yet fortunately shallow, gash on his arm. Such sudden violence, right in the middle of urban Chicago, trips Quinn's memories of Vietnam, and, more specifically, a fear he has cultivated strangely *after* his homecoming, what he calls a "conspicuous undisciplined fear of enormous injury" (88). Such fear haunts Quinn, and well after his encounter with the junkie in Chicago, he starts awake at night, sure that disaster is about to befall him. In those moments, he remembers "not the junkie who cut him on Kenwood Avenue . . . but the snowman in the train yards at South Bend, standing erect and by himself, smiling out at some disaster rising up on the horizon" (88). This strange image both comforts and disturbs Quinn; the snowman's smile is perhaps too perfect, too vacant, too oblivious, even as it scoffs at destruction.

Any reader of Wallace Stevens will also think of his poem called "The Snow Man," published originally in the 1923 volume, *Harmonium*. The poem suggests that anyone who has contemplated a winter landscape for a long time and been cold in the midst of icy trees may also find it difficult not to think of misery. The bare landscape, the wind, the cold all find their way back to the one, the poem says, "who listens in the snow, / And, nothing himself, beholds / Nothing that is not there and the nothing that is."[4] The observer, the listener, becomes part of the barren landscape, seeing there what is lacking in himself as well as what is lacking outside of the self. He is nowhere, a "no man" emptied out by the blank white vacancies around him. The poem is unquestionably modernist in theme.

Though Ford himself is an admirer of Wallace Stevens, there is no evidence to suggest that he had this poem in mind during the construction of his snowman scene. The resonances with the poem, however, are interesting, for Quinn also deals with some hollowness in himself, something that is subject to disappearance. This bleak and unredeemable interior place corresponds to the exterior landscape presided over by the dapper and goofily grinning snowman, an image strikingly at odds with its location.

Quinn frequently imagines himself balanced precariously on the edge of some gaping space, rather like the snowman, gaining a strange kind of adrenaline kick from such a risk. As he observes the Mexican landscape, beautiful yet treacherous, he thinks, "It was like a *National Geographic,* a stricken landscape that appealed to you the moment you realized you'd never be there. Only, he thought, he was there now, and it made him feel on the edge of something dangerous, as though a sense of lucklessness swam in the air around him" (*UGL,* 125). The ultimate good luck, as Quinn will explain later, always involves transcending the present landscape, and it's best if that instance of transcendence entails more than the "celestial moment" or "loop" he has experienced in Vietnam. Some kind of vivid self-awareness must also occur. Quinn often considers the consequences of being without luck, and he fears becoming luckless, marooned in that state without an escape route. He acknowledges nonetheless that "everybody lives in some relation to the luckless" (127). Living life successfully involves finding the right balance between protecting one's self and letting go, or, as Quinn thinks, "when you *tried* to protect yourself completely and never suffer a loss or a threat, you ended up with nothing. Or worse, you ended up being absorbed right into nothing, into the very luckless thing you were most afraid of" (127). The concept of "nothing," then, becomes synonymous with lucklessness, the emptiness one must avoid at all costs. It is no wonder that the image of the snowman, its absence of color heightened by its jaunty blue and gold cap, haunts Quinn.

Rae's relationship with the landscape differs markedly from Quinn's. For one thing, she seems supremely adaptable. Any place that she and Quinn move is "just another place to her" (43). Wherever they are, she can sit outside, painting or drawing landscapes that she copies out of *National Geographic*s or *Audubon*s. While she "simply adapted right" (43), Quinn notes a hollowness in himself where only Rae can "[make] a feeling come" (43). Rae confesses that she has never found a place that she liked (129), and when she leaves Quinn the first time she does so in deep winter in Michigan, where Quinn is a game warden. Quinn believes that Rae is "locked in present time" (43), "with a view of the world she had learned to put herself into with ease" (44). Such a state is at once desperate and liberating, in Quinn's opinion, since he is constantly battling time and place to make both yield something beyond themselves.

Talk Is Risky

Quinn, a Michigan native, is anything but at ease with the world around him. He finds himself among people but isolated nonetheless. He resists easy integration into his surroundings. He eschews what the narrator calls "nonessential conversation" because, simply put, "Talk was risky" (1). Eerily like Jake Barnes, who tells Brett that she'll lose the moments with Pedro Romero if she talks about them, Quinn believes in stripped-down, utilitarian language, and, to some extent, in relationships conducted under similar provisions. As the novel opens, he picks up a girl in a cafe, and before returning to his apartment for the inevitable one-night stand, he takes her to the fights, where two young Zapotec boys jab stiffly and timidly at each other until the crowd goads them to real and bloody violence. It is this nonverbal language with which Quinn is most comfortable and which he has anticipated with pleasure: "[Fights between boys] were stand-up and correct fights, and the punches drew blood precisely" (4). Unlike words, which can be sloppy, hit or miss, punches are precise, unquestionable signifiers of some emotion: power, aggression, fear, anger.[5] Sex, though somewhat more imprecise than a punch, is still preferable to conversation, so after the fight Quinn takes his date, who by now is quite drunk and prone to hallucination from imbibing too much mescal, back to his room. With physical contact always a more sure thing than emotional connection, Quinn opts for the carnal over the cerebral, for the time being better able to protect his body than his mind.

　　Quinn, who usually avoids the company of women because they "pushed things out of shape too fast" (*UGL,* 3), thinks in this case that "sometimes you had to adjust your routine to serve the circumstances, and the circumstances added up that he wanted the girl to stay" (3). After the sex is over and before she leaves, the girl says to Quinn, quite rightly, "Well I think you're an asshole" (12). From this moment, Ford conveys Quinn's propensity to use others to serve his own desires, and in the early chapters of the novel, Quinn's character materializes as a tough guy, a loner unlucky in love and with no ties to anyone or any place, just the sort who could spring his old girlfriend's brother from a foreign prison.

Quinn operates under the assumption that he is in danger, and his instincts, in fact, prove to be correct. He has paid Bernhardt to get a judge to arrange for a document of release for Sonny, a transaction that will require $10,000, the money that Rae is bringing with her to Mexico. Sonny has been imprisoned for drug trafficking, for being the mule who smuggles cocaine from one place to the other, but he has also been accused by his contact of skimming the cocaine before letting himself be arrested. This latter accusation complicates Sonny's release and sends Quinn into the underworld of Mexican drug smuggling, despite Bernhardt's promised protection.

A Modern Predicament

Such circumstances only confirm Quinn's perspective: he is an outsider and should trust no one. Ironically, the words of his one-night-stand haunt Quinn. She has said that Quinn suffers from the problem that plagues "foreigners in a strange country"; she says, "you lack a frame of reference that allows you to take the right mental picture" (12). Nonetheless, Quinn resolves to distance himself from his surroundings and from others because, as he believes, "intimacy just made things hard to see, and he wanted things kept highly visible" (21). His wartime experiences become relevant again: "In the war you maintained your crucial distance from things and that kept you alive, and kept everything out in front of you and locatable" (44). In this instance, by "locatable" Quinn means something tangibly present, easily seen. (Later, as Quinn gives into his need for Rae, he will surrender the visible for what cannot be seen or named.) Although Quinn is not physically impotent like Jake Barnes, the war has left its own emotional scars. Quinn fears involvement because, from his experience, being intimate means literally risking your life. Rae left Quinn, in fact, because Quinn was unable to commit to her even though he loved her, and this emotional impotence has left a gap, an emptiness, that Quinn can name but cannot fill. He knows what he calls a "feeling of detachment and impairment" (132), but he has isolated himself for so long that he doesn't know how to avoid the pressure of "empty space . . . closing down around him" (132). All of his contacts in Mexico are impersonal connections, relationships established through and for the exchange of goods and services, commercial in venture. Not only does Quinn lack a frame of reference because he is a stranger to Mexico, but he also establishes a very rickety frame of relationships. At any time, any one person could pull out of the structure, rendering it flimsy and collapsible. This is, in fact, exactly what happens; the impersonal network of exchange is a fragile one.

In one last effort to regain Rae's trust and perhaps to combat his own tendencies toward isolation, Quinn has agreed to help her brother. In so doing he becomes more deeply embroiled in Bernhardt's world of bribery and betrayal, strangely reliant upon people he doesn't even know, and ironically more alienated as a result. Bernhardt, it turns out, has been sleeping with Susan Zago, the wife of the man who heads the drug smuggling operation, and whose man, Deats, Sonny has allegedly cheated out of part of the cocaine. These bizarre relationships lead Quinn to define his own modern predicament:

> It was nuts . . . to be tied to somebody, two counting Bernhardt, you had no feeling about, but who somehow made all the difference. That was the essence of the modern predicament. The guy who had it in for you was the guy you'd never seen. The one you loved was the one you couldn't be understood by. The one you paid to trust was the one you were sure would cut and run. The best you could think was maybe you'd get lucky, and come out with some skin left on. (*UGL,* 35)

When Bernhardt is murdered, Quinn realizes that he has gone "all the way inside" (196), as Bernhardt had said he had to, but that he is too far in.

Susan Zago sends for him to work out another deal; the family's employees are young boys with whom Susan conducts trifling affairs, and one of these boys has a brother who is a guard at Sonny's prison. When Quinn goes to see Susan Zago, he is frisked by a young boy, heavily armed, who misses the gun Quinn has hidden in the small of his back. As the boy runs gentle hands over him and looks him in the eyes, Quinn ponders the strange intimacy created between those who know they hold each other's lives in their hands: "It felt odd, Quinn thought, always to be intimate with strangers, never with people you cared about. Kids with guns. . . . It had to be another phase of the modern predicament" (190). Once Quinn is inside, Muñoz, the boy whose brother is a prison guard, tries to strike the deal. For $5,000, he says, he can get Sonny out that very night. The catch is that Quinn must give him the money up front, despite Quinn's negotiation that he would give half now and half when Sonny is free. As a gesture that is supposed to communicate sincerity and trust, Muñoz shows Quinn the dead body of Deats, the man whom Sonny has allegedly cheated. But by now Quinn is skeptical; he has trusted Bernhardt for nothing, and he is not about to risk losing his money. Jumpy and quick to point their guns at Quinn, the young boys make sudden moves. The scene erupts in violence, ending with the deaths of Muñoz, Susan Zago, and Bernhardt's assassin, the young boy whose inexperience has allowed Quinn to keep his gun.

Almost cinematic in its effect, Ford's prose here captures the urgency of the situation with one movement ricocheting off another: "A body came into the frame very low, and there was a yellow and red flash and the room was full of noise, and Susan Zago was in silhouette, then knocked sideways as though someone had grabbed her shoulder and flung her out of the way" (195). Even the description suggests Quinn's powerlessness to stop the action: the body suddenly appearing in the door frame, Susan Zago being "flung" aside. Only through his own violent action can Quinn exit this place. Moments after, he muses, "He wondered . . . if he'd perfected something in himself by killing three people he didn't know, when he had come at the beginning, simply to save one, and if now he had pleased anybody anywhere. Though he thought if he hadn't pleased anybody, at least he'd tried to, and had performed it under control, and he hadn't coped so bad all by himself at the end. He thought, in fact, that he'd done fine" (197). Espousing a hybrid theory of stoicism and existentialism, Quinn justifies his decisions. He has done the best that he could do, under less than pleasant circumstances, and if his attempts have actually made no difference, then at least he's survived, and done so only by virtue of himself.

Quinn's understanding of this modern predicament, then, depends upon the factors of eventual violence, of circumstances being out of his control, of death staring him in the face. It is possible, however, that Quinn seeks violence to startle him out of another kind of modern predicament, and that is his inability to connect with others except through meaningless sex and overt aggression. Quinn's wartime skills serve him well in the midst of danger and quite poorly when confronted with love. Despite his epiphany in the wake of the killings, he still misses the point of human intimacy, that which is based on love, and, as such, is always subject to loss.

Quinn does not deal well with risk, particularly risk that concerns what remains unseen and undefinable, off limits to his total control. In his post-Vietnam mindset, he cannot fathom any kind of surrendering of the self, even though he longs for some connection with Rae, one that, this time, will last. Ironically, Quinn does not escape his modern predicament deliberately; instead, his experience of intimacy is somewhat accidental, resulting from a haphazard synchronicity of time, place, and circumstance.

Locatedness

What redeems Quinn from his modern predicament and from his own solipsistic shortcomings is his desire to be "located." But by this term he does not mean being secure in a particular place or having a particular place even mean something to him. His particular brand of expatriation, in fact, will not interfere with his quest for location, even though Bernhardt has already described "the American experience abroad [as] the long decline in expectation until you could see the immediate world like a native, but without the native's freedom. It should be a great unburdening, Bernhardt said, but to Americans it was always a hardship" (10). Quinn has glimpsed the "immediate world like a native," and he has done so as a conspicuous outsider whose one contact, Bernhardt, is murdered before Sonny's release can be settled. As Quinn fails to do what he has come to Mexico to do, he begins to succeed in becoming "located."

This moment is more apt to occur in solitude, when one is free to exist without the distractions of other people. After Vietnam, Quinn experiences locatedness in his work as a game warden, out in the woods at night watching for deer poachers, "the high density sensation of solo work at night," as Quinn puts it; "It made you feel out of time and out of real space and located closer to yourself, as if located was the illusion, the thing he'd missed since he'd come back, the ultimate good luck" (77). Quinn's use of the verbal "located" in the phrase "as if located was the illusion" seems significant here, as if the process of experiencing this moment necessitates more than passive thought. The moment seems to require a projection of self beyond the self; at the same time, the sense of being located is illusory, just out of reach, something requiring the "ultimate good luck." In other words, being located is not an experience that one can will into existence; the sensation depends on circumstance and upon the mind being *involved* with circumstance in a certain way. In this sense, then, being located contradicts being alienated; the two sensations are mutually exclusive. And, most importantly, being located requires self-engagement and self-abnegation, both at once.

It is not surprising, then, that Quinn experiences locatedness again as he tries to protect Rae after they witness Bernhardt's murder. But it is not in the act of protection that Quinn achieves this feeling; rather, it is in the act of empathy, trying to feel what she feels and, more significantly, trying to communicate his calm to her. To do so, Quinn leans his forehead next to Rae's on a store window and measures his breathing to

coincide with hers; as they exhale and inhale together, "by degrees
[Quinn] heard the soft suspiring night sigh of the city begin again, and
Rae became erect and cool in his arms, and he could smell her breath
hot and not sweet, and, for a moment, with her close to him, his cheek
on the cold glass, he felt himself fully located for once, and in a world in
which time couldn't pass" (157). The passage is oxymoronic: only when
time stops can Quinn and Rae hear the sounds of the city *begin again;*
only when Quinn and Rae breathe does the city also sigh; only in a transient moment of "locatedness" can the illusion of eternal belonging be
sustained. Clearly, part of what makes the sensation of "locatedness"
powerful is the fact that it is so terribly fleeting and ineffable.

As Quinn begins to surrender to the possibility of being "located," he
continues to develop his definition of luck, eventually letting his mind,
rather than some contemplation of an actual place, play the trick of
removing him from present circumstances. After Bernhardt's murder,
for example, the sensation of being solely responsible for the present
gives Quinn that pushed-to-the-edge feeling; furthermore, in the actual
moment described below he is literally sitting across the room from Rae,
observing her, not regarding some landscape where light and shadow
might transport him as if by legerdemain.

> He imagined separate faces, Zago and Deats, but they seemed to lose
> ground irretrievably and be replaced by a vista over pale grey water, at
> the perimeter of which tiny dots didn't move, like boats too far out to
> picture. Bernhardt's absence made him feel marooned close to the clean,
> satisfied edge of exhausted possibility, beyond affection or sorrow, the
> stalemate edge of all losses, the point where time froze on whatever was
> present, and nothing could be longed for or feared or protected against,
> where luck was not the thing you played. It was the best luck there was.
> (*UGL,* 161)

Such circumstances engender that balance that Quinn has defined
before: the delicate art of protecting yourself, but not too completely,
the risk of which is ending up with nothing. Here, "nothing could be
longed for or feared or protected against"—"nothing" suggesting no
thing as well as the abstract concept of nothingness. Being pushed to
the edge at last permits Quinn's surrender to the present; what he discovers is that all he cares about is Rae, and "that would be all that mattered anymore, an intimacy that didn't need an outside frame" (161).
With these thoughts, Quinn defies the cautionary words of his one-

night-stand, that he lacked a frame of reference. Being in a different country and living by unfamiliar rules both become irrelevant, as do his surroundings. His mind *creates* the vista that makes him feel marooned yet connected to Rae.

Quinn must come to terms with risk, specifically as it applies to love, before he regains Rae as his companion and escapes his modern predicament. What he must accept, then, is the uncertainty of the moment, the fact that most strange forces in our lives, including luck and love, have at their core the possibility of loss, of exposure, of termination. It seems to take this odd journey from Michigan to Mexico, from being a deer-protector to being Sonny's last hope for an unjustified release, to begin to free Quinn from his self-consumedness, his utilitarian view of others. This quest to do something, not because he wants to do it, but for the sake of someone he has loved in the hopes that she still loves him, is not purely selfless. Quinn, after all, agrees to help because he hopes to inspire Rae's forgiveness, and, realistically, at novel's end, he is not a completely changed man. But at the very least his relationship with Rae is more logical than those he has defined as integral to the modern predicament. He even concedes that "love seemed to him like a place to be, a place where nothing troublesome could come inside" (201), and he and Rae are together when the novel ends.

Quinn's yoking of love with a place would seem significant: love, unlike place, is intangible, possibly fleeting, off limits to property lines and territorial claims. In fact, love weakens under the threat of possessiveness. However, Quinn's definition of location and of being located, already established as the "high density sensation" not at all dependent upon physical place, makes his coupling of love and place not so incongruous. The fact that Quinn conceptualizes love as a place frees both words from their usual definitions and Quinn himself from the idea that somehow he can own Rae or control everything that will happen in their lives.

Finally, however, the novel does not guarantee the relationship's success. Rae, after all, has been holed up in the hotel room, worrying, sleeping, and drinking. Quinn himself may be in a heightened state because of his brushes with death. In short, the narrator makes no promises about Quinn and Rae's future, further emphasizing the novel's focus on the present. Without excessively sentimentalizing Quinn and Rae's desires, the novel documents their reunion only in its immediate relevance to their lives.

Redefining Place and the Modern Predicament

Stung by reviews of his first novel that likened it to a weak attempt at
Faulknerian prose, Richard Ford no doubt removed himself from such
possibilities in *The Ultimate Good Luck*. In this novel, however, he seems
to acknowledge his American literary heritage, using terms deliberately
that would resonate with and, most importantly, expand certain con-
cepts in southern and American fiction. It is not for the critic to ascribe
intent to the writer (though it happens all the time), but it is possible to
read this novel as a kind of metafictional comment upon certain facets of
southern literature and signatures of modernist fiction. Ford's choices of
"locatedness" and the "modern predicament" as the cruxes of Quinn's
interior and exterior worlds allow the author to offer an antidote to the
southern or modernist novel. Freeing his main character from the con-
strictions of place and isolation-induced, postwar despair, Ford suggests
that becoming unmoored from place may not be such a bad thing after
all, that identity drawn only from the landscape may prove as blank and
doomed as a snowman's grin. In "An Urge for Going: Why I Don't Live
Where I Used to Live," Ford has written that "I've tried to contend that
locatedness is not some science of the ground but rather of some quality
with us" ("Urge," 67). Appropriately, in *The Ultimate Good Luck*, locatedness, not place, redeems Quinn. Through an intimacy with Rae that
doesn't "need an outside frame," Harry Quinn escapes a modern
predicament defined by meaningless relationships, violence, and ensuing isolation.

Chapter Four

Truth Versus Fiction in
The Sportswriter

In *The Sportswriter*'s Frank Bascombe, Richard Ford creates a speaker whose efforts at truth-telling result mostly in further obfuscation, whose voice at once beguiles and bedevils the reader.[1] Frank begs us to question his "frankness" as he describes not only who he is but also how he thinks. Frank *is* frank, but he insists upon seeing the truth from many angles. He is the title character, of Haddam, New Jersey, who cites his own failed imagination as the primary reason that he has abandoned the avocation of story writing for the more clear-cut existence of sportswriting. As a first-person narrator who is more than capable of spinning a good yarn, Frank consciously constructs his persona and admits to telling his story as a deliberate act; even as he protests his loss of imagination, he engages some faculty remarkably like it. And of course Ford himself used his imagination to create Frank, a fact that imparts another layer of irony to the novel. As Frank refers to "literary" and "novelistic" devices at times with disdain, he himself employs such strategies (as does his creator, Ford). Even a presumably more reliable record, such as history, Frank admits, presents only a partial story, since it also depends upon the historian's credibility. Built into Frank's narrative, then, is the possibility of untruth, a slight fabrication or embellishment of an event—the inherent danger, or challenge—of the first-person, mostly present-tense narrative.

Such a risk is not at odds with Ford's thematic concerns in *The Sportswriter*. Through his characterization of Frank Bascombe, Ford assesses the distance between what is real and what is artifice and how language—or other means of disclosure—may bridge or widen that rift. Recently separated from his wife (whom he dubs simply X) after the untimely death of their son Ralph from Reye's Syndrome, Frank certainly knows the perils of loneliness and loss. The novel opens with Frank's meeting with X, predawn on one Good Friday morning, to observe their lost son's birthday. From this still point Bascombe wanders into a turning world, traveling to interview a former sports great who is now crippled and anticipating Easter dinner with his girlfriend Vicki's midwestern family. He'll also have a meaningful encounter with his friend and fellow member of the Divorced Men's Club, Walter Luckett, who, anything but lucky, later commits suicide. As Frank ponders his place in a fateful and fickle universe, his mental journey, a secular pilgrimage with a wayward pilgrim, becomes the novel's text.

The Unburdened Southerner?

The musing narrator prone to self-diagnosis and enthralled with language is no stranger to Western literature. One thinks of William Shakespeare's Hamlet, T. S. Eliot's Prufrock, John Updike's Harry Angstrom, Walker Percy's Will Barrett, among others, but this character type has also been yoked with southern fiction, whose pages are filled with white male voices at once embracing and denying their pasts, nostalgic and ashamed. Such impulses possibly find their origins in the complicity imparted by prior generations of white males who subjected other human beings to an inhuman existence, that is, slavery. Such guilt over the sins of the fathers, critic Fred Hobson has explained, manifests itself in the voices of male characters who can't let go of their pasts in part because they don't want to but who nonetheless feel great shame for this attachment. These conflicted feelings give rise to a particular need to tell a story, the "rage to explain," as Hobson has put it in the title of his *Tell About the South: The Southern Rage to Explain*.[2] Such a desire also manifests itself in the work of real-life apologists for the South, such as W. J. Cash, whose *The Mind of the South* (1941) attempted to explain the region's complexities without condemning the place entirely.[3] The apologist—whether fictional or real—finds himself in the awkward position of acknowledging the indefensible, and to do so he depends upon language to soften the blow. To put it another way, he uses language to tell the truth but gently, relying upon words both to reveal and conceal his own self-consciousness about his origins.

The white male character who confesses his deepest desires, secrets, longings, and griefs via his own history—a history deepened by the conflicts that have plagued his region—has thus become a character type in southern fiction. Critics have located such a voice in novels by William Faulkner, Robert Penn Warren, William Styron, Walker Percy, and Peter Taylor, among others. Ever battling the perception that, because he is from Mississippi, he is a "southern writer," Richard Ford finds himself in this company. His creation of Bascombe, then, is precisely what some critics needed to situate him in this "southern tradition." But as he has asserted, Ford takes issue with this label, finding regional categories far too limiting for the kind of writing he aspires to do.[4] Furthermore, Bascombe's ambivalence about the past's significance, at least to him personally, does liberate him from the company of his southern literary antecedents, and in Bascombe's creation, Ford seems to make this break quite deliberately. As Frank muses,

> All we really want is to get to the point where the past can explain nothing about us and we can get on with life. Whose history can ever reveal very much? In my view Americans put too much emphasis on their pasts as a way of defining themselves, which can be death-dealing. I know I'm always heartsick in novels (sometimes I skip these parts altogether; sometimes I close the book and never pick it up again) when the novelist makes his clanking, obligatory trip into the Davy Jones locker of the past. (*SW,* 24)

Via Bascombe's thoughts, Ford comments here on the uselessness of looking back as the primary way of defining the self. Instead, a character needs to be accountable for his or her actions, rather than blame personal or regional history for his or her shortcomings. As Bascombe puts it, "The stamp of our parents on us and of the past in general is, to my mind, overworked, since at some point we are whole and by ourselves upon the earth, and there is nothing that can change that" (24). Bascombe, of course, expresses his own share of personal regret, but he doesn't blame hundreds of years of history for his predicament. He finds the present more mysterious.

Nonetheless, that Frank Bascombe is from the South, confesses to a dislike of history, and wields language carefully inspired Fred Hobson to label him the "unburdened Southerner":

> not only do family and the past mean nothing to him, the South and his identity as a Southerner, he insists, mean nothing to him either. The South of his remembrance—and this is Mississippi, remember—isn't mysterious, isn't violent, isn't savage, isn't racially benighted, isn't Gothic or grotesque, isn't even *interesting*. In fact, it is not the South that fascinates Frank but . . . it is the Middle West. . . . Here we have, then, the southern expatriate for the eighties, with no interest in past, place, family, religion, community, guilt, and burdens of history, family or regional or otherwise. Or do we? . . . the more Frank protests he is not interested [in these things], the more we are convinced that he is. (Hobson 1991, 48–49)

Arguing that Bascombe simply transposes issues traditionally associated with the southern imagination into a midwestern context, Hobson finds evidence that Ford writes within certain parameters of the southern novel even as he parodies it. According to Hobson, Ford parodies the southern male type, creating in its stead a character preoccupied by all the same things even as he denies his preoccupation and disavows its origin. Hobson speculates that the same is true of Ford himself, who has long protested that he has nothing new to say about the South and whose reasons for thinking so I examine in chapter 2.

Ford may parody the southern novel here, but he does so through a text within the text, erstwhile writer Frank Bascombe's unpublished novel; Frank's *Night Wing* has as its protagonist a "bemused young southerner" who contracts a "mysterious disease . . . and loses himself in a hazy world of sex and drugs" (*SW,* 36); the book "climaxed in a violent tryst with a Methodist minister's wife who seduces him in an abandoned slave-quarters" (36). Ford gets in all of the requisite themes: Frank's character struggles to reconcile *past* with present, deals with wartime *guilt* (he was discharged); he succumbs to *violence* and sex in a *place* (slave-quarters) redolent of violent memories (*slavery*) with a woman who's married to a minister (*religion*). Frank's novel sounds overwrought, and deliberately so, and does not resemble *The Sportswriter.* Such subjects have outlived their usefulness, Ford suggests humorously through Frank, whose manuscript is lost in the mail and never seen again. However, setting his own book in New Jersey is not enough to get Ford off the hook of readers searching for southern literary paradigms in his work.

The issue of southernness, finally, may depend upon Bascombe's truthfulness as he discounts his southernness. Certainly, the reader questions just about every claim that Frank makes, at least after the first 50 pages or so, as his penchant for prevarication becomes clear. For example, while Frank listens to X talk at the graveyard, he wonders what his voice will sound like to her and in so doing also characterizes himself: "Will it be a convincing, truth-telling voice? Or a pseudo-sincere, phony, ex-husband one that will stir up trouble? I have a voice that is really mine, a frank, vaguely rural voice more or less like a used car salesman: a no-frills voice that hopes to uncover simple truth by a straight-on application of the facts. I used to practice it when I was in college" (11). No one trusts a used car salesman, as Frank must be aware, and he rarely applies the facts "straight-on." It is no surprise that Hobson doubts his truthfulness. Ford surely uses the pun on "frank" deliberately. No doubt Ford intends for the reader to find artifice in Bascombe's voice; after all, Frank is a constructed fictional character, not a real person upon whose veracity anything depends. He can be both reliable and unreliable as a narrator, as the very nature of first-person narration ensures. Later in the novel, he contradicts himself, conceding that a past is, after all, a good thing to have: "And truthfully . . . I am usually (if only momentarily) glad to have a past, even an imputed and remote one. There is something to that. It is not a burden, though I've always thought of it as one. I cannot say that we all need a past in full literary fashion, or that one is much useful in the end. But a small one doesn't hurt, especially if you're already in a life of your own choosing" (371). Even here Frank qualifies himself with a parenthetical aside "(if only momentarily)" after he uses "truthfully" to describe what he is about to say. His words could in fact inspire distrust; his use of "truthfully" suggests that he has not always told the truth. So is he the unburdened southerner, as Hobson finds? Maybe, and maybe not: Bascombe's equivocation is his protective device, and language is the cloak in which he wraps himself. For this reason, he may appear arrogant, self-consumed, obtuse, and in fact he is all of these things at one time or another. What may redeem Bascombe for the reader who grows impatient with him is a degree of wry self-consciousness that creeps out of his voice; perhaps Bascombe, too, knows how insufferable he occasionally sounds. Surely he is that self-aware, his narrative would imply (and if he isn't, then Ford certainly is). Ford's narrator, then, is not always reliable; he often fails to explain himself fully. As in *The Ultimate Good Luck,* redemption resides momentarily in the most unlikely places, and nothing can be pinned down and kept, except through recreation by language, itself a faulty tool. In his creation of Frank Bascombe, Ford seems more preoccupied with these existential and epistemological quandaries than with Frank's regional origins.

Frank himself pursues the truth, exploring the degrees to which a person should reveal bits of his or her life, pieces of his or her history or present. He finds the truth to be a rare commodity, experienced in fragments and at times best left alone. Thus he can tell about the "glistening one moment" that he experiences at novel's end, but even his telling obviates the "real" moment, already relegated to the irretrievable past. But this moment, not the Eastertide, is his redemption, that which now, in the novel's present, eludes him and the reader as he retells the events which lead up to it. Now he must construct the imagined, not the real, and in so doing he may miss other realities, other moments for the tak-

ing, the plain sense of things, regular old blackbirds, to recall Wallace
Stevens's poem. Finally, Frank's problems are not due to his southernness, or possible lack thereof, but to his humanness, not to those things
that make him unlike others of different regions but to those that make
him similar.

Dreaminess, Mystery, Factualism, and Literalism

Frank, however, constructs himself in such a way as to exaggerate his
differences. After all, Frank *is* a construction: first, and most obviously,
of Ford's, and second, of his own making within his fictional world. As
he confesses above, he has *practiced* his voice. Despite his admission that
he aspires "to speak in a plain, truth-telling voice" (209), Frank wants to
be complicated without appearing to be so, and he devises a philosophical system that explains his mental stages. Literally building a persona
as he goes, Frank explicates himself rather formally, coining specific
terms by which to label his various states of mind, which far outnumber
the three confessed by Stevens's speaker in "Thirteen Ways of Looking
at a Blackbird" who addresses another group of thin men from Haddam
(though not of New Jersey). Frank's vocabulary includes the notions of
"dreaminess" and "mystery," "factualism" and "literalism." Ford himself
admits that the lines between the terms may deliberately blur.

> I don't know if, even if I sat down with the books [*The Sportswriter* and
> *Independence Day*], I could completely plot them all out. But I would
> think if you were an ardent and skillful philosopher that you'd be able to
> make all of those things dovetail. I might could. It could be that at one
> time I had them all nicely dovetailed. . . . I can explain "dreaminess." As
> concepts they're provisional ways of getting experience released from
> mute sensation and giving them a name. That's what writers are sup-
> posed to do. (Walker, 133)

Ford concedes the abstraction of these terms, the tendency of each definition to be slippery and somewhat inaccurate, rather like language's
inherent imprecision. The word often fails to describe the thing completely. But the reader concerned with understanding these terms might
come up with the following theories. The onset of "dreaminess," a vague
dissatisfaction with the present that results in "seeing around" the current circumstances to what may lie beyond them, often accompanies the
experience of too much "factuality," that which occurs irrevocably, such
as death, taxes, delayed airplanes. A factualist differs in degree from a

"literalist." A factualist is apt to get distracted by the basic facts, as the term would suggest, and lose all other awareness, whereas a literalist lets those things go in order to be content within a given moment. A literalist is usually not a seeker; nor is he or she prey to much dreaminess. "Mystery"—the unexplained, the ineffable, the satisfying twinge of the unknown—is the state that Frank seeks most avidly. For a literalist, mystery may or may not be desirable; usually a literalist needs mystery, though, to redeem the more mundane moments of a simplified existence. Some literalists actively seek moments of mystery. A small degree of literalness, in so far as a place or a person is predictable, for example, is comforting. On the other hand, if one reveals too much about one's self, one is guilty of "full disclosure," a state that rapidly devours all the mystery available in a given moment and often results in the retreat of the person to whom too much has been exposed.

Through Frank's voice, Ford offers these terms as "provisional ways" (Walker, 133) of releasing experiences from the realm of the undefined and unspoken and providing instead a name for them. To name experience is to dispel isolation; one person can then recognize the experience of another in the epiphany of "yes, that's exactly what I have felt but have never had the words to describe." The adjective "provisional" bears some importance, too; even language falls short of capturing experience completely, a fact that resonates with the dichotomy of the imagined versus the real. Frank learns this lesson as he struggles to navigate the treacherous seas of self and other. His obsession with these terms reveals his fundamental dilemma: Just how much should one person disclose to another? Just how much does one person *want* to know about another? The line between what needs to be known and what should not be is incidentally the boundary of Frank's narrative, the territory of his story. He seeks to balance himself there in the telling of his tale and in the relationships that he describes. Perhaps here resides the reason that Frank's character and degree of truthfulness prove so difficult to analyze. He simply doesn't know how much to tell, whether he should tell what he does, and what difference it all makes anyway. At times he discloses too much; at others he keeps too much to himself. As readers, we accept Frank's "reality" within the novel that houses him, but Frank isn't a real person, obviously, and it is critically fallacious to pretend that he is. For this reason, it is helpful to remember that Ford has made certain decisions as he has created Frank's voice, decisions that make Frank at times confounding. This strategy also easily coincides with the novel's crux: the question of how deeply one person can be connected to another, can know another, and be known, themes that Ford will continue to explore in *Independence Day* (1995).

Dreamy Digressions: Frank's Musing Narrative Style

As Frank uses his coined terms to identify emotional states, he seeks the essence of the very things that so often resist definition. Usually a catalyst, something external that impinges upon his internal world, propels Frank from one of these states to the next. He numbers his son Ralph's death and his ensuing divorce as two of these externals: events that have fundamentally changed his life and his way of viewing the world. He blames himself, in fact, for the kind of "dreaminess" that allowed his marriage to slip out of his hands.

To understand any one of the terms that Frank uses, one must also grapple with the others, for Frank often juxtaposes them or employs one to illuminate the other by contrast. Furthermore, he cannot simply tell one piece of his story at a time; instead he resorts to a kind of stream of consciousness that allows him to define his terminology and relate the quotidian events of his life simultaneously. The effect, though, is that one event may lead him off into a tangential discussion of its accompanying state of mind, and the discussion of that state of mind may remind him of another unrelated event, and so forth and so on. Finally, then, it takes Frank many pages to conclude one portion of his history, and between one fact and another are lines and lines of recorded thoughts that may or may not have anything to do with the plot of his life.

So he does as he describes the dreaminess that assaults him after Ralph's death: "I launched off into the dreaminess his death may or may not have caused but didn't help, and my life with X broke apart . . ., causing her to send her hope chest chuffing up the chimney stack" (*SW*, 41). Frank goes on to discuss the relative merits and demerits of history as a way of understanding the self and the world, concluding that each person's history is unique; "nobody's history could've brought another Tom, Dick or Harry to the same place" (42), a fact, Frank says, that "limits the final usefulness of these stories" (42). In other words, he questions what possible good use one's personal history is to another person, since each person's history depends on that individual, and there is nothing that one could glean from hearing the sad tales of someone else's life that would always guarantee one's own happiness. By making this point, Frank utilizes a strategy to which his audience should be alert: he undercuts himself. Clearly his assessment of history's relative uselessness does not stop Frank from relating *his* history. Nonetheless, Frank argues, *again* skillfully undercutting his previous concern, "history can make mystery" (42)—which is a desirable experience—simply because sometimes history may be understood incorrectly, or only partially told, or a downright lie. Mystery, to Frank, is in short supply; unlike dreaminess, it is a positive state and is arguably what he pursues with relative single-mindedness throughout the novel's course. But he attempts to define dreaminess here, and these other musings, though typical of Frank's narrative patterns, digress from his intended point.

> Dreaminess is, among other things, a state of suspended recognition, and a response to too much useless and complicated factuality. Its symptoms can be a long-term interest in the weather or a sustained soaring feeling, or a bout of the stares that you sometimes can not even know about except in retrospect, when the time may seem fogged. . . . when you get to my age, dreaminess is *not* so pleasurable, at least as a steady diet, and one should avoid it if you're lucky enough to know it exists, which many people aren't. For a time—this was the period after Ralph died—I had no idea about it myself, and in fact thought I was onto something big—changing my life, moorings loosed, women, travel, marching to a different drummer. Though I was wrong. (*SW*, 42)

Even here Frank can't help but include a reference to factuality, the seeming antithesis of dreaminess and mystery. The reference to "too much useless and complicated factuality" includes precisely what the term might suggest, those things that have happened that can't be undone, that are incontrovertible and irreversible, such as Ralph's death. It is of no use to dwell on these things, since no amount of pondering them can change the end effect. Dreaminess, however, can provide a brief respite, a way of viewing the world that necessarily includes distraction. Even if such a retreat is finally irresponsible, it may also be necessary, if only for brief periods, especially in grief's face. But for Frank, dreaminess has propelled him too far from his wife and the realm of his marriage. It governs his decisions; his decisions affect his wife's life. Finally she can no longer ignore his means of distraction: travel, other women, a job that requires him to leave their home and the other two children behind.

But before Frank tells that part of the story, he digresses once again, in this instance to characterize his decision to quit being a "real" writer and to become a sportswriter instead. The simple reason that he quit writing fiction, Frank says, is that he lost his sense of anticipation, the "sweet pain to know what comes next" (43). Obviously, to write about sports would be to recapture anticipation, since one never knows how the game ends until it does, and some other game always takes the place of the one that has just ended. The more complicated reason, Frank admits, is that he just got too "gloomy." In this self-assessment of his stories, Frank's wryness certainly appears.

> It was also true, though, that there were a good many descriptions of the weather and the moon, and that most of [the stories] were set in places like remote hunting camps on Canadian Lakes, or in the suburbs, or Arizona or Vermont, places I had never been, and many of them ended with men staring out snowy windows in New England boarding schools or with somebody driving fast down a dark dirt road, or banging his hand into a wall or telling someone else he could never *really* love his wife, and bringing on hard emptinesses. (*SW,* 46)

Ford's own sense of humor also manifests itself, since many of his works that preceded *The Sportswriter* could themselves only be called gloomy, and Frank could very well be describing some of Ford's short fiction.

Frank concludes that another barrier to his writing fiction was that he really didn't know "how people *felt* about most things"—again raising the issue of recognition, of knowing—and that to complicate this failure he also could not *imagine* the material necessary to take the place of knowing. This "failure of imagination" coupled with what he calls his loss of "authority" (46) convinced Frank that it was time to make a change, to substitute the grandness of life, where he "could get somewhere" (47), for the more sterile world of literature, where he couldn't (but which he, as a character, so easily inhabits).

Of course Ford evokes humor here; he's a writer writing about a writer who has quit writing because the literary life failed him. Frank says, "It is no loss to mankind when one writer decides to call it a day. When a tree falls in the forest, who cares but the monkeys?" (47). These wry digressions undercut the high seriousness of Frank's voice and also remind the reader that Ford has not lost *his* authority. The humor gently mitigates *The Sportswriter*'s graver moments, its preoccupation with mortality, and Frank's own shortcomings. Indeed, this chapter of the novel comes to an end with Frank's remarks about the monkeys. He has not gotten back to dreaminess; he has not gotten back to X's burning of her hope chest. When Frank does get around to telling about the job he takes, the move that requires him to live apart from X and that in many ways directly precipitates their divorce, 178 pages have passed.

The Lie of Literature

Frank uses this phase of his life to illustrate several of his own discoveries about language, truth and falsehood, literature and life. About a year after Ralph has died, Frank receives a call from a friend of a friend, inviting him, out of the blue, for a visiting term in the English department at Berkshire College, as a kind of writer-in-residence. The department's chair has read Frank's book of stories, been impressed, and called him to replace the "usual" writer, who apparently has gone literally crazy. Somewhat to his own surprise, without consulting X or giving it more than a moment's thought, Frank agrees to come. In retrospect, he confides to the reader, "I decided to go teach at Berkshire College—I know now—to deflect the pain of terrible regret" (215). Though perplexed, X is surprisingly understanding, and off Frank goes to teach, only to discover that he has "nothing to teach," except perhaps that "love is transferable; location isn't actually everything" (217).[5] Already guilty of conducting affairs, Frank embarks upon another liaison, this time with a colleague, a Lebanese woman named Selma Jassim, with whom Frank sleeps shortly after his last visit with X while at Berkshire. Upon this occasion, the second weekend that Frank is at the college, X has pleaded for him to come to his senses and return with her to Haddam. Frank says, "I told her, of course, that I couldn't just leave. (Though if I had I might still be married, and I had the feeling she was dead right about my staying: that another failed writer would crawl out of the woodwork and be in my place in less than twenty-four hours. . . .)" (224–25). Ironically, it is not his affair with Selma—or any current sexual dalliance—that sends X's hope chest up the chimney but X's discovery of a rather innocuous letter correspondence between Frank and another woman. X draws the wrong conclusion from Frank's platonic relationship, and their marriage ends, ironically, over the one truth that Frank is telling, that there is nothing between him and Peggy Connover, his far-flung correspondent from Kansas. To X, perhaps, this evidence is superfluous to Frank's other literal and figurative absences from their life together. At any rate, Frank ends up at Berkshire College for one term, where he reiterates his prior claim about the "minor but pernicious lie of literature" (119).

The "lie of literature" encompasses the idea that emotions are simply and purely felt, one at a time, that one can be entirely rooted in a response as pure as one of James Joyce's epiphanies. (Frank himself uses this allusion.) The lie suggests,

> after significant or disappointing divulgences, at arrivals or departures of obvious importance, when touchdowns are scored, knock-outs recorded, loved ones buried, orgasms notched, that at such times we are any of us altogether *in* an emotion, that we are within ourselves and not able to detect other emotions we might also be feeling, or be about to feel, or prefer to feel. If it's literature's job to tell the truth about these moments, it usually fails, in my opinion, and it's the writer's fault for falling into such conventions. (I tried to explain all this to my students at Berkshire, using Joyce's epiphanies as a good example of falsehood. . . .) (*SW,* 119)

Frank goes on to confess what he is feeling at that particular moment, a statement, "What I feel, in truth," (119), that he again qualifies with a protestation of his veracity. He also expects literature to tell the truth, but of course it doesn't; the reader must discern truth from falsehood or, better yet, acknowledge the artifice inherent in any story's telling. After all, even if it records events that actually happened, the story itself is once removed from its subject. The story is not the thing itself but rather the imagined version of what happens or a mere reflection of the life that it describes; furthermore, the story only *attempts* to describe its subject. But Frank ignores the artifice in art, desiring instead for there to be a seamless union between truth and fiction. Of course human emotion is never as simple (or perhaps even as complex) as it may appear to be in novels or stories, but language's limitations prevent the complete emergence of what it describes. Another way to conceptualize this tension is to note the differences between a painted apple and a real one. The fruit conveyed in art may look like the real thing; depending upon the artist's skill, the proportions may be accurate, the light and shadow perfectly rendered in paint and texture and depth of field. But the painted apple can never be cold or crisp; such is the limit of its reproduction in art. By this same argument, Frank himself, as a character, will not be as fathomable, or by contrast as unknowable, perhaps, as a real person. This fact makes his own protestations slightly comic; prone to use phrases such as "of course" and "in truth" and "truthfully," Frank invites his audience, whomever they may be, to believe him, suggesting that while he may be impenetrable (or even cold, dishonest, manipulative) to his fellow characters, to his audience he is faithful, truthful, and concerned with getting it right. As Ford obviously knows, every time Frank makes a crack about the perniciousness of literature, Frank takes a crack at himself—and his creator.

Where literature fails, Frank believes, is in not allowing for the phenomenon of "seeing around," or the precise notion that he has described above in terms of never being completely *in* an emotion. Not necessarily a positive act, "seeing around" also refers to being distracted by other possibilities, thinking about what one might be doing rather than what one *is* doing. Such a state prevents one from being completely in the moment. Frank falls prey to it himself, or, at least, he has in the past. If one is in the throes of seeing around, one finds it impossible to reduce anything to an easily contemplable size. Such a state would obviously be a problem for a professor who seeks to compose a syllabus, give a lecture, explicate a poem. Frank explains,

> this has a lot to do with "seeing around," which I was in the grip of then but trying my best to get out of. When you are not seeing around, you're likely to speak in your own voice and tell the truth as you know it and not for public approval. When you *are* seeing around, you're pretty damn willing to say anything—the most sinister lie or the most clownish idiocy known to man—if you think it might make someone happy. Teachers, I should say, are highly susceptible to seeing around, and can practice it to the worst possible consequences. (*SW*, 217–18)

Since Frank is presumably speaking in retrospect, the reader only hopes that he is not still seeing around, but even raising these issues should alert Frank's (and Ford's) audience that Frank may have been known to "say anything" for "public approval." At Berkshire, Frank found literature to be "wide and undifferentiatible—not at all distillable—" (218), although he admits he was capable of waving his arms around and telling jokes in Latin, both nice parodic examples, on Ford's part, of the professoriat. One key disadvantage of teaching, as Frank sees it, is that literature and its critics seek to explain too much, thereby violating the mystery of things. Of Berkshire, he remarks, "the place was all anti-mystery types, right to the core—men and women both—all expert in the art of explaining, explicating and dissecting, and by these means promoting permanence" (222). As Frank warms to his topic, he refines his criticism, focusing it on the teachers and not necessarily the books themselves. Even so, he will, before he is through, contradict himself again.

On the one hand, Frank claims that literature, as an eternal art form, perfectly suits teachers seeking permanence. He confides, "Teachers, let me tell you, are born deceivers of the lowest sort, since what they want from life is impossible—time-freed, existential youth forever. It commits them to terrible deceptions and departures from the truth. And literature, being lasting, is their ticket" (222). On the other hand, he expounds further, "Literature's consolations are always temporary, while life is quick to begin again. It is better not to look so hard, to leave off explaining" (223–24). Despite this apparent inconsistency, Frank is right: literature is both lasting *and* evocative of only temporary consolation. The text itself achieves a permanence that organic, or living, beings never attain, but for these living beings, the act of reading a book is but a temporary one. The book will end; the reader's life will resume again. Whatever solace the book may provide then also dissipates, though it may not disappear completely: the paradox of art as an "eternal" form. The problem, as Frank sees it, is that too often teachers miss this point. "Real mystery—the very reason to read (and certainly write) any book—was to them a thing to dismantle, distill and mine out into rubble they could tyrannize into sorry but more permanent explanations; monuments to themselves, in other words. . . . Explaining is where we all get into trouble" (223). But even Frank must admit that the teachers were only doing "exactly what I was doing—keeping regret at arm's length" (223). The more Frank talks, the more he explains to X, for example, the deeper into trouble he also gets, but such a fate certainly doesn't silence him for long. Frank's rather long-winded analysis ends, finally, with simplicity, "Some things can't be explained. They just are." (223), and in these two succinct sentences this narrator encapsulates one of Ford's many philosophical preoccupations. The lie of literature, more precisely defined than in Frank's digressions, is that often language simply cannot do justice to experience, making the imagined, at least sometimes, less perfect than the real.

The Literal: Real or Imagined?

On the other hand, Frank can hardly describe the literal without resorting to the imaginative. His preoccupation with the "literal" would suggest a desire to strip away the nonessential in order to see the thing itself, and he finds such promise in the simple town of Haddam, New Jersey, which is "as straightforward and plumb-literal as a fire hydrant, which more than anything makes it the pleasant place it is" (103). Significantly, Frank uses a metaphor here—the fire hydrant—to explain Haddam's literalness. Haddam resembles a fire hydrant in that it is commonplace, dependable, apparently permanent. But Haddam is not *literally* a fire hydrant, as Frank's audience understands; it is not red and it does not contain water. Blithely using the figurative to describe the literal, Frank seems unaware of the irony: Haddam's literalness cannot be explained well without resorting to metaphor. Frank's actual words often belie the gist of what he is saying, and Ford deliberately engages these contradictions through Frank's voice. Frank takes pleasure in the literal, but he cannot leave what is literal to its literalness. Instead he employs figurative, or imaginative, language as a descriptive tool. Frank nonetheless goes on to say, "we all need our simple, unambiguous, even factitious townscapes like mine. Places without challenge or double-ranked complexity. Give me a little Anyplace, a grinning, toe-tapping Terre Haute or wide-eyed Bismarck, with stable property values, regular garbage pick-up, good drainage, ample parking, located not far from a major airport, and I'll beat the birds up singing every morning" (103–4). Of these traits, only the need for a major airport would seem unlike the others. Such a requirement suggests that even the happiest denizen of this literal place might want to leave town on occasion, perhaps in search of mystery.

Other sources of uncomplicated literalness are the pages of glossy catalogs, which he and X page through nightly after Ralph's death, almost ritualistically projecting themselves into the perfect lives of tanned models lounging on boat docks in crisp khakis and white tennis shoes. Such pictures evoke the very thing that is missing in Frank's life, what is "knowable, safe and sound" (196). A shopper can participate in the life promised in the catalogs simply by ordering from their pages, which provide a "perfect illustration of how the literal can become the mildly mysterious" (196). The fact that the shopper may have an inkling that the catalog does not reflect reality may provide the soupçon of mystery to which Frank refers. The illusion comprises ordinariness and literalness—"some things outside my life were okay still" (196), as Frank puts it—even if once the items arrive, reality sets in.

While Frank is at Berkshire College, he sights an old acquaintance modeling in the pages of such a catalog, a discovery that sends him reeling with possibility. Mindy Levinson, a former college love interest, gazes at Frank from "almost every page" (198) of an exclusive outdoorsy catalog that Frank has picked up in the faculty lounge. He proceeds to track Mindy down to a place not far from the college, to which he drives to see her, based on his presumption that a "certain kind of mystery requires investigation so that a better, more complicated mystery can open up like an exotic flower. Many mysteries are not that easy to wreck and will stand some basic inquiry" (199). The ensuing encounter is everything that Frank hopes that it will be, simply because the excursion removes him, if only momentarily, from his current reality and lets him into a "perfect, crystalized life" (202) that he and X cannot possibly have at this moment. He gets his glimpse, as he puts it, of "a nearly perfect life of a kind, as literally perfect as the catalog promised it would be" (202). Frank knows that such instances are at best rare and always temporary, but he craves exactly what the philosopher Kierkegaard would call a "rotation," a means by which to escape his own life for another person's, which may be accomplished through having love affairs, traveling, or as in Frank's case, perusing catalogs. Ideally, a rotation would allow one to return to his own life empowered by a new way of seeing it. Frank has not really grasped this possibility, and the literalness he seeks cannot be sustained because no one lives a simple life, no matter how symmetrical one's town streets are.

Another way that Frank escapes his own life is by trying to "simulate full immersion" (129) into someone else's (ironically, the very act that reading a book makes possible). For Frank, this can entail sleeping with other women, as many as 18, in fact, while he is prey to dreaminess and loosed in his moorings with X "without even noticing the slippage" (128). He counts teaching and buying a Harley among his other actions committed while in this same state of dreaminess. In short, what Frank describes is simply the need to escape reality, but the escape is of course only temporarily achieved. Unfortunately, Frank's frenzy to escape comes at X's expense. Blind to her needs, Frank imagines that she knew everything about his affairs but failed to ask him embarrassing questions out of supreme consideration of his feelings, so that he wouldn't be "so miserable" (128). Prey to the worst kind of solipsism here, Frank goes on to recount what he considers his main mistake, and that is this hope for "full immersion." What he means is that while talking to these other women he experienced a need to become part of their lives, to share their realities, a need that inspired him to say all sorts of things that later he knew he did not mean, the most dangerous of which was "I love you." He demanded "full disclosure when [he] had nothing to disclose in return" (130). Only in retrospect does he realize that he has succumbed to the "worst, most craven cynicism," and at least he is suitably hard on himself. Frank explains that "What I was doing, though I didn't figure it out until long after I'd spent three months at Berkshire College . . . was trying to be within myself by being as nearly as possible *within* somebody else. . . . it doesn't work. In fact, it leads to a terrible dreaminess and the worst kind of abstraction and unreachableness" (130). Frank attempts to know himself by knowing others, a failed enterprise, he can later concede, on two counts. One, knowing the self first may better prepare one for knowing another. Two, no one else can ever be known completely. He even admits that "Married life requires shared mystery when all the facts are known" (131).

Ironically, this realization leads Frank to embrace literalness, the understanding that he should have been having a "whale of a time" and forgetting "about everything else" (132) when instead he was "bound up creating and resolving a complicated illusion of life" (132). In a literal state of mind, the distance closes between what one is feeling and what one might feel; "seeing around" is no longer a problem. Emotions become pleasurably simple. Only then, Frank says, "your instincts can be trusted" (132).

> It is the difference between a man who quits his job to become a fishing guide on Lake Big Trout, and who one day as he is paddling his canoe into the dock at dusk, stops paddling to admire the sunset and realizes how much he wants to be a fishing guide on Lake Big Trout; and another man who has made the same decision, stopped paddling at the same time, felt how glad he was, but also thought he could probably be a guide on Windigo Lake if he decided to, and might also get a better deal on canoes.
>
> Another way of describing this is that it's the difference between being a literalist and a factualist. A literalist is a man who will enjoy an afternoon watching people while stranded in an airport in Chicago, while a factualist can't stop wondering why his plane was late out of Salt Lake, and gauging whether they'll still serve dinner or just a snack. (*SW*, 132–33)

Being a literalist is just another way of being completely in a moment and happy there, which as a goal seems perfectly reasonable. Its danger for Frank, though, is that he confuses such contentment with being absolved of a certain kind of responsibility for the future, so that he can go on to say "I love you" to his girlfriend Vicki Arcenault without worrying about creating a lasting attachment. "Who cares if I don't love her forever?" Frank questions rhetorically. "Or she me? Nothing persists. I love her now, and I'm not deluding myself or her. What else does truth have to hold?" (133). Frank's line of thought displays a certain logic even as it fails to acknowledge the potential for pain. Vicki, though, takes ample care of herself and dumps Frank before he can dump her, so Ford does not seem to want the reader to fret over Vicki's feelings.

What emerges again as a central conflict is delusion versus truth, which by now the reader knows is important to Frank and to Ford. To be a literalist is on the one hand to subject one's self to truth's brutality while on the other to simplify life so that its truths are correspondingly simple. To seek mystery is to long for some delusion, some trick of displacement, that mitigates current circumstances, a reality, such as grief for Ralph, that may bear forgetting, at least for a while. When such a reality becomes almost too much to bear, dreaminess may set in, keeping one from seeing things as they are (in Frank's marriage, for example) and making one more apt to focus only on one's self and chase after mystery irresponsibly. Finally, the literal may too often verge upon the banal, making that reality also something from which to flee, as Frank discovers when he tries to live in the moment without regard for others. The other, in fact, is the variable that can set the equation right, the embodiment of mystery: the strange blend of the knowable and the unknowable. But the only way to succeed in a relationship with others is to have achieved a certain kind of self-understanding, which Frank spends most of his story trying to find.

In Search of Mystery

Set on Easter weekend, *The Sportswriter* raises inevitable associations with the Christian story of Jesus' resurrection from the dead. However, Ford adamantly states otherwise, "it's not a Christian book. The kind of redeeming that goes on in that book is entirely unreligious" (Bonetti, 85). *The Sportswriter* nonetheless shares a longing for mystery with the Easter story. To quote Frank, certain things can't be explained; they just are. In the novel, it's simply a different kind of mystery, something that might be felt today, not tomorrow or after death. In spite of Ford's protestations to the contrary, Frank's quest is, in some sense, religious, or to use a less loaded word, spiritual; it's just not Christian. In keeping with the novel's other instances of redemption from self and circumstance, any moment that Frank finds potentially healing is just that: momentary. Redemption, especially the religious kind, occurs only temporarily, as Frank experiences in the Presbyterian church's sanctuary on Easter morning: "A rare immanence is mine, things falling back and away in the promise that more's around here than meets the eye, even though it is of course a sham and will last only as far as my car" (SW,

238). Frank argues, "[I] am 'saved' in the only way I can be (*pro tempore*), and am ready to march on toward dark temporality" (238). In other words, Frank denies the possibility of eternal salvation or existence after death—the "sham," as he puts it. He remains focused on what can happen in the present, and in the present such salvation occurs only fleetingly.

Despite its humor, the novel certainly addresses issues of loss: deaths that can't be undone, bodies that remain unresurrected. "Death, after all, is a mystery Christians can't get cozy with" (204), as Frank says, hence the need for the miraculous to counterbalance the "severe and unequivocal" (204) nature of mortality. Frank implies that for him death is more mysterious than the possibility of resurrection, and here he betrays another inconsistency in his thinking. Death is *factual* and mysterious, whereas resurrection is only mysterious. For Frank even the mysterious must have its roots in the factual, although he worries that X may be turning his children into "perfect little factualists" (204). Since Frank himself can't get around, beyond, or over the paucity of proof for bodily resurrection after death, he cannot partake in Christianity's salvation. For him what is important is that his son Ralph is dead and not to return on this earth: "My only wish is that my sweet boy Ralph Bascombe could wake up from his sleep-out and come in the house for a good Easter tussle like we used to, then be off to once-a-year services. What a day that would be! What a boy!" (204). This is Frank at his most poignant. Going to church has been a "once-a-year" thing, almost strictly to revel in that most mysterious of Christian observances, Christ's resurrection, but that particular mystery has failed him, been rendered insignificant by the *fact* of Ralph's death, that, in the here and now, can't be undone. Ironically, Frank recounts that what made him stop going to church in the first place, earlier in his marriage when he and X lived in Michigan, was that "Christianity, like everything else in the Ann Arbor of those times, was too factual and problem-solving-oriented. The spirit was made flesh too matter-of-factly. Small-scale rapture and ecstasy (what I'd come for) was out of the question." (104). Frank has since attended First Presbyterian in Haddam every now and then "to lift [his] spirits with a hymn" (104), so he seeks mainly that instance of well-being, a momentary high that he can also find elsewhere. Unable to believe in what finally can't be proven, Frank falls prey to a factualism that allots no room for any kind of coming of Christ who, to Frank, is as unreal and irrelevant as his son Ralph was otherwise. Thus Frank turns elsewhere for what might be called spiritual relief.

He regularly visits Mrs. Miller, a palmist, for evidence of mystery, strange workings beyond his control that can affirm his tentative belief in the inexplicable although he suspects—or even knows—that Mrs. Miller has no more idea of what the future holds than he does. Rationalizing, Frank can only muse, "I have learned over time that when her answers to my questions have been wrong, the best thing to think is that somehow it's my fault things didn't turn out" (100–101). Mrs. Miller's advice usually takes on such a general character that Frank's careful interpretation of events can make her words seem on the mark. Frank seeks her out precisely for the mystery that she imparts, not through her advice, but through her being, all the unanswered questions that hang about her life: "Who is this Mrs. Miller if she is not a Gypsy? A Jew? A Moroccan?" (102). She simply admits Frank into "the mystery that surrounds her own life," allowing him to go home "with high hopes, as warm with curiosities and wonder on the very lowest level" (102). For Frank, sometimes just being in her driveway is enough to impart the high of vicarious connection; he can see the light beyond her curtains and imagine what might be going on inside. He wants to remain unseen himself, so that the ugly fact of voyeurism will not dispel the pleasant mystery of being so close to the mundane goings-on behind veiled windows. Frank's relationship (though it is hardly that) with Mrs. Miller contrasts with his disaffection for organized religion. As a human being, Mrs. Miller offers what Frank longs for, some vestige of connectedness with another person's world. However, for a good part of his story, he, as its subject and not its narrator, obviously hasn't quite realized his desire to be emotionally intimate with another person.

Frank persists in characterizing mystery as the most desirable state he can imagine and aspire to experience. He confides that mystery is "the *only* thing I find to have value at this stage in my life" (101). Here he defines the term: "Mystery is the attractive condition a thing (an object, an action, a person) possesses which you know a little about but don't know about completely. It is the twiney promise of unknown things (effects, interworkings, suspicions) which you must be wise enough to explore not too deeply, for fear you will dead-end in nothing but facts" (101–2). Frank's exemplary instance of a typical mystery, which he goes on to describe, entails meeting a beautiful woman in a city where you find yourself only for a few days, having a good dinner, discussing old lovers and locales where you've both been, and ending up in bed to "woggle the bejesus out of each other" (102). Frank's diction here comically undercuts the eloquent tone of his first definition, a clue from Ford that this narrator can be rather dilettantish at times. Frank dabbles in language, at once relying upon what passes for erudition and what might be called colloquialism. He both talks over the heads of and complicitly to his possible audience: in his learned way he may define abstractions and in the next breath conjure the image of buddying up to a guy in a bar over a drink, sharing stories of sex in hotel rooms. Frank clamors to be taken seriously while he also reveals his weaknesses, which are primarily triggered by needing to be desired by women. As other of Frank's passages have shown, the problem with such encounters is that they can quickly turn from being spots of mystery to moments inviting full disclosure, depending upon the participant's mindset at the time.

Missing the Connection with Men (Herb, Wade, and Walter)

One of Frank's problems is that he seeks intimacy via sex and not friendship, and most disclosure between friends, full or not, scares the "bejesus" out of him. Nonetheless, three men impose their stories on Frank over his narrative's course: Herb Wallagher, the former athlete, now crippled from a water skiing accident, whom Frank is assigned to interview; Wade Arcenault, girlfriend Vicki's father; and Walter Luckett, an acquaintance from the Divorced Men's Club to which both he and Frank belong. In all three encounters, Frank becomes the listener, a reluctant confidant who hears confessions that are not particularly welcome. In Herb's case, of course, Frank knows that he faces some potential unpleasantness. After all, Herb lost his career as a professional ballplayer and lives his postinjury life from a wheelchair. Frank's task in interviewing Herb is to coax inspiration from circumstances that on a daily basis may not leave much room for awe.

Frank's trip to interview Herb is one of the few places in the novel where Frank's career as sportswriter becomes central. In fact, finding himself once again in a cab en route to a community where he is nothing but a stranger, Frank speculates that his choice of vocation is by definition isolating. He imagines that neighbors watch out for each other, calling in advance at the first sighting of him, the intruder come to expose what should be left private. "All of which," Frank muses, "makes me realize just how often I am with people I don't know and who don't know me, and who come to know me—Frank Bascombe—only as a sportswriter" (152). Likewise, as he realizes that Herb can't provide him with the kind of story he is seeking, he ponders what being a sportswriter has taught him, namely that "you can't go into these thing [*sic*] thinking you know what can't be known" (158). Here, Frank's repetition of "to know" verbs indicates his preoccupation with that act: how deeply he, Frank, can be known and how completely he can know others. He'll continue to pepper his musings with the verb. Here, too, Frank deals with issues of disclosure. In truth, as Frank would say, he doesn't really want to deal with Herb's sorrow; it reminds him too much of his own. As Frank listens to Herb ramble on about reading Ulysses Grant's thoughts about dying, he concludes that "It's pretty clear to me that Herb suffers from some damned serious mood swings and in all probability has missed out on a stabilizing pill. Possibly this is his gesture of straight-talk and soul-baring, but I don't think it will make a very good interview. Interviews always go better when athletes feel fairly certain about the world and are ready to comment on it" (157). Frank distances himself from Herb's story as he detects the "sadness of elusive life glimpsed and unfairly lost" (164), a sadness very like the regret that Frank seeks to avoid. He literally backs away from Herb, as eager to get into his waiting cab as he can be to stave off that terrible regret, leaving Herb behind, "his sad face astream with helpless and literal tears" (164). Despite his efforts to the contrary, Frank carries Herb's sadness with him. Back at the hotel in Detroit with Vicki, Frank finds himself in the grips of the "sad old familiarity from the dreamy days after Ralph died," acknowledging that he is "lost in strangerville with a girl I don't know well enough" (168). Vicki is, of course, the same young woman he professed to love 30 pages or so earlier, there in the throes of literalness and not dreaminess. Literalness does not seem like the same refuge now, having become yoked with Herb Wallagher's tears.

Easily infected by the sorrow of others, Frank avoids such encounters when he can, and usually he feels quite comfortable in the company of athletes. However, Herb fails to resemble Frank's archetypal athlete, who, by and large, is unlikely "to feel the least bit divided, or alienated, or one ounce of existential dread" (62). Frank explains, "athletes at the height of their powers make literalness into a mystery all its own simply by becoming absorbed in what they're doing" (63). Athletes don't find themselves worrying about other people, according to Frank; they don't "see around." They are able to live completely in the moment, like a practiced literalist, and as such are the objects of Frank's envy. Though since Frank himself raises the issue of existential dread, it is appropriate to remark that, according to at least one philosopher, the worst kind of despair occurs when a person does not recognize that he or she is in despair. Despair, in other words, is the catalyst for some higher state of mind because it makes its host seek something beyond the self. These athletes would then be in the worst kind of despair, if Frank's perception of them is accurate, which is another issue entirely. Herb Wallagher, however, defies Frank's assumptions, and Frank, who is afraid to get to know Herb, misses out on what might make for a very good interview. In fact, Frank has complained about a sameness to athletes who share "unsurprising and factual" (65) lives. For this reason, Frank has confessed, he "sometimes tells less than [he] know[s]" (65) for the sake of a better article. But Herb threatens to tell too much, and in his case, Frank doesn't really want to *know*. Frank can't get the story he's assumed that he would get, so he doesn't get a story at all, at least, not for his magazine. He hears enough of Herb's story to know that Herb's dividedness mirrors his own.

Frank feels similarly trapped by and uncomfortable with Wade Arcenault, Vicki's father, who proudly escorts Frank to the basement of his home in the Jersey suburbs, where the family has converged for Easter dinner. Even though Wade is not a "full-disclosure kind of man" (273), Frank "know[s] exactly what he's discovered" (273), a kind of pleasure that comes from knowing something completely, in and out. In Wade's case, the knowable thing takes the form of a Chrysler, "a big box-safe of a car with fat whitewalls, ballistic bumpers, and an air of postwar styling-with-substance that makes my Malibu only a sad reminder" (264). What's odd about the car is that it resides permanently in Wade's basement where Wade can tinker with it to his heart's content, know every inch of its wiring, start it up and hear it purr. However, the car can take its passenger nowhere but back and forth over the same ground. Wade can "drive it a foot one way and a foot or two back," since "There isn't much room down here" (264). Symbolically, then, the car suggests confinement, dead ends, predictability. Though a powerful vehicle, it never achieves momentum, never performs the function it is so perfectly prepared to perform. Wade's obsessive attention to it in the dark cave of his basement also suggests the isolation and sterility inherent in the suburbs, where houses are close together and presumably neighbors know one another. As Frank talks in the basement with Wade, "The hum [of an electric organ upstairs] sinks through the rafters and fills the basement with an unavoidable new atmosphere. Despair" (274). All of a sudden, Frank visualizes Wade in the hospital for tests, not puttering around in his basement; he glimpses Wade's mortality, longs to tell him to "stay out of hospitals" and "to hug him now" (274), but he cannot do those things, afraid of what Wade might think. They've had such a man-to-man kind of talk; Frank doesn't want Wade to "get the wrong idea" (274). The hum in the air may evoke despair for Frank, but Wade simply glances at the ceiling as if he expects such a noise, which, to him, Frank imagines, signifies that "his house is in superb working order" (274). Frank recognizes Wade as "a man completely without subtext, a literalist of the first order" (274), but obviously Wade's life does not appear to be very desirable. He goes on to tell Frank that he feels like he's seen him before; " 'Isn't that strange?' " (274), he asks Frank. Frank cannot bear to tell him that Wade, who has been a toll-taker for years, actually took Frank's money on Route 1 South approximately "four hundred times" (274). Frank believes that "Wade is after mystery here, and I am not about to deny him" (274). Wade prefers to believe that somehow Frank is a kindred spirit, someone he recognizes as if he has always *known* him, but the truth is that he *has* seen Frank before, many times, under the most banal of circumstances. Frank's assessment of Wade is as gloomy as his assessment of Herb Wallagher, but of course to some extent Frank is not sharing in their despair; he is projecting his onto them.

According to Frank's paradigm, the archetypal athlete and Wade Arcenault thus share a kind of literalness, a lack of "subtext" that renders them unable to detect terror in the air, catch a whiff of mortality, or feel the cool shadow of death lurking around every corner. Although he professes to be a literalist, Frank is not really, and when confronted by others who are, more often than not he flees the scene. As he puts it, when "the facts are made clear, I can't bear it, and run away as fast as I can" (83). Later in the narrative, Frank will make his distinction between factualism and literalism using the example of the two men stranded in the airport, one of whom (the literalist) settles down to watch people and the other of whom (the factualist) wonders what caused the delay and whether a snack will be offered on the next flight. Finding Herb to be as "dreamy as a barn owl" (158) and Wade to be an exemplar of literalness, Frank's thoughts and actions betray the truth, and that is that there is something wrong with all three of these stances, dreaminess, factualism and literalism, as ends in themselves. Any state locks its host into one way of seeing the world and narrows the possibilities for genuine closeness to others. Governed by its own rules, each way of knowing is in and of itself flawed and incomplete.

Walter Luckett's story exemplifies the perils inherent in closing off possibilities. Acquainted with Walter through the Divorced Men's Club,

Frank nonetheless has not felt comfortable with him. Although they've had conversations, they've also experienced silences so terrible that once Walter just got up from the table where they were having coffee and "walked out without ordering anything or saying another word" (85). On other occasions, Frank has "ducked" Walter, and Walter, having walked into the door at a bar that the Divorced Men frequent and having seen Frank, has twice "walked out again" (85). The unspoken boundaries of conversation in the Divorced Men's Club prohibit personal questions, so it comes as some surprise when Walter asks Frank on the night before he leaves for Detroit if he has anyone he confides in. Frank responds, " 'I guess I don't, to tell the truth' " (87), qualifying himself again. Confessions of feelings are of course off limits between men such as Frank and Walter, who should instead be talking about the weather, sports, politics, anything but emotion. But Walter goes on to tell Frank that in a bar in New York a couple of nights before, he "let a man pick [him] up" (92). He says, "Then I went to a hotel with him—the Americana, as a matter of fact—and slept with him" (92). Although he is obviously surprised by this revelation, Frank does not condemn Walter, but he wonders why Walter picked him, in particular, to hear his confession. Walter reveals that he has read Frank's book and decided that Frank could hear such a tale without making a big deal out of it. He does not want Frank to think of the conversation as a confession, because, as he says, "I don't really want a response from you. And I know you don't like confessions" (93). Despite such intimate conversation, Walter dodges Frank's questions about how he feels, acknowledging only that he doesn't really feel any better for having told anyone. Walter just didn't want to possess a secret: "I don't like secrets" (94), he tells Frank. So here Frank finds himself the unwitting confidant, a role he plays again with Herb and then Wade. But his experience with Walter fails to prepare him for those subsequent moments, because Frank, perhaps understandably, misses Walter's cues, which to complicate matters, don't necessarily come in the form of uttered words but rather in what remains unspoken. After all, Walter often deflects Frank's direct questions. But ironically Frank completely fails to detect Walter's despair, the state he fixates on so readily in the cases of Herb and Wade, who, arguably, are in fact coping better than Walter is, at least for the time being.

Typically, Frank finds fault with Walter's confession based on Frank's categorization of mind states. Walter's tale of coupling with another man is finally, according to Frank, just a set of facts. There's no mystery to it, and there will never be. Frank muses, "By disclosing an intimacy he absolutely didn't have to disclose (he didn't want advice, after all), Walter Luckett was guilty of both spoiling my superb anticipation [of a trip to Detroit with Vicki] and illuminating a set of facts-of-life I'd have been happy never to know about" (98). Frank interprets Walter's words solely in relation to himself, a selfish approach, to be sure, but Frank already feels noble for having stayed longer than he planned to have a drink with Walter when instead he wanted to be speeding along the highway toward Vicki's place.

Frank, however, is not yet free of Walter. When he returns from Detroit, he finds Walter standing in his living room; Frank's boarder has let him in. Tired and depressed after his encounter with Herb and ensuing strangeness with Vicki, Frank again is loath to listen to Walter, let alone stay up and have a drink with him. But Walter has more to tell, more sadness to impart, and this time he assures Frank that he feels better for having spoken. In a gesture of trust, he gives Frank a key to his house that he can use "anytime." Frank speculates *"Himself* is what Walter's trying to see! If some old-fashioned, conventional Walter Luckett-ness is recognizable in conventional and forgiving Frank Bascombeness, maybe things won't be so bad. Walter wants to know if he can save himself from being lost out in the sinister and uncharted waters he's somehow gotten himself into" (192). Knowing the self via knowing another is a treacherous enterprise, but Frank truly believes that this exchange is exactly what has occurred. Thus he can usher Walter cheerfully out into the night certain that he has done Walter some good, absolved of the guilt that might otherwise occur from unplugging his phone: "Don't call, my silent message says. . . . Don't call. Friendship is a lie of life. Don't call" (195). This is the last time that Frank will see Walter alive.

"Truth" continues to be a vexed term in *The Sportswriter.* Walter tells Frank the truth, but Frank believes that "Too much truth can be worse than death, and last longer" (139), a thought that he utters before he learns of Walter's suicide. Then there are the many disadvantages to "full disclosure," of which Walter is certainly guilty via his nonconfession. Furthermore, so many subjects, including literature and friendship, promise truth but deliver lies. Even truth poses its own risks: "Full disclosure never does anybody any favors, and in any event there are few enough people in the world who are sufficiently within themselves to make such disclosure pretty unreliable right from the start. All added to the fact that this constitutes intrusion where you least need to be intruded upon, and where telling can actually do harm to everyone involved" (77). Frank's thoughts here only confound the issue further.

After all, he goes on spinning his own tale, but he has revealed upon more than one occasion that he is rarely completely "within" himself. Only the "sufficiently within themselves" can tell it right anyway; a divided self, like Frank, for instance, invites his audience immediately to question his reliability, according to Frank's *own* ponderings. Furthermore, he heartily resists being intruded upon, but he expects his audience to bear with his own confessions, his meandering definitions of abstract states of mind, his strange chronicle of regret.

Even Walter finally rejects full disclosure, albeit posthumously. He leaves a suicide note for Frank in which he instructs Frank to look up his long-lost daughter. "No way" is Frank's response. "I have my own daughter. . . . What happened to Walter on this earth is Walter's own lookout. I'm sorry as hell, but he had his chance like the rest of us" (351). Despite this promise, the reader later will learn that Frank looks her up anyway, only to discover that she does not, in fact, exist. "Walter's story about a daughter born out of wedlock and grown up now in Florida was, it turns out, not true. . . . [it] was just his one last attempt at withholding full disclosure. A novelistic red herring" (367). Frank believes that part of Walter's problem was that his life held too few secrets; he became desperate for mystery yet could not locate it. As Frank tells X, "Walter gave himself up to the here and now," as any good literalist would do, "but got stranded" (334), and he lost his "authority" (350). Frank questions with sorrow, "Whose life ever has permanent mystery built into it anyway?" (350); he is sorry that Walter never found his own version of Mrs. Miller, the palmist, and admits, angrily, "If Walter were here I'd shake the bejesus out of him" (351). Walter's concocted story about the illegitimate daughter becomes his final concession to Frank, the gesture that shows that he has known Frank better than Frank has known him. He knew that Frank hates confessions, so he sends him off on a wild goose chase after the truth and in the process shows Frank that he was capable of telling a lie. This untruth is Walter's "story" within his story: "you thought you knew me, but you didn't." All ways of telling about things are but "provisional" after all, to use Ford's word. Frank will never write the piece on Herb Wallagher, he will never again find himself in the cavernous and humming basement swapping car stories with Wade Arcenault, and he will never get to tell Walter Luckett that no life has "permanent mystery built into it." These stories intersect with Frank's narrative to show just how tenuously language connects one person to another. Frank literally rushes out of such situations, terrified of the truth.

On the Verge of Losing Himself Entirely:
Frank's Relationships with Women

Frank's search for himself has for a time involved sinking as completely as possible into the life of someone else, namely a woman, who is willing, at the very least, to be physically intimate with him. As Frank has said, this process entails "full immersion," the attempt "to be within myself by being as nearly as possible *within* somebody else" (130). Frank does not mean this literally, though at times literally he *is within* someone else. But Frank is not after physical closeness, necessarily; in his narrator's voice he acknowledges that as a "new approach to romance" (130), such a strategy does not work. Not surprisingly, he argues that mystery plays a central role in a successful relationship with a woman, but again and again, he recounts episodes of sexual intimacy that have inspired moments of verbal intimacy, confessions of love and so forth, that give way to full disclosure and subsequent discomfort. Significantly and ironically, these confessions aren't true, either. Such circumstances characterized Frank's series of affairs after Ralph died, when he "romanced all those eighteen women in all those major sports venues" (228). Presumably he learns from these experiences, moving on to conduct affairs based on other, but nonetheless, still shaky foundations.

For example, his relationship with Selma Jassim, with whom he sleeps while at Berkshire College, depends solely on "anticipation" (228) for its energy. In other words, he and Selma deliberately keep their relationship in what is usually an early stage, nurturing the excitement of their time together and making no attempt to progress toward something more permanent. With no expectations of each other apart from the time they both enjoyed, Frank acknowledges that they "thrived," though they "never talked about it" (228). They have little in common, finally, except a desire for each other, which they capably satisfy. Their relationship boils down to what usually are but temporary and insignificant sensory moments: "The sound of cigarette smoke against a telephone, the tinkle-chink of ice cubes from a caressing silence" (229). Frank reveals, though, that he has told Selma he loved her, but she responded strangely: " 'I'll always tell you the truth, unless of course I'm lying to you.' Which at first I didn't think was a very good idea; though. . . after a while I realized that it was actually a piece of great luck. I was being promised truth *and* mystery—not an easy combination" (77). No full disclosure here, Frank reminds his audience, though his recollections also make clear that there was also not much basis for trust between him and Selma. Selma knows "how much of someone you can actually get to know about. Very little" (77), and Frank finds this attitude refreshing at the time. However, prone to recall, more than once, what "a woman I met at the college where I briefly taught" (7) told him, Frank's own narrative suggests that, for him, the relationship had more of a lasting influence on his life than he had planned. Although Frank calls this interlude with Selma "a life briefly perfected" (229) and accepts the relationship's limitations and eventual end, later he finds himself calling her from a pay phone in New Jersey, on his way back to Haddam to identify Walter Luckett's body. Clearly he thinks that he needs something that she can provide, and thus he renders his earlier protestations of their relationship's welcome superficiality somewhat hollow. Their subsequent conversation, during which Selma laughs frequently and inappropriately, suggests how little Selma has thought about Frank. Significantly, and despite her intelligence, Selma is still alone, having found all of her suitors "idiots and very poor" (302), so perhaps her attitude about knowing others, though apparently refreshing, results merely in further isolation. Unable to tell her what is really on his mind, Frank asks, desperately, if he can come and see her; Selma of course refuses him, and the only thing evocative of their earlier intimacy is the familiar clink-clink of an ice cube against her glass.

On the other hand, Vicki, Frank's current girlfriend in his narrative's present, is not his intellectual equal, but she possesses more self-assurance than Frank gives her credit for. Frank describes her as a displaced Texan and hospital nurse, a "sweet, saucy little black hair with a delicate width of cheekbone, a broad Texas accent and a matter-of-factness with her raptures that can make a man like me cry out in the night for longing" (6). Also apt to call her his "little bundle" (7), Frank objectifies Vicki; he clearly acts superior to her in a way unjustified by his being eight years her senior. He *needs* to feel more sophisticated than she, and he is. He also wants to be in control of the relationship, certain of exactly what it is that she provides. Like Selma, Vicki offers him physical intimacy and vicarious literalness. A "literalist from the word go, happy to let the world please her in the small ways it can" (128), Vicki stabilizes Frank, but only temporarily. Wiser in practical matters than she may seem in appearance, Vicki has endured divorce and witnesses daily trauma in the emergency room where she works; nonetheless, Frank concedes that "it is possible to see her as sixteen and chaste instead of thirty and divorced" (59). A "sweet" girl, Vicki possesses valuable traits of kindness and spontaneity. Although not prone to analysis and self-reflection like Frank is, she knows enough to anticipate Frank's mood swings, and she cares enough about herself to withdraw from him before he can withdraw from her. She accomplishes this feat after Easter dinner at her parents' home, where she gives Frank a deserved blow to the head. At the Arcenaults, Frank receives the news of Walter's suicide and the request to identify the body. Taken totally by surprise, Frank has not expected Walter to meet such an end. After all, he never diagnosed Walter as a victim of despair. As Frank departs, he tries to persuade Vicki that he does in fact love her; he coaxes her to the car, rather condescendingly. Upon that occasion, Frank recalls, she "busts me full in the mouth with a mean little itchy fist that catches me midstride and sends me to the turf" (295). Vicki, ironically, utters the novel's most accurate and resounding indictment of Frank: "You're liable to say anything, and I don't like that" (295). Frank acknowledges that in that moment "Words, my best refuge and oldest allies, are suddenly acting to no avail, and I am helpless" (294). In fact, it is Vicki who succeeds in using language for her protection; she lies to Frank about X, telling Frank that X has been having an affair with one of the doctors at the hospital, a statement she makes perhaps simply to turn the tables on the man whose words she can no longer trust. Vicki sees right through Frank's persona, revealing herself to be smarter than she looks.

Frank makes the same mistake with Catherine Flaherty, whom he meets close to novel's end and who is also different from the way she first appears to be. Like Vicki, Catherine is sure of what she wants, and she doesn't mind manipulating Frank to get it. Thinking that she truly admires him and needs a mentor, Frank succumbs completely to her flirting. But he ends up acknowledging that Catherine really doesn't need him to help her in her nascent career as a sportswriter (it turns out she is really interested in medicine); in fact, she needs no mentoring at all. Finally, Frank admits, "I am too old for her; she is too smart for me. . . . I have been wrong altogether about her attitudes toward love and lovemaking, and have also been pleased to find out she is a modern enough girl not to think that I can make things better for her one way or another, even though I wish I could" (372). Some may interpret Frank's desire to make the world better for women whom he cares about as an endearing trait; others may find it patronizing. At least here, though, Frank appears to have learned something about his own limitations and his propensity to label women based on his own desires. For not only has Frank wanted at times to immerse himself completely in another's life, but he has also longed even more to view the world through her eyes, as a literalist, while still sustaining the mystery he values so dearly.

Frank's friendship with X differs markedly from his experiences with other women, including magazine model Mindy Levinson and platonic correspondent Peggy Connover. Both Frank and X keep themselves intact after the divorce; although "there is a resolute sadness between X and me that our marriage is over," it is a "sadness that does not feel sad" (10). With X, Frank does not risk losing himself by desperately hoping that X will provide what he by himself cannot summon to his aid. One could even argue that at one time or another Frank has taken X for granted; Frank admits, as he recounts his surrender to dreaminess, "toward the end of our marriage. . . . I would wake up in the morning and open my eyes to X lying beside me breathing, and not recognize her!" (10). Nonetheless, she is the only woman with whom Frank shares significant history—and common grief—and for whom he expresses genuine respect. He confides, "Sometimes I see her on the street in town or in her car without expecting to and without her knowing it, and I am struck by wonder: what can she want from life now? How could I have ever loved her and let her go?" (11). He never resorts to characterizing her solely through a physical description, though he does describe her carefully. Even through the lens of Frank's occasionally faulty eye, X seems infinitely more mature than Frank's other partners, his marriage to her more meaningful than these other encounters.

Frank's mistake, the problem that precipitates his affairs, resides in his inability to concentrate on his marriage to X, along with many other things. Deep in the throes of dreaminess, he floats from one notion to the next, his mind spinning around infinite possibilities: where to go, with whom to be, what to do. For X, finding the letters to Peggy Connover propels her to action. The platonic nature of the relationship achieves little significance; what she notes is that Frank focuses his energy elsewhere, and the "good sense and breezy humor" (148) that characterize the letters fail to occupy Frank in their home. By this point in Frank's story, one recognizes that Frank is probably less "real" in this correspondence; no doubt he's constructed a persona here, too. However, the fact remains that he neglects his relationship with X by letting his dreaminess overcome him. Frank interprets X's response: "And she began to think, then, that love was simply a transferable commodity for me—which may even have been true—and she didn't like that. And what she suddenly concluded was that she didn't want to, or have to, be married to someone like me a second longer—which is exactly how it happened" (148). Frank's aside here, "—which may have even been true—", is significant, a concession to X's perception. Here, he speaks in the past tense, as narrator, not subject of the story. At the time love may have been easily "transferable," but Frank's long-term relationship with X, which so far surpasses any of his other liaisons, suggests at the very least that something lasting—whether the lives of their other two children, or their mutual grief over Ralph, or just some basic sense of responsibility—binds them to each other.

Furthermore, Frank grants a weight to X's opinions that his other dalliances fail to inspire. She never hesitates to tell him what she thinks, even in the slightly uncomfortable predawn hour of their meeting at Ralph's grave. Frank has chosen part of a poem, Theodore Roethke's "Meditations of an Old Woman," to read: "'I have gone into the waste lonely places behind the eye. . . .' X has already begun to shake her head before I am to the second line, and I stop and look to her to see what the trouble is. . . . 'I don't like that poem,' she says matter-of-factly" (18–19). Frank concedes, "It is possible that reading a poem over a little boy who never cared about poems is not a good idea" (19). Frank relies on X perhaps more than he realizes, often spending the night on her couch after being with his children, at least until he begins his relationship with Vicki. But it is X who meets him upon his return to Haddam after Walter's death, and it is X who accompanies him over to Walter's apartment. Despite the fact that words have failed between them and promises have been broken, their actions testify to some lasting devotion.

Any reader wonders, of course, about the significance of "X" as the letter denoting her identity. Some readers may speculate that Frank, or Ford, intends for this letter to be demeaning in some way, a signifier of her status as an ex-wife, rendered nameless, identity-less, and punished for her leaving. According to the author, however, precisely the opposite is true: "I couldn't find a name that I liked. I decided quite early on to put X on the page because I didn't have a name for her and I thought, eventually I'll come to a name. So all along as I was writing the book, I would write X. And finally X is who she became. Looked at in other ways, Frank can't bear to say her name; he can't—it's an intimacy he doesn't have anymore" (Bonetti, 86). Ford's words imply that Frank has known real intimacy with X, a privilege that he loses after their divorce. The novel confirms this notion: "Genuinely good conversations with your ex-wife are limited by the widening territories of intimacy from which you're restricted" (328), Frank explains. Ironically, true intimacy is what he has been seeking with all of these other women. He realizes he has had such closeness with X, and as the novel ends he suggests that perhaps all is not lost. After all, he and X speak from time to time, keeping each other informed about their decisions. This fact of communication becomes the defining characteristic that sets Frank's relationship with X apart from his other forays into love. Frank even stays in touch with X's parents and mediates between them, because they, too, live apart. As Frank says, "It is possible to love someone, and no one else, and still not live with that one person or even see her" (374). Although he has thrown the word "love" around easily, his manner of speaking about X testifies to the indescribable nature of that emotion, something that the word cannot really capture. The failure of language; the missed cues and signals; the times when X needed Frank and did not realize he had tried to offer consolation; even later when they discuss these moments and Frank admits, "I didn't have the heart to say I'd spoken, but she hadn't heard me" (374): all of these instances betray, again, that human relationships depend on imperfect symbols, the words that human beings use to create those very connections.

In Truth

As *The Sportswriter* ends, Frank claims, "The only truth that can never be a lie, let me tell you, is life itself—the thing that happens" (374). And life, not the story about it, but life itself, often resists the advances of language to characterize it. "Some life is only life," Frank says, "and unconjugatable, just as to some questions there are no answers. Just nothing to say" (369). The unconjugatable does not prevent Frank from trying to make sense of things; he concludes that he "has something to tell that would be important and even interesting" (369). So Frank engages in the attempt to pull experience up out of the depths of the unknowable and give it a name, just as a writer would do, not incidentally, and that attempt, probably more than anything else, is what enables Frank to deepen his understanding of himself and others. Furthermore, the attempt provides him the ballast to face "up to an empty moment in life without suffering the usual terrible regret— which is, after all, the way I began to describe this" (369). The "empty moment" encompasses the whole of Easter weekend, which culminates in Walter's death, the rupture with Vicki, and Frank's spoken request to go home with X after their time at Walter's apartment, an idea that X rejects. Frank then finds himself completely alone, and in that state he recognizes that he is in "a neighborhood where I am not known, a man with no place to go in particular—out, for the moment, of any good ideas, at the end of a sad day that in a better world would never have occurred at all" (338). But this occasion is not a "genuinely" empty moment, Frank concedes, just part of the larger picture.

What he becomes, at that instance of knowing no one and having no place to go, is "invisible":

> Just to slide away like a whisper down the wind is no small freedom, and if we're lucky enough to win such a setting-free, even if it's bad events that cause it, we should use it, for it is the only naturally occurring consolation that comes to us, sole and sovereign, without props or forbearance of others—among whom I mean to include God himself, who does not let us stay invisible long, since that is a state he reserves for himself.
> God does not help those who are invisible too. (*SW,* 339)

Frank describes a kind of self-sufficiency here that has eluded him too readily before. He has sought this kind of consolation many times with women, desiring to be free, escaping the mind through the body, evoking the doom of the Cartesian split. But in this kind of moment he is "loosed from body and duty" (339) and made ready for what is next, having survived what has come before. Without knowing it, he prepares himself for a moment that might be called spiritual, and to some extent it is only by losing himself, almost literally, that he finds it. Frank does not feel visible again until another person turns and sees him, pointing him out while he lurks near the train station (itself a useful symbol of journey, flux, and motion) as a possible ride home. Frank senses "a connection being made. . . . I am unexpectedly visible!" (344).

Such visibility still does not last, even after Frank ventures into New York City, which he calls Gotham, tries to write his piece on Herb Wallagher, which he doesn't finish, and meets Catherine Flaherty. Perhaps Frank loses his figurative visibility again here because he casts himself as a literalist, all for Catherine Flaherty's benefit; he tells her, " 'I just try to arrange things the best way I know how according to my abilities.' I glance around my desk as if I'd just remembered and wanted to refer to something important—a phantom copy of *Leaves of Grass* or a thumbed-up Ayn Rand hardback" (362). Frank loses himself precisely because he is making himself up, contriving his glance around the desk, donning an air of what verges on stoicism. He just does the best that he can, he protests, modestly. As Frank waits for Catherine to go to the ladies' room, he gazes out of his window, across to some other building with lighted windows, and he looks for something he's seen there before. A moment earlier, he's seen another man in an office building, also looking out the window, who for a moment is contemplative, then turns clearly at the sound of someone's voice, knocked from his reverie when "someone I cannot see speaks to him or calls his name" (364). It is no surprise, though, that just a short time later, when Frank looks back out of his own window, he sees no sign of his counterpart across the street. Nonetheless, "I step closer to the glass and try to find him through the dark, stare hard, hoping for even the illusion of a face, of someone there watching me here. Far below I can sense the sound of cars and life in motion. Behind me I hear a door sigh closed again and footsteps coming. And I sense that it's not possible to see there anymore, though my guess is no one's watching me. No one's noticed me standing here at all" (365). At one time, the whisper of a door closing and footsteps coming would be enough to send him soaring into anticipation (cf. Selma Jassim). Frank demonstrates that he has changed even as he comes to terms with his ultimate isolation. Here, Frank reckons with a fundamental fact: that we are ultimately alone upon this earth, responsible only for ourselves. Frank, for a moment, loses his audience; there is no one there, watching him here. Furthermore, he can no longer see his mirrored self, someone he once was but is no longer. Rendered invisible again, he is stranded with only himself to blame. Thus this chapter closes, suggesting that by trying to be other than what he is in order to impress Catherine Flaherty, Frank does risk the loss of himself, or more precisely, the possibility of knowing himself via another.

There is certainly consolation to be had with others; Frank admits as much: "To take pleasure in the consolation of others, even the small ones, is possible" (341). However, Frank's lesson in *The Sportswriter* centers around finding something within himself that can sustain him, throwing off the pain of regret, or "possibilities misconstrued, for consolation not taken" (335), phrases that easily characterize Frank's mistakes with both X and his friend Walter Luckett. Frank alone can reconcile himself with these choices. Perhaps more than anything, *The Sportswriter* is the story of how Frank misses the cues that others send, leading him to the very regret that he has begun his story trying to deflect. Frank's narrative indeed becomes a paean to regret, but at its end he emerges, if not entirely cleansed of its effects, at least partially so. Frank explains, "I thought that one natural effect of life is to cover you in a thin layer of . . . what? A film? A residue or skin of all the things you've done and been and said and erred at?" (374). Telling his story is one way that Frank accepts responsibility for his actions and words, even if he cannot

help but complicate the truth by questioning it. Fittingly, then, he ends
the tale in this way:

> Only suddenly, then, you are out of it—that film, that skin of life—as
> when you were a kid. And you think: this must've been the way it was
> *once in my life,* though you didn't know it then, and don't even really
> remember it—a feeling of wind on your cheeks and your arms, of being
> released, let loose, of being the light-floater. And since that is not how it
> has been for a long time, you want, this time, to make it last, this glis-
> tening one moment, this cool air, this new living, so that you can pre-
> serve a feeling of it, inasmuch as when it comes again it may just be too
> late. You may just be too old. And in truth, of course, this may be the last
> time that you will ever feel this way again. (*SW,* 375)

Frank transcends the world here in a redemptive moment that is by definition temporary, a Wordsworthian spot of time that recreates something akin to childhood purity and freedom. What Frank documents, of
course, is a time during which he is completely within himself, a feat
achieved seemingly only in the best kind of solitude. As Richard Ford
emphasizes in an interview, the moments of clarity that "come to you
with somebody else are different. At least from my particular philosophical Emersonian view (see, I think that's who my great influence is:
Emerson), the kinds of rapport you have with others are totally supported by some kind of wholeness of self" (Walker, 143). Frank partakes
of such wholeness in this "glistening one moment." And, "in truth,"
Frank says, never letting the reader forget his earnestness, he may never
feel this way again.

Frank's freedom here differs from the kind of invisibility he's described
before. It takes root in what Richard Ford is fond of quoting Emerson to
explain: the "infinite remoteness" that underlies us all. Only the attempt
at communication with others can temporarily dispel the infinite remoteness. Such communication succeeds best, though, after individuals
reckon with and accept their own isolation, taking from that state some
experience from which to speak. In other words, self-reconciliation pre-
cedes reconciliation with others. Even in the novel's conclusion, however,
Ford will not let his readers forget what he has called the "provisional"
nature of naming, of storytelling, of speaking to dispel loneliness. After
all, in his final passage, Frank describes precisely what he has said happens *only* in literature: that Joycean epiphany, that sudden realization
that one occupies a moment completely and undistractedly, blessedly
rapt in a singular emotion. This sort of description, Frank himself has

claimed earlier, comprises the great "lie of literature." How does one know the truth about these things? Perhaps it would be fair to say that such a "glistening one moment," when it does happen in life beyond the page, can never be contrived or willed into existence. Always unexpected, it comes unasked for, undeservedly, like grace or serendipity, and resists all attempts to classify it for posterity via language. But Frank, like Richard Ford, has to try.

Chapter Five

Redeemed by Telling in "Great Falls" and *Wildlife*

Several of Richard Ford's works are classic coming-of-age tales in which a teenage boy must witness a parental failure, experience sexual desire and disappointment, pose questions that have no obvious answers, and, like William Faulkner's Sarty or the narrator of James Joyce's "Araby," choose justice over kin or feel his eyes burn with anguish and shame. Ford's male narrators in the short story "Great Falls" (included in *Rock Springs* (1987)) and the novel *Wildlife* (1990) experience loneliness that accompanies self-knowledge gained despite, or perhaps because of, the inscrutableness of others. Although Ford leaves his narrators in isolation at each narrative's end, he reveals the heightened awareness that has projected them into the act of observation. Told in the past tense, each text is narrated by an adult speaker who structures his story carefully, editorializing and revising the incidents that changed the course of his teenage years and shaped his attitudes toward others. Significantly, this mature perspective confirms each speaker's ability to recast an emotionally volatile time as an open-ended story.

Philosophical Questions: Knowing and Being

Through the scaffolding of each narrator's quest to know himself and his parents, Ford bolsters what on the surface are spare narratives with an underlying philosophical complexity, and his propensity to quote Jean-Paul Sartre outside of the frame of his fictional universes suggests the author's fascination with being, knowing, and nothingness, words that also occur frequently in Ford's fiction. His narrators pose epistemological and existential questions that defy easy answers, finally discovering not only the frailty of human nature but also the frailty of language. Paradoxically, language's instability also provides its magic, its capacity to transform and transcend the ordinary. Ford's narrators in both "Great Falls" and *Wildlife*, in fact, embark upon quests not unlike that of Sartre's own fictional and epistemological seeker, Roquentin, the narrator of

Nausea who discovers that only art may transform loneliness and transcend existence and time.[1]

Resisting notions that his often-musing narrators liken his fiction to Walker Percy's or other southern works dominated by intellectual male voices, as Fred Hobson has observed (Hobson 1991, 54–58),[2] Ford prefers to situate his work in the context of a Western literary canon that can lay claim to writers and texts far exceeding the geographical boundaries of the South.[3] To limit certain kinds of characters by a regional frame is to ignore a much vaster sphere of influence, Ford argues. Rather than grouping Faulkner's Quentin Compson, Wolfe's Eugene Gant, Warren's Jack Burden, Percy's Will Barrett, and his own Frank Bascombe as "southern male intellectuals" whose thoughts stultify their actions, Ford observes that southerners have no such corner on this market (Walker, 133). Ford is much more apt to quote Sartre than Faulkner, as he does in an interview: "To name something is to take it out of the well of the unmediated and bring it up to the level of notice" (Walker, 132). It is in this context that his narrators' choices to tell their stories in "Great Falls" and *Wildlife* become significant.

Stylistic Connections Between the Narratives

Both narratives depend upon a voice that interrupts time, gliding past the intervening years and back to a season, a day, or even an hour when life as the narrator knew it changed. The texts are in fact quite similar in tone and exposition, and each narrator's self-conscious phrasing indicates his deliberate plan to tell these events as crafted story rather than angst-filled confession. "Great Falls" opens with Jackie's words: "This is not a happy story. I warn you. My father was a man named Jack Russell, and when I was a young boy in my early teens, we lived with my mother in a house to the east of Great Falls, Montana" (29). The turning point for Jackie takes place in 1960, when he is 14. Joe, *Wildlife*'s narrator, begins, "In the Fall of 1960, when I was sixteen and my father was for a time not working, my mother met a man named Warren Miller and fell in love with him" (1). Each narrator locates the memory by place and time and his own age, the past tense removing him from the scene even as he participates as central character.

Furthermore, each son sets the mother at some emotional (or physical) distance between himself and his father, either through the judicious use of "we" or simply by yoking himself with his father: "when I was sixteen and my father was for a time not working," for example. The past tense also hints that this connection between father and son is a temporary link, one determined not so much by kinship as by sheer circumstance: time, place, and action. These syntactical details suggest the rifts that will only widen between the speaker and his parents, so that, by each narrative's end, the "I" has become unquestionably singular.

The disappearing mother further connects these narratives thematically. Both sons witness marital disjunction, usually initiated as an easing of communication between father and mother that develops into a full-blown and profound rupture, often precipitated by the mother's pursuit of another man and followed by her departure. Interestingly, several other of Ford's stories include sons with absent mothers or mothers who have taken up with boyfriends, such as "Children," "Optimists," and "Communist," all published along with "Great Falls" in *Rock Springs,*[4] as well as the more recent "Jealous," published in the collection *Women with Men* (1997). This recurrence of fictional circumstance would seem to suggest the author's fascination with familial dissolution, or, perhaps, echoing a metaphysical poetic lesson, the predictability of woman's inconstancy. Some readers might seek to identify the death of Ford's own father in 1960, when the younger Ford was 16, as some psychological impetus for exploring themes of abandonment. Ford's own life, however, testifies to his mother's consistent presence in it, as the author himself documents in "My Mother, In Memory." Ford himself has been married to the same woman for 30 years. These facts may undercut attempts to psychoanalyze the author as well as refute unjust charges of sexism on Ford's part. Careful readings of these narratives would also preclude the latter, since the father characters emerge as self-absorbed and somewhat oblivious to the marital problems that precede their wives' departures, while their subsequent behavior is revealed as immature at best.

What seems most significant is that in each narrative the sons must deal with *both* parents as frail human beings rather than authority figures possessed of prudence and wisdom. The parents tumble off their pedestals; the sons meanwhile clamber for some purchase on adult ground precisely as that territory becomes defined as mysterious, unpredictable, unreliable. In these works, parents become demythologized when their sons are hardly pubescent (not in itself an uncommon occurrence), and the role reversals that ensue determine each narrator's perspective thereafter. The collapse of parental structure, these texts suggest, is not a phenomenon that necessitates explication; in fact, such circumstances will resist rather than yield to studies thereof. That resistance is what captivates each son. Literally being the only one left out of and with no control over the father-mother relationship, even as he exists as one point of the triangle connecting them, the narrator drifts into his role as outsider before the reader's very eyes. Simultaneously, his parents become ghostlier demarcations of their former selves, now suddenly unknowable. The question that inhabits each narrative is an epistemological one: What can I know when I cannot even know my parents?

Parents as Unknowable Entities in "Great Falls"

This question is succinctly posed by "Great Falls." Early paragraphs in the story indicate that Jack and his wife, who is never given a first name at all and in fact is called "Mrs. Russell" only once over the story's course, have long had different ideas about how their lives would proceed. "[My father] had been an Air Force sergeant and had taken his discharge in Great Falls. And instead of going home to Tacoma, where my mother wanted to go, he had taken a civilian's job with the Air Force, working on planes, which was what he liked to do" (29–30). Jackie's mother married Jack because he was "young and wonderful looking" (30), and because she wanted to escape her present life and see the world, which Jackie assumes they were able to do for a while. "That was the life she wanted, even before she knew much about wanting anything else or about the future" (30). Acknowledging his mother's thwarted or buried desires, Jackie intimates that his mother possessed some internal life that even she was not yet privy to at that age. That internal space seems to grow larger and larger, so that by the time he tells the story, his mother is someone with whom he and his father "lived" (29), almost a stranger.

Jackie more explicitly characterizes his father's passions: hunting and fishing. In so doing, he subtly reveals his father's faults: "It is a true thing that my father did not know limits. . . . he would catch a hundred fish in a weekend, and sometimes more than that. It was all he did from morning until night, and it was never hard for him. . . . It was the same with ducks, the other thing he liked" (30–31). Jackie describes taking these trips with his father and later selling—illegally, of course—the excesses of wild game that he has caught to the Great Northern Hotel. Afterwards, often they would stop for Jack to get a drink, arriving home late. Jackie never wonders what his mother is doing during these weekends or attempts to assess her degree of loneliness. Jack senior emerges as a man who does what he wants, when he wants, and who disregards the rules if they don't suit him. Such descriptions suggest some insensitivity to his wife's needs and desires as well as a nature that defies any external boundaries that don't coincide with his own. Jack is a man of excesses whose passions apparently exclude his wife, at least most of the time.

One night, however, after one of these hunting trips, Jackie and his father depart from routine, a change that instigates an unusual conversation between father and son as well as foreshadows the incident that alters the family dynamic. Jack suggests that they go straight home from the Great Northern and "surprise your mother" (33), cook the remaining ducks on the grill, do "something different" (33). On the way home, Jack adopts a different manner with his son, telling him things that Jackie finds a little odd, such as that his mother had said, "Nobody dies of a broken heart" (33), and asking him questions about himself. " 'What do you worry about, Jackie,' my father said" (34). Pushing his son for an answer, he suggests a few himself: girls, his future sex life, all of which Jackie denies. " 'Well, what then?' my father said. 'What else is there?' 'I worry if you're going to die before I do,' I said, though I hated saying that, 'or if Mother is. That worries me' " (34). Although his father makes a joke out of his response ("If I were you, I'd worry that we might not" [34]), Jackie describes the conversation poignantly: "He smiled at me, and it was not the worried, nervous smile from before, but a smile that meant he was pleased. And I don't remember him ever smiling at me that way again" (34). From his future vantage point, the narrator can cast these moments as fleeting and significant, his younger self as poised unwittingly on the brink of change. He tells the reader that his father then says, " 'I want to respect your privacy,' . . . for no reason at all that I understood" (35). The exchange dramatizes Jackie's awareness of his parents' mortality, foreshadows broken hearts and his father's own inscrutable behavior (his sentence uttered "for no reason at all that I understood"), as well as the son's inability to imagine a reason that makes sense at the time. Only in retrospect can this editorializing occur ("And I don't remember him ever smiling at me that way again," for instance), suggesting the narrator's careful reconstruction of the scene and the dialogue.

Language's Failure in "Great Falls"

Meanwhile, the circumstances—departing from the usual routine, surprising the mother—set up the story. The mother will not be expecting them. Father and son will arrive home to find a strange car parked down the road from their house and a young man—not much older than Jackie—in the kitchen. Several confrontations and conversations ensue. The young man, whose name is Woody, and Jackie wait outside while his father and mother talk. When his father comes out of the house, he "looked roughed up, as though he had hurt himself somehow" (39), and soon he pulls a gun from his pocket that he brandishes foolishly in Woody's face, repeatedly asking him, "What's the matter with you?" (40). All four characters end up in the yard, publicly displayed. Jackie observes that no one really thought that his father would shoot Woody, except perhaps his father himself, who "was trying to find out how to" (41). With his mother standing by ineffectually, trying to assure Jack that Woody doesn't love her, Woody unflinching and nonchalant before his father's gesticulations and rapid-fire questions, and Jackie standing by as a spectator, the tableau depicts failed communication on several fronts. Jackie's preoccupation with knowing others has begun as he tries to make sense of the scene.

The verb "to know" dominates many of Jackie's sentences. Woody "*knew* nothing about anything that was here" (38; italics mine). While talking to Woody, Jackie finds himself wondering "what Woody *knew* that I didn't. Not about my mother—I didn't *know* anything about that and didn't want to—but about a lot of things, about the life out in the dark, about coming out here, about airports, even about me. He and I were not so far apart in age, I *knew* that. But Woody was one thing, and I was another" (39; italics mine). Jackie appears certain of what he does know, and he knows enough to realize just how much is left unknown. Talking to Woody in the yard will not reveal Woody's secrets, or explain "life out in the dark." But Jackie wonders what Woody knows about him, as if now he has to see himself—and indeed the entire realm of his family life—through someone else's eyes. The retrospective narrative voice transforms the teenage Jackie's encounter with Woody into a fundamentally existential moment; Jackie knows he exists and that Woody exists, but he cannot make the common fact of existence pull them into each other's sphere of knowing. In other words, the presence of an "other," while confirming one's own being in the world, does nothing to dissipate isolation. In this encounter, "*l'enfer, c'est les Autres,*" as Sartre has written, because Woody's gaze does nothing but alienate Jackie from himself and what he has previously assumed about his world. Jackie's last sentence—"Woody was one thing, and I was another"—asserts the basic separateness that characterizes all human beings, the very notion dramatized moments later by the scene in the yard.

Furthermore, all of the words exchanged in that scene become emptied of meaning. Jack's threats, Woody's response, and Jackie's mother's denial of Woody's love finally effect nothing: " 'Are you in love with her, too? Are you, crazy man? Are you? Do you say you love her? Say you love her! Say you love her so I can blow your fucking brains in the sky.' 'All right,' Woody said. 'No. It's all right.' 'He doesn't love me Jack. For God's sake,' my mother said. She seemed so calm" (41). Woody's contradictory and passive response to his father, his mother's unemotional resignation and imminent departure with Woody, and his father's hollow gesture of violence all conspire, presenting these adults as isolated individuals doomed to utter meaningless phrases. Hell *is* other people, this passage implies, especially when the one supreme isolation-defying instrument, the very thing that sets human beings apart from all other creatures—language—fails.

When language fails, Jackie can only know the circumstances empirically, through hearing and watching, paying attention to the signs that make this place familiar to him: "The wind rose then, and from behind the house I could hear [the dog] bark once from far away, and I could smell the irrigation ditch, hear it hiss in the field. . . . It was nothing Woody knew about, nothing he could hear or smell" (38). Though present in the same surroundings, Jackie and Woody exist in different worlds of knowing. What is "nothing" for Woody assumes significance for Jackie, further assuring each's alienation from the other. Jackie knows these things because, for him, these sensations actually signify something, that is, that this place is his home; for Woody, the same events fail to register, and certainly fail to signify. However, even for Jackie, his awareness of his own being in the world, what the philosopher Martin Heidegger would call *Dasein,* will not be enough. Jackie cannot know others through the signs of the wind blowing, the dog barking, the water hissing; rather he must rely on words, symbols, the very things that his parents and Woody cannot summon effectively.

Woody even lies inexplicably to Jackie, telling him that his mother has been married before. Later, when Jackie asks her if this is true, she says, "No. . . . Who told you that? That isn't true. I never was. Did Jack say that to you? Did your father say that?" (47). Jackie never tells her who has made this statement, and his mother's surprisingly defensive response suggests some past of which his father has not approved, but Jackie will never, of course, know the real truth. Likewise, his mother will never know who spoke those words.

Under these circumstances, language is a slippery instrument. In its purest use, language may function semiotically as a symbol connecting an object with a word and, via the word, the person with the object, just as the word "wind" denotes that which is blowing, that Jackie hears and recognizes as "wind," and also connotes other meanings, associations of familiarity, security, knowledge of a place. Drawing upon the writings of American philosopher Charles Peirce, Walker Percy has distilled this semiotic concept into a simple triangular diagram; the speaking person, the word, and the thing the word signifies each make up one point of the figure.[5] The picture becomes somewhat more complicated when another person is introduced into the exchange; then the word must signify the same thing to both speakers in order for communication to occur. If words lose their meanings or fail to signify, as they have in the conversation that takes place out in the yard in "Great Falls," then language, Jackie discovers, may not be an effective conduit for knowledge.

Knowing, Being, and Nothingness: Making Jackie's Story Yield to Language

As the story ends, Jackie continues to frame the memory in terms of some epistemological search; he says that he thought to himself, "my life had turned suddenly, and that I might not know exactly how or which way for possibly a long time. Maybe, in fact, I might never know" ("Great Falls," 49). He goes on to question,

> why wouldn't my father let my mother come back? Why would Woody stand in the cold with me outside my house and risk being killed? Why would he say my mother had been married before, if she hadn't been? And my mother herself—why would she do what she did? In five years my father had gone off to Ely, Nevada, to ride out the oil strike there, and been killed by accident. And in the years since then I have seen my mother from time to time—in one place or another, with one man or other—and I can say, at least, that we know each other. But I have never known the answers to these questions, have never asked anyone their answers. ("Great Falls," 49)

The adult voice wrestles with the same questions, this passage attests. Despite claiming to know his mother (perhaps meaning here that they are at least acquainted), Jackie suggests that he does not feel comfortable enough with her to talk about these puzzling events. As he has observed about Woody, he "was one thing, and I was another" (39). The story's closing passage only confirms this observation: "Though possibly it—the answer—is simple: it is just low-life, some coldness in us all, some helplessness that causes us to misunderstand life when it is pure and plain, that makes our existence seem like a border between two nothings, and makes us no more or less than animals who meet on the road—watchful, unforgiving, without patience or desire" (49). A "coldness," a "helplessness," keeps one person distinct from another, so that two lives cannot really meet, so that "our existence is a border between two nothings" (49). In this passage, the speaker synthesizes his epistemological and existential inquiries: we can never know each other, he claims, and, furthermore, we exist in the face of nothingness; others may remind us not only of our being but also of our isolation, our existence in the face of what is not, and of our own consciousness that is impossible to explain. Whatever it is that makes us misunderstand each other, the "coldness," the "helplessness," and whenever language fails us, we are no more (or less) than animals, the speaker finally theorizes.

These are the philosophical conclusions that the narrator of "Great Falls" draws, sounding finally much more like Jean-Paul Sartre than a product of Montana.[6] Thematically such a detail is appropriate; the narrator may take the reader by surprise with his existential thoughts. His observation about the human predicament may seem a bleak and unpredictable one, but he has warned the reader from the beginning that this will not be a happy story. Despite such a grim analysis, the narrator's own attempt to make the circumstances yield to language is important, and his Sartrean preoccupation with being and nothingness no accident on Richard Ford's part.

Continuing the Search in *Wildlife*

Ford makes the same point in his novel *Wildlife* (1990), which chronicles another narrator's witnessing of familial dissolution: his mother leaving his father for another man, his father's outraged act of arson as a consequence, and then the strange reconciliation between his parents. Also set in Great Falls, the narrative centers around Joe's attempt to know his parents. Like Jackie, he embarks upon an epistemological search, though he acknowledges early in his telling that "when you are sixteen you do not know what your parents know, or much of what they understand, and less of what's in their hearts" (18). Again, however, Ford provides an adult narrator, one who looks back over his life and relates the details in a certain way. Such a perspective makes the father's words to his son—"When you get older. . . . If you want to know the truth don't listen to what people tell you" (15)—particularly resonant. Language will fail here, too, and here, too, the son will fail to know his parents.

Wildlife, in fact, seems to be an extended exploration of the themes first dramatized in "Great Falls." Just as Jackie suspects that his mother has not been happy with his father's decisions, so Joe speculates about his mother's unfulfilled desires. In *Wildlife,* the Brinsons have moved to Montana because Joe's father Jerry had hoped to partake in the area's economic boom. Jerry has been a golf pro, working at small country clubs mainly in eastern Washington state, though the family lived in Idaho preceding their move to Montana. Joe thinks perhaps his mother has followed his father simply out of love, but says "I do not think she ever wanted to come to Montana" (4), where the weather was harsher and the people less friendly. Joe presents his family as outsiders in the town, a fact only exacerbated after his father loses his job at the club and his mother takes a position as a swim instructor at the YWCA. Meanwhile, timber fires rage west of Great Falls, figuratively suggesting the tension smoldering in Joe's own family as his father goes weeks without seeming to look for work. At last a position fighting the fires opens, a chance Jerry enthusiastically takes, despite his wife Jean's vocal opposition of her worries that he knows nothing about fighting fires. Thus Jerry leaves Joe alone with his mother, whose behavior will become increasingly erratic. Almost overnight, in the three days of his father's absence, Joe's assumptions about his family will be questioned; the adult narrator observes: "It should've been a time when I cared about more things—a new girlfriend, or books—. . . . But I only cared about my mother and father then" (25). The "then" punctuates the narrator's perspective, implying that since that time he has learned something about himself and his parents and the boundaries between them.

To See Is Not to Know in *Wildlife*

In her husband's absence, Jean takes up with another man, Warren Miller, who has played golf at the club, entering a dalliance that will set Joe apart from his mother and cause him to see her differently. Seemingly oblivious to her son's feelings, Jean flaunts this relationship, taking Joe with her to Warren's house where she dances drunkenly with him and kisses him. Even after she and Joe go to the car, she returns to Warren's house one last time, leaving Joe cold and watchful in the car, where through the window he can see that "Warren Miller had pulled my mother's green dress up from behind her so that you could see where her stockings were held by white elastic straps, and you could see her white underpants. . . . he was holding my mother outside her underwear, and pulling her toward him so hard that he picked her up off the floor and held her against him while he kissed her and she kissed him" (97). Forced into voyeurism, Joe sees his mother as he never should see her: a sexual object whose garters he cannot even call by name, resorting instead to the innocent and descriptive "white elastic straps." Later that same evening, his mother has sex with Warren Miller in her own home, where Joe will see Warren naked in the hall. Again Jean will leave Joe alone while she walks Warren out to his car in the morning's wee hours. Joe waits, *again* looking out the window, forced to watch for something as yet unknown, identifying with a magpie that he catches in the dim light of his flashlight through the window.

Contemplation of this object makes Joe himself like the bird. The bird seemed to be looking at "nothing" (111), and "It wasn't afraid simply because it knew nothing to be afraid of" (112). When it finally flies at the glass, Joe fears that it will crash against the window, but strangely it veers without hitting anything, "leaving me there with my heart pounding, and my light shining onto the cold yard at nothing" (112). Confronted with "nothing," Joe likewise becomes invisible, literally and figuratively speaking, as the bird regards the nothingness where he is, glassed in by his own isolation.[7] The repetition of "nothing" recalls the ending of "Great Falls," and Joe's moment in the dark with the bird may be likened to the strange exchange between Jackie and Woody in that story. Only here it is the bird's gaze, not Woody's, that renders the boy aware of what he does not know and of the emptiness that surrounds him and fills him. At first even his mother does not see him when she returns to the house, but finally catching a glimpse of him in the shadows, she slaps him inexplicably, not once but twice, with each hand. Again he catches sight of her in a way that makes her strange to him, her stomach "and all of that" (114) visible through her open bathrobe. He wishes that "she had her clothes on" (114).

Both Joe and his mother are objectified here; the son can see his mother only as the consummate "other," but her confrontation of him makes him see himself through her eyes to such an extent that he actually apologizes to her, ashamed of having witnessed the scene. As Sartre writes in *Being and Nothingness,* "the Other is the indispensable mediator between myself and me. I am ashamed of myself as I *appear* to the Other. By the mere appearance of the Other, I am put in the position of passing judgment on myself as on an object, for it is an object that I appear to the Other."[8] Later, in the dark of his room, Joe admits, "what I felt like was a spy—hollow and not forceful, not able to cause anything" (*WL*, 116). Literally incapacitated by this encounter, forced to see himself through his mother's gaze (and she also is ashamed, though she expresses this emotion through anger), Joe can only ponder the futility of it all: "And I wished for a moment that I was dead" (116).[9] Robbed of his subjectivity and "not able to cause anything," Joe contemplates not existing and the nothingness that threatens to erase his own being.

Being, Knowing, and Why Words Fail in *Wildlife*

Faced with what is fleshly and carnal (his mother) and with the emptiness without and within (symbolized by the vacant stare of the bird and Joe's own invisibility), Joe confronts evidence of being and nonbeing, states that defy the use of language to describe or dispel them. Appropriately, Joe offers no explanation of his mother's behavior and describes his own silence in his mother's presence as deliberate. These extremes—his mother's visible nakedness versus his own strange bodily emptiness—render him speechless. He describes her angry countenance, his awareness that she might hit him again, his recognition that he is actually afraid. His mother continues to talk to him, asking him if he wants to leave, telling him that he can tell his father that she's "not up to" (115) making things better. But Joe cannot say a thing, worried that if he speaks his mother will not answer back and that he will then be left with his "own words . . . to live with, maybe forever" (115). This thought reminds the narrator, who now intrudes in his adult voice, that certain words should not be said and are useless under certain circumstances. "And there are words, significant words, you do not want to say, words that account for busted-up lives, words that try to fix something ruined that shouldn't be ruined . . . , and that words can't fix anyway" (116). Here, then, is Joe's acknowledgment of language's failure.

Confronted by this same failure when his father comes home from fighting the fires, Joe knows that his father wants to know the truth about his mother and Warren Miller, but he cannot bring himself to tell his father the whole story. After answering several of his father's questions, Joe again lapses into silence, because, he says, "I did not say anything else because even though I could see it all in my mind again. . . I didn't think I knew everything and did not want to pretend I did, or that what I'd seen was the truth" (150–51). Joe makes a distinction here between something that he can see and something that he can know, suggesting that the act of knowing is not based sheerly on empirical evidence but rather on something that defies rational explanation. The "truth" about his parents—their different ways of being unfaithful to each other, and the relationship that persists between them—is something that Joe will concede he has never known by the novel's end.

Arguably, the novel's climax centers around Joe's father's own irrational attempt to burn down Warren Miller's house, an act that, like the strange scene that Jackie witnesses in the yard in "Great Falls," becomes very much a public spectacle. A crowd gathers as Warren Miller emerges from the house with another woman who is wearing silver high-heeled shoes that Joe has seen in a closet in Miller's house. After setting the porch on fire, Jerry remains stationary as Warren strides toward him, cursing him, and finally hitting him squarely in the face. During all of this commotion, Joe notices more people coming out of their houses and younger boys angling for better views, a fact punctuated by Warren's angry inquiry, "What do you think all these people think of you? A house-burner like this. In front of his own son. I'd be ashamed" (167). Jerry replies, "Maybe they think it was important to me" (167). But Joe suspects that all of the spectators, including the firemen who have by now arrived, know Warren Miller, whereas "we, my father and I, and my mother, didn't know anyone" (167).[10] Acknowledging that they had only themselves to "answer for us" (167) if things went wrong, Joe presents his family as self-contained, unbelonging, "strangers" (167). Faced with a crowd of people whose stares can only intensify his family's shame, Joe experiences real isolation, another Sartrean moment when the presence of others only certifies one's loneliness.

In the narrator's own words, "not very much happened" (167) after that. Miller tells the firemen that there has been some misunderstanding; a fireman scolds Jerry harshly for starting such a senseless fire in dry weather, reminding him of the smoldering wild fires that Jerry himself has battled. Joe ends up living with his father when his mother moves out. Warren Miller eventually dies. Joe acknowledges not really having any friends but believing that his life "*was* like other boys' lives" (175). He has to admit, however, that he "did not have a life except for the life at home with [his] father" (175), a fact that he does not find strange "even now" (175), in his adult voice and from his adult perspective. He does include the detail that the wildfires have continued to burn, that "they did not die out easily" but instead "smoldered all winter" (175), that they could not be put out the way that one would think that they could. The narrator only alludes to the fires' symbolic overtones; he resists the explication himself, leaving the image open to his audience's interpretation.

What Joe does do is to admit his wonderment about the world that has enfolded him so tightly. "I wondered . . . if I would ever see the world as *I* had seen it before then, when I did not even know I saw it. . . . [if] that when you faced the worst and went past it what you found there was nothing. Nothing has its own badness, but it does not last forever" (174). The crisis makes him see the world with a keener eye; he suggests that prior to these events he "did not even know" that he saw the world. Pursuant to this new awareness, though, is Joe's suspicion that he has also encountered something that is not so concrete as the world, a "nothing," not a something, in fact. Existence and nothingness seem inextricably bound; to know one is to know the other, Joe suggests. Furthermore, the act of knowing is itself a tricky enterprise. After his parents' eventual reunion, Joe can only admit that "God knows there is still much to it that I myself, their only son, cannot fully claim to understand" (177), and with those words the novel ends. This admission is striking, given Joe's own assertion throughout the text that his entire world has consisted of his parents and his close observations of the rifts and reunions between them. Despite his rendering of the story, he finally must accede to something that resists explanation: the unknowableness of the two people who were closest to him in the world.

Telling as the Redemptive Act in *Wildlife*

Joe's conclusion, and that of the novel, makes no attempt to explain, to analyze, to interpret; rather, it suggests that the mere telling of the story is enough. His transformation of the events into story does not, Joe must admit, make the events make more sense, but he tells it anyway, as if the act itself assumes some significance and in itself redeems the memory of his isolation. Richard Ford has acknowledged his own fascination with loneliness and what he calls its "cure":

> It's what Emerson in his essay on Friendship (interestingly enough) calls the "infinite remoteness" that underlies us all. But . . . [the] predicament is a seminal one; that is, what it inseminates is an attempt to console that remote condition. If loneliness is the disease, then the story is the cure. To be able to tell a story like [*Wildlife*] about your parents is in itself an act

of consolation. Even to come to the act of articulating that your parents are unknowable to each other, unknowable to you, is itself an act of acceptance, an act of some optimism, again in that Sartrean sense that to write about the darkest human possibility is itself an act of optimism because it proves that those things can be thought about. (Walker, 141)

In both "Great Falls" and *Wildlife,* the events that occur are not spectacular events that require theorizing or explanation. But it is the narrator's way of grappling with his life that transforms it into story material while at the same time allowing the narrator to transcend his past through the self-conscious fashioning of the story. He is at once the present "I" and the future "eye" who sees the events at some distance. The adult perspective, in fact, allows the speaker to frame his search as an epistemological one, and the existential reckoning with the surrounding world accompanies this quest for knowledge about others and the self. In the passage above, Ford provides a lens through which to view his narrators' searches while the texts themselves provoke a Sartrean examination of loneliness and ways of redeeming that state.

The Sartrean Connection

In *Nausea,* Sartre's novel that expounds upon many of the same points that he makes in the more complex *Being and Nothingness,* the main character, Roquentin, tells his story through a diary that records his efforts to discover something about himself in relation to other people and objects. His epistemological search is essentially a mental one, revolving around his thoughts rather than events that happen to him. His sensation of nausea derives from the notion that he is simultaneously alienated from his consciousness of himself and yet unable to escape it. Doomed to failing relationships with other people as well, Roquentin becomes more and more repulsed by his own body. Finally, though, he experiences a revelation while wandering by the sea and into a garden, and that is that any attempt to categorize a thing using abstract language is a false attempt to understand its being. Language, in fact, is simply imposed on the world by human beings in an attempt to make the world orderly.

Instead, Roquentin discovers the disorderliness of the world, the characteristics that defy groupings and namings by species and kind. In the famous contemplation of the chestnut tree, Roquentin offers this explanation,

This root . . . existed in such a way that I could not explain it. Knotty, inert, nameless, it fascinated me, filled my eyes, brought me back unceasingly to its own existence. . . . "This is a root"—it didn't work any more. I saw clearly that you could not pass from its function as a root, as a breathing pump, *to that,* to this hard and compact skin of a sea lion, to this oily, callous, headstrong look. The function explained nothing: it allowed you to understand generally that it was a root, but not *that one* at all.[11]

Roquentin himself resorts to metaphor in his description ("breathing pump," "skin of a sea lion"). The irony of course is that he still must use language, but here he employs it differently, not to categorize. The root itself brings him back over and over again to its individual properties, its essence that defies generalizations about roots. When he ponders that the root has been called black, he exclaims, "Black? I felt the word deflating, emptied of meaning with extraordinary rapidity" (175). In other words, the thing will defy the word that normally describes it. Confronted by the root's unrelenting existence, Roquentin must instead use words that are not usually associated with the root in order to even approach capturing its being in language.

What Roquentin ultimately realizes is that only art escapes the realm of existence; art objects—a painting, a song, a novel—are unreal and ideal, transcendent of time. As he hears a voice sing, "Some of these days / You'll miss me, honey" (234), he acknowledges that the record can be scratched, even destroyed, but the song will not cease to exist. Such a thought inspires him, not to commit suicide, as he has already contemplated, but to write a novel that would require its reader to "have to guess, behind the printed words, behind the pages, at something that would not exist, that would be above existence" (237). Likewise he has had to guess at the essence of the root, at what lies behind the words that normally would fail to describe it.

Roquentin's search may also clarify Jackie's search in "Great Falls" and Joe's similar quest in *Wildlife,* demonstrating how each narrator's discovery of language's failure will not prevent him from telling his story. Time after time in these two narratives, words themselves are emptied of meaning, as quickly as Roquentin cites the deflation of the word "black." This phenomenon, though, does not obstruct the more complicated effort to create a story that will actually require a probing beyond the words on the page, to get at what the words point to, not just what they say but what they symbolize. To describe that which exists requires metaphor, the deliberate and creative misuse of language that allows the language-user to compare two things that are not usually likened. Significantly, Ford and his narrators do not call attention to moments in their stories that might be named metaphorical or symbolic, as if to suggest that meaning must be derived from language, not dictated by it. Only the repeated patterns of certain words—"knowing" and "nothing," for example—invite what Sartre would call the "guess" at something beyond the printed page.

Sartre is certainly not the only philosopher or intellectual to find some sort of redemption in art. Heidegger praises the poetic voice; Kierkegaard notes the importance of the aesthetic reversal. If one is alienated, to read (observe a painting, hear a song, etc.) about another's alienation may to some extent relieve the alienation. Modernist writers including Ezra Pound and Wallace Stevens find art the only ballast against an unstable world; Stevens goes so far as to replace religion with art. Regardless of its name, whether it is called despair or anguish by philosophers such as Kierkegaard and Heidegger, or simply "the border between two nothings," as the narrator of "Great Falls" pronounces, loneliness spurs its host to contemplate something beyond the self. In fact, some cognizance of loneliness in the face of an unyielding universe of the self, the world, or the other seems to be required for art to perform its transcendent function. In this way, then, loneliness is redeeming even as (or precisely because) it necessitates a redemption from its state.

Rendering Life into Art

Despite their realizations of language's potential for failure and the frailty of human beings, the narrators of Richard Ford's "Great Falls" and *Wildlife* decide to reconstruct something that has happened to them and to tell it in such a way that it becomes a deliberate rendering of a specific time in their lives, a time that continues to open into the future, as their adult voices testify. By the inclusion of remarks that explicate and interpret the past (or that acknowledge that the past cannot be explained), the narrators expose the artifice of their constructions even as they participate in the narratives' unfolding. This process entails forays into musings beyond the simple facts of what has happened, contemplations of senses and objects that in themselves suggest something other than themselves, as the magpie and the fires do in *Wildlife*. In other words, each narrator transforms a traumatic event into a constructed story: life into art.

Jackie and Joe experience bereavement, disappointment, and betrayal at the hands of their parents, and in both texts, a painful rift between father and mother leaves the son caught between the two but able to name the unknowableness that characterizes human beings, even those bound by blood. In the ever-widening gap between self and other, these narrators locate the reader, offering some consolation that even that which resists understanding gives way to telling. "If loneliness is the disease, then the story is the cure" (Walker, 141), Richard Ford asserts. But loneliness itself is also redemptive, its evocation of nothingness the very state that invites transcendence through art. Language's paradoxical role complicates this endeavor; in fact, each narrator must first realize that there are things that "words cannot fix anyway," as Joe observes, and times when words cannot even be uttered. As Jean-Paul Sartre explains, language is an imperfect tool, but the attempt to use language figuratively, to force meaning from the unwieldy word despite its inherent imperfection, is itself an act of creativity that reaches beyond the mire and blood of existence. In this sense Richard Ford makes these narrators creators of their own worlds, sovereign over their lives if by nothing else than words and their calling to something beyond their presence on the page.

Chapter Six

Infinite Remoteness in *Rock Springs*

Richard Ford's *Rock Springs* (1987) includes stories published in magazines and journals between 1982 and 1987. A bleak and uncompromising look at lives changed by choice and circumstance, the collection features many first-person male voices whose stories evoke themes present in Ford's other works. For example, Russ, the narrator of "Sweethearts," acknowledges another character's empty moment (see chapter 4 on *The Sportswriter*) and discusses how words may fail (see chapters 4 and 5 on "Great Falls" and *Wildlife*). Though certainly not in any kind of southern literary sense, place exerts some influence here; the wildness of the physical landscape corresponds to the unwieldy lives of the characters. Cars, trains, and other means of transit figure prominently in these narratives set in the western part of the United States, often in Montana. By traveling, the characters seek to escape the poor decisions they've made in the past, but often they find themselves stuck in the same predicaments that they flee, if only because of their own repeated mistakes. They do not adopt Frank Bascombe's more rarefied tone; instead they speak of evading jail, hating their parents, committing meaningless sexual acts to stave off loneliness. In short, they occupy a different societal space; lacking money and opportunity, the protagonists here have little leisure time to mull over philosophical quandaries, but somehow Ford evokes their desires to know, do, and be more than their lives may permit them. Faithful to the details of each scene, Ford opens wide the worlds of the dispossessed, the criminal, the bereaved, and the disappointed. These stories are, in fact, the ones that earned Ford the title of "dirty realist." Despite the spare prose that describes the empty lives that fill these pages, the questions that plague these characters find their origins in the complexities of existence. Even as he casts a cold eye on these sometimes sordid lives, Ford continues to probe the depths of loneliness and assess its effects on those whom it strikes.

Loneliness Realized in "Children," "Communist," and "Optimists"

All three of these stories share themes and stylistic traits with "Great Falls" and *Wildlife,* the two works that I examined in the previous chapter. Each narrator speaks in retrospect—in two cases here the narrator is in his early forties—recounting some moment in his youth, usually when he was about 16, when he suddenly grasped the magnitude of each person's isolation on this earth. Accompanying this realization is the understanding that the adults he knows have failed, sometimes professionally *and* personally, to conduct themselves responsibly when faced with difficult circumstances. Such knowledge contributes to the narrator's isolation, his awareness of his relative smallness versus the universe's incomprehensible breadth, and his concession that much about life exceeds the boundaries of his control. As I suggest in the previous chapter, the very act of telling his story in some sense functions as the character's redemption from an otherwise desperate state; this act allows him to reconstruct this particular time with poignancy but without regret.

In "Children," the narrator George recasts part of his sixteenth year in 1961, when he and Claude Phillips, who is half Blackfoot Indian, take a strange fishing trip with Claude's father Sherman's prostitute, a young girl—just 16—named Lucy. Sherman is a full-blooded Indian, violent and unpredictable, and both George and Claude avoid him whenever possible. The story takes place near Great Falls, Montana, where wheat farmers have found themselves broke and cropless, and a general air of desperation reigns. The place's remoteness complements the lives of its inhabitants. George speculates that "I have thought possibly it was the place itself, as much as the time in our lives or our characters, that took part in the small things that happened and made them memorable."[1] George and Claude have met in an amateur boxing club; they spend a lot of time together, but George acknowledges that there is much about each other that they do not know: "You did not learn much of other people in that locality, and though Claude and I were friends, I would not say I knew him very well, because there was no chance for it" (70). As George remembers this time and tells the story, he characterizes Claude as a boy remarkably like his father, prone to small acts of violence and sudden outbursts of temper. Sherman has in fact been in prison twice before the events that George describes. Casting himself more as an observer, George tells how he begins to grasp youth's transience and his own tenuous relationship to the world around him.

Sherman's request starts the story in motion. He orders Claude to go to a motel where Sherman has spent the previous night and pick up the Canadian girl Lucy. Sherman has to get home to his wife, and he wants to keep Lucy off the streets. Meanwhile, George reveals that his own father works on the railroad and is gone two nights at a time; his mother has left some time ago. When Claude stops at his house on the way to the motel, George gets in the car to accompany him, even though both boys are supposed to be in school. Parental supervision is noticeably absent, but seeing Sherman with Claude does not arouse any longing in George. Instead, he watches in fear as Sherman hauls Claude around by the hair, trying to command respect through sheer physical force. Finally, Sherman gives Claude some "shut up" money and tells him to take the girl fishing, and the boys' adventure begins.

The trip reveals the differences between the boys, finally suggesting that their friendship arises primarily out of their shared circumstances rather than any true kinship. Drinking from a bottle of Canadian gin that they find in Sherman's car, they are already slightly drunk when they pick Lucy up for their excursion. Claude adopts a tough-man pose, making fun of Lucy, ridiculing George's parents, and telling her that George's father also was unfaithful to George's mother. George does not believe that this is true. The only truth he acknowledges in Claude's words is the statement, "This is wild country up here. Nobody's safe" (82), a dire pronouncement. Nonetheless, George knows that people have left that part of Montana, and he figures his mother has felt the same way: "She had never liked it, and neither my father nor me ever blamed her" (82). Claude continues to show off when they get to the water, where he proceeds to brag about causing the fish pain. Oddly, he makes George kill and clean the first one, and as Claude attempts to clean the second, it twists around so that its fin jabs into Claude's hand. Angrily, he curses it, aware of Lucy's gaze, and making George think that perhaps he will do "something terrible—say something to her or do something to the fish that would make her turn her head away. . . . He was able to do bad things easily" (91). But instead Claude gives the fish to Lucy, who without flinching jabs it with the knife and heaves it through the air and back into the water, where it will be too maimed to survive.

Claude attempts to command Lucy's attention through small but violent acts, but George demonstrates more of a willingness to talk to her

and figure out what exactly has brought her to this moment. Their conversation, however, leads to little communication. While Claude has been
showing off his fishing skills, Lucy tries to coax secrets from him and make
him admit things he's done that have made him feel shame. George cannot think of anything, except for not caring when his mother left: "We
didn't need her. She didn't need us either" (89), he tells Lucy, though he
admits in his narrator's voice that neither of those statements was true.
When Lucy invites him to kiss her, he does, and their exchange—like
Lucy and Claude's will also be—is simply physical. George acknowledges
that their words bear little relevance to what each is thinking. For example, Lucy utters meaningless endearments to George even as she turns her
attention to Claude the next minute. Claude threatens to kill her, since no
one knows where she is, but fearlessly she offers to take off her dress, a
gesture that Claude accepts. Soon George realizes that he should leave the
two alone, and he retreats to the truck, where he waits for them to finish
whatever sexual activity they have engaged in. In spite of George and
Lucy's attempt at conversation, the level of intimacy between the boys
and Lucy stays very superficial.

George concludes several things about his experience. One, he knows
that for Lucy shame is just a feeling like any other; the word does not
mean the same thing to her that it does to him. He detects that Claude
uses the word in another context also, wishing that he could marry Lucy,
believing that he could love a woman better than his father, a fact that is
a "shame" (98), he says to George. When he sees Lucy naked, George
also realizes how young she is, "But it did not matter because she was
already someone who could be by herself in the world" (94). This ability
does not characterize himself or Claude, he knows. He does not want to
be alone. As he waits for Claude and Lucy, he tries to think about something other than himself; "I realized that was all I had ever really done,
and that possibly it was all you could ever do, and that it would make
you bitter and lonesome and useless" (96). Instead, he focuses on Lucy
and his mother to involve himself in some selfless act. All of George's
efforts to understand others suggest that he does not want to grow up to
be like the adults whom he knows, their lives narrowed by their own
selfish points of view.

As George admits, the story ends up better than it might have, but
his accompanying realizations offer little protection against loneliness.
The two boys decide to drive Lucy to Great Falls so that she does not
have to go back and wait for Sherman, who probably wouldn't show up
anyway. There they give her their money and the "shut up" money that

Sherman has given Claude. As they drive back, George experiences another realization: "I thought Claude was a fool then, and this was how you knew what a fool was—someone who didn't know what mattered to him in the long run" (97). As Claude talks on about what he could provide for Lucy if only he were older, George recognizes the separateness that divides them even as they have been united momentarily in their one act of kindness to Lucy. George remembers that at that particular moment, he began to be aware of his life going by, "fast and plummeting—almost without my notice" (98). He wonders how he and Claude will fare in the world and how they will get out of that place and those circumstances, thoughts that inspire him to observe that "Outside was a place that seemed not even to exist, an empty place you could stay in for a long time and never find a thing you admired or loved or hoped to keep. And we were unnoticeable in it—both of us" (98). He concludes his tale by acknowledging that he and Claude were "simply young"— mere "children" as the story's title reminds the reader—and did not know even as much as they thought they did at the time. Presumably in retrospect he speaks from another place, at least figuratively, where he has not been overcome by the wide emptinesses around him and between him and those he counts as friends.

The vast and unfriendly spaces that divide one person from another exert a kind of pressure akin to the landscape's emptiness, and the fear sponsored by this kind of emptiness leads to violent impulses in some and deeper introspection in others. The narrators of these three stories all encounter these divisions, finding themselves forced deeper into their thoughts even as they witness strange and unaccountable acts by others. In "Communist," the speaker Les also recounts a time in 1961, when he was 16 and his mother 32, and when his mother had taken up with a boyfriend named Glen Baxter, the communist of the story's title, whose greatest joy was hunting. Just like the fishing trip in "Children," the hunting scenes in this story inspire certain realizations by its narrator. When Glen startles an entire flock of geese, he fires recklessly into the air. The scene is at once beautiful and gruesome as the sky is filled with birds whose feathers fly like snow. When the flush is over, Glen realizes that he's wounded a bird, but he refuses to go after it even as Les's mother begs him to. Finally, he makes a great show of killing it, firing repeatedly at it with a pistol. Les recalls, "A light can go out in the heart. All of this happened years ago, but I can still feel now how sad and remote the world was to me. Glen Baxter, I think now, was not a bad man, only a man scared of something he'd never seen before—something soft in himself—his life going a way he didn't like."[2] Les himself wrestles with this awareness: "And what I felt was only that I had somehow been pushed out into the world, into the real life then, the one I hadn't lived yet" (233). He reveals that he's never gone to college, he's had a series of bad jobs, and he's done hard-rock mining. When the story ends, he tells the reader that he's 41 years old, and that he "has not heard [his] mother's voice now in a long, long time" (235). Nonetheless, like other of Ford's narrators, he remembers that time "without regret" (235). This story is the final one in the *Rock Springs* collection, and its conclusion echoes the endings of most of the other stories. Here, the world's remoteness has not abated, but Ford's narrator speaks into its void.

In "Optimists," Frank tells a similar tale. He describes a time in 1959 when he was 15, and he tells the story because, he says, the events were so unimaginable to him before they actually happened. This was "the year my parents were divorced, the year when my father killed a man and went to prison for it, the year I left home and school, told a lie about my age to fool the Army, and then did not come back. The year, in other words, when life changed for all of us and forever—ended, really, in a way none of us could ever have imagined in our most brilliant dreams of life."[3] Once again, the narrator sees what turns out to be a senseless but irrevocable act of violence, an act that seems to startle its witnesses into the rest of their lives. Intimacy having failed, violence seems to supplant it. And Frank, like Les and George, finds himself alone in the face of what seems to be an empty and unpredictable world.

Despite the fact that both Frank's parents, Roy and Dorothy Brinson, were optimists (as in the story's title), both find their lives taking turns for the worst. Suspicious that his wife has been having an affair with acquaintance Boyd Mitchell, Roy punches Boyd out one night when Boyd and his wife are playing cards with Dorothy. Drunk, Boyd has insulted Roy, a gesture that Roy takes personally. The narrator acknowledges sadly that when Boyd is drunk "he did not even know what he was saying, or what had happened, and that words just got loose from him this way, and anybody who knew him knew it. Only my father didn't" (178). The blow that Roy delivers happens to hit Boyd just right in the chest, killing him almost instantly. Frank says, "I began to date my real life from that moment and that thought. It is this: that situations have possibilities in them, and we have only to be present to be involved" (181). Thus his father's actions implicate Frank in this drama that he has not chosen for himself.

Roy had had a bad day when he punched Boyd Mitchell in the chest; earlier he had seen a man killed on the railway and had not been able to do anything. This regret and his feeling of impotence haunt him. Frank feels similarly paralyzed. He's watched his father commit this act and has not been able to do a thing to stop him or change the end result. Later he sees a picture in the house that he has always assumed to be an image of himself with his parents, but he figures out in the wake of Boyd's death that it is actually his father with *his* parents, whom Frank has never known. To some extent, then, he must see his father differently from that moment on, as a man who has had a life that Frank could not influence much, despite his desire to help him. "What mattered was, I felt, that my father had fallen down now, much as the man he had watched fall beneath the train just hours before. And I was as helpless to do anything as he had been. I wanted to tell him that I loved him, but for some reason I did not" (185). Doomed thereafter to observe his parents' lives from a distance, Frank knows that the way he views the world is forever changed.

In spite of his father's explanation to his mother, which is intended to be hopeful, "It's just a coincidence, Dottie. It's wildlife. Some always get left back" (187), and his mother's exhortation to Roy to "Be an optimist" (187), their life together disintegrates. Roy's words prefigure the title of Ford's 1990 novel *Wildlife,* offering some kind of evolutionary explanation for his predicament. Through those words, Roy abdicates, at least in some sense, his control over his own life. What Frank must then witness is the death of his parents' relationship and the eventual drunkenness of his own mother, whom he encounters in the street when he is 43 years old, and who tries to tell him then, of all times, that Boyd Mitchell never loved her. Her words, like so many other gestures in the story, are finally futile, mistimed, and misplaced. But she wants Frank to believe her, and he promises that he does. "And she bent down and kissed my cheek through the open window and touched my face with both her hands, held me for a moment that seemed like a long time before she turned away, finally, and left me there alone" (191). Thus Frank concludes his story, told many years later, of this one year in his life that changed everything.

Like "Children," "Communist," "Great Falls," and the novel *Wildlife,* this story pivots on a retrospective male voice that describes the moment its speaker found himself thrust into adulthood. The adult speaker tries, somewhat ironically, to make sense of adult actions that resist explication. Failed by his parents, each of these sons learns firsthand that he faces life primarily alone and that he alone is accountable for the choices that he makes. Even this perspective, as harsh as it may seem, renders these stories more hopeful than others in this collection, which feature grown men—adult versions of Claude Phillips, perhaps—who continue to make poor decisions, seemingly unable to put together the obvious strands of cause and effect to see the whole picture.

On a Road to Nowhere in "Rock Springs," "Sweethearts," and "Empire"

Earl certainly fits the profile of the adult male who cannot make his life productive in "Rock Springs," the first and title story of the volume, which he narrates. Heading south to Florida to make a new start with Edna, his girlfriend of eight months, and his daughter Cheryl, Earl makes a mistake and knows he's making it. Rather than ditching the stolen car that he is driving in a timely fashion, he holds on to it one more day. Already having been in prison for stealing tires, Earl cannot afford to get caught again, and he knows it. But swept up in what feels like good fortune, he drives the car one day longer than he should, at which time the car begins to overheat, leaving him, Edna, and Cheryl with no other option than to stop in the next town, Rock Springs, Wyoming.

Two events occur that change Earl's outlook. First, Edna tells him a story about a monkey that she won in a bar one time while she was rolling dice. She liked the monkey fine until the day that a Vietnam vet came into the bar where she worked as a waitress and told her that monkeys kill people. Strangely influenced by this customer's passing words, Edna submits to her fear and ties the monkey to a chair that night with a piece of clothesline. Sometime during the hours that follow, the monkey falls off the chair and hangs herself because Edna has made the cord too short. Edna refers to the story as a "shameful" one, and an "awful thing that happened to [her]."[4] Preoccupied by the car and hoping to get to Rock Springs soon, Earl fails to respond to the story with as much sympathy as Edna has expected, leaving her to comment, "You've got a character that leaves something out, Earl" (9). The conversation seems to mark a turning point in their relationship. Earl senses Edna's waning interest in him, her impatience for a better life, and he suspects that it won't be long before she leaves him.

The monkey's story reveals some things about Edna, too: first, that she is prey to irrational fears; and second, that she believes that this "awful thing" has happened *to* her. In other words, she fails to accept responsibility for the choices that she has made that have helped the monkey to its fate. Furthermore, the monkey's story mirrors Earl's life: he, in effect, hangs himself, not literally, of course, but figuratively. One bad decision leads to the next, and the next, and the next.

When they finally reach a trailer park in Rock Springs, Earl encounters an African American woman whose strange kindness also affects him. She lets him use her phone even though her husband is not home, trusting that he won't harm her. As she tells him about her life, Earl finds himself lying to her, making his life better than it is and casting himself as an ophthalmologist relocating to a practice in Florida. She commiserates with his "bad luck" with the car; "We can't live without cars, can we?" she asks (13). Indeed, in many of these stories, the car (or train) suggests at once freedom and entrapment, speed and the mechanistic grooves into which modern lives get stuck. Earl phones a cab and thanks her for "saving" him, to which she replies, "You weren't hard to save, . . . Saving people is what we were all put on earth to do. I just passed you on to whatever's coming to you" (17). Of course the cab does not prove to be Earl's salvation, but he remembers the woman, later comparing his life to hers even though he knows very little about her. For the time being, he must acknowledge that there is always "a gap between [his] plan and what happened" (17), but that is as close as he comes to taking responsibility for his mistakes.

At story's end, as he is about to steal another car in the Ramada Inn's parking lot, Earl speculates that in truth not much separates him from any other regular guy except the ability to dodge trouble and forget the trouble that occurs anyway. He poses final questions to the eyes behind motel room curtains that might be watching him and wondering what he was doing as he peered into cars: "Would you think his girlfriend was leaving him? Would you think he had a daughter? Would you think he was anybody like you?" (27). It is his humanity—and fallible human nature, at that—that connects Earl to others whom he encounters. But to Earl there is also some crucial difference. As he explains,

> I thought that the difference between a successful life and an unsuccessful one, between me at that moment and all the people who owned the cars that were nosed into their proper places in the lot, maybe between me and that woman out in the trailers . . . was how well you were able to put things like this out of your mind and not be bothered by them, and maybe, too, by how many troubles like this one you had to face in a lifetime. Through luck or design they had all faced fewer troubles, and by

their own characters, they forgot them faster. And that's what I wanted
for me. Fewer troubles, fewer memories of trouble. ("Rock Springs," 26)

Of course Earl can't really know the nature or number of troubles that
have befallen those whom he's met only briefly, such as the woman at
the trailer park, but to speculate in this way relieves him of some measure of accountability. Like Edna, he embraces the notion that to some
extent life has just happened *to* him. And like many of the adult characters in *Rock Springs,* Earl gives up sovereignty over his own life without
even realizing it, ascribing what happens solely to "luck or design."
Thus he ends up where he began: in trouble.

These stories often target the thin line between criminal and law-
abiding behavior, in each case finding the origin of the slip from the latter to the former in the moment a man allows control over his life to be
loosed from him. Such a moment can sneak up on a man the minute he
ceases to be aware of others and his environment. Russ describes it well
in "Sweethearts," which chronicles his and his girlfriend Arlene's trip to
take her former husband Bobby to jail. As Russ observes Bobby, he realizes how easily he, too, could find himself lost:

> Somehow, and for no apparent reason, your decisions got tipped over and
> you lost your hold. And one day you woke up and you found yourself in
> the very situation you said you would never ever be in, and you did not
> know what was most important to you anymore. And after *that,* it was
> all over. And I did not want that to happen to me—did not, in fact,
> think it ever would. I knew what love was about. It was about not giving
> trouble or inviting it. It was about not leaving a woman for the thought
> of another one. It was about never being in the place you said you'd
> never be in. And it was about not being alone. Never that. Never that.[5]

Russ describes here what his fictional cousin Frank Bascombe would call
"seeing around": the peril inherent in not being in a moment but
instead imagining yourself in another moment, maybe with a different
woman, in a different life, as if that life would be better than the present
one. Before one knows it, Russ speculates, a man has let go of one thing
for another of dubious value, finding himself where he never thought
he'd be. Originally published in 1986 in *Esquire,* "Sweethearts" came
out during the same year as *The Sportswriter,* so it's not surprising, then,
that Ford had these notions on his mind. Thematically, "Sweethearts"
picks up other motifs of the *Rock Springs* collection, including the dangers of being alone and the somewhat transferable nature of love. Not

much is impervious to time, these stories suggest, leaving the individual to make sense of his life under circumstances that constantly change.

"Empire" finds its characters in transit once again, this time from Spokane to Minot by train. Told in the third person, this story centers around Vic Sims, an Army veteran, and his wife Marge, who are on their way to visit Marge's sister Pauline, who is suffering from mental problems and has been institutionalized briefly in Minot. As the story unfolds, it becomes clear that Vic is a kind of compulsive adulterer, a man who commits the very acts that Russ warns against in "Sweethearts." Although he loves Marge, Vic can't help but wonder what other women will be like. Repeatedly skirting the consequences of many poor decisions, Vic somehow has managed to avoid exposure, even after he slept with his next-door neighbors' friend Cleo while Marge was in the hospital and the neighbors were out of town. Cleo turned out to belong to a biker's group, Satan's Diplomats, whose members later threaten Vic. Nothing comes of the threats, and Vic goes on with his life and his infidelities, concluding that "Things you do pass away and are gone, and you need only to outlive them for your life to be better, steadily better."[6] So when Vic decides to sleep with a female Army captain on the train while Marge rests in their cabin, the reader is not surprised. Their encounter is typically meaningless and desperate, the captain echoing Vic's shaky philosophy: "you can do a thing and have it mean nothing but what you feel that minute" (143). This kind of attitude allows Vic to write off his brief affairs as momentary lapses of judgment, finally insignificant compared to his love for Marge. Upon his return to bed with her, Vic traces the scar from her surgery, finding there some measure of life's unpredictability: "This can do it, he thought, this can finish you, this small thing. He held her to him, her face against his as his heart beat. And he felt dizzy, and at that moment insufficient, but without memory of life's having changed in that particular way" (148). Unlike Earl in "Rock Springs," Vic *can* look away from trouble and forget it, shedding his own insufficiencies in the process.

The story's ending provides the only clue that Vic's life is slipping from his control, just as it threatens to do for many of these characters: "Sims felt alone in a wide empire, removed and afloat, calmed, as if life was far away now, as if blackness was all around, as if stars held the only light" (148). Like many passages in *Rock Springs,* this one closes the story without judgment or censure. Ford's language, though precise, does not impart goodness or badness upon this moment that Vic Sims experiences, leaving its meaning somewhat ambiguous. He is calm, but he also feels alone in the dark. The conclusion's other significant image is that of a fire moving across the railroad tracks ahead of Vic and Marge's paused train, its heat reaching them nonetheless, and them powerless to staunch its flames that "moved and divided and swarmed the sky" (148). Often Ford leaves these characters isolated at story's end, facing an inscrutable sky or open space, and pondering their tiny lives dwarfed by the universe's vastness. Here, too, Ford contrasts the train with the wilder place that surrounds it, pitting the man-made against that which defies human control. As the character George remarks in "Children," the location itself sometimes exerts as much pull upon its inhabitants as their fellow characters do; like gravity, these landscapes work upon the characters in ways that they cannot control. Constricted by the circumstances that befall him and the choices he's made, Vic, like Earl and Russ, seems unable to transcend his life except momentarily, even then made dizzy by the mere sight of Marge's scar, a reminder of all the forces that keep him earthbound.

A Matter of Trust in "Winterkill," "Going to the Dogs," and "Fireworks"

The moments of connectedness between one person and another prove brief and fragile in *Rock Springs*. In "Winterkill," "Going to the Dogs," and "Fireworks," all three male protagonists find themselves changed by encounters with others that they have not expected. "Winterkill" takes place primarily in two of Ford's favored locales in this volume: in a bar where speaker Les first drinks with his wheelchair-constrained buddy Troy and meets Nola, and then by a river where the three go to do some late night fishing after a few drinks. In the bar, Troy begs Nola to tell them a love story, and she proceeds to recount details of her husband's death of heart failure after she discovers that for quite some time he has had a mistress. Despite this turn of events, Nola claims that "*you* need to be trusted. Or you aren't anything."[7] But like other characters in this collection, she is able to say to Les, "I'll. . . . Just do a thing. It means nothing more than how I feel at this time" (162). The significance of each decision is thus measured relative to the moment it occupies, a code of conduct that surely leads often to betrayal. The three embark, though, on a relatively innocent fishing trip that culminates in Troy hauling in a large, cold, dead deer from the water's depths. Later, back at the place that Les shares with Troy, Les hears his friend's wheelchair bump as it rolls into Troy's room, accompanied by Nola's drunken laughter. He concludes, "I thought we had all had a good night finally. Nothing had happened that hadn't turned out all right. None of us had been harmed. And I put on my pants . . . and with [my fishing rod] went out into the warm foggy morning, using just this once the back door, the quiet way, so as not to see or be seen by anyone" (170). Les's words, though on the surface more optimistic than many uttered by characters in this volume, expose his desire "not to see or be seen." Keeping to himself seems to be the stance he has adopted; he has already confessed that he would just as soon lie if it would prevent some-one from being unhappy. He concludes he's trustworthy nonetheless, thinking of Nola's words and pondering the "matter of trust" (169). He knows that he can be counted upon to behave a certain way in a certain situation, that he can be *trusted* to respond appropriately. And so he does as he leaves Troy and Nola alone, having realized that "though my life . . . seemed to have taken a bad turn and paused, it still meant something to me as a life" (169–70). Possessed of himself, Les can leave the two to their coupling; his trust in his own life redeems what would otherwise be a lonely moment.

The speaker in "Going to the Dogs" does not fare so well. His wife has left him, and he's already bought a train ticket to Florida to "change [his] luck."[8] As he waits for the snow to end on the day before Thanks-giving, he becomes the host for two female hunters who come to his door looking for his landlord. Glad of the company, he talks with them a while. They both are heavy women, but he finds one, Bonnie, vaguely attractive, enough so that when she attempts to seduce him, he consents readily. Although he thinks it odd that she should make such an offer in front of her friend Phyllis, he observes that Phyllis seems used to it. In fact, Phyllis offers to tidy up the place while he and Bonnie are in the bedroom. For this narrator, the matter of trust proves a matter of loss, for of course Phyllis steals his train ticket while she "tidies up." Trusting these two, mainly because he is desperate for company, leaves this speaker with no way out of his current misfortune. When he sees that there is "nothing but some change and some matchbooks [where his ticket should be], . . . [he realizes] it was only the beginning of bad luck" (108). Having made the decision *not* to think beyond the current moment, as so many of these characters do, he loses at least one possible future.

"Fireworks" focuses on the momentary redemption provided by its main character's decision to trust his wife. Out of work for a while, Eddie Starling meets Lois at the bar where she works for a drink after a long day right before the Fourth of July. Earlier, she has met with her former husband who was just passing through, and Eddie has had to fight off jealousy over their encounter. Meanwhile, he has received a collect call from someone he doesn't know, a young man named Jeff who begs for help from his "Dad" and pleads for the charges to be accepted. Eddie's decision not to take this call haunts him all day and is only momentarily relieved by the sight of Lois dancing in the rain with a lit sparkler when they get home after her shift. Her movements make "swirls and patterns and star-falls for him that were brilliant and illuminated the night and the bright rain and the little dark house behind her and, for a moment, caught the world and stopped it, as though something sudden and perfect had come to earth in a furious glowing for him and for him alone—Eddie Starling—and only he could watch and listen. And only he would be there, waiting, when the light was finally gone."[9] The way that Lois's fireworks "caught the world and stopped it" here recalls the "glistening one moment" that Frank Bascombe describes at the end of *The Sportswriter.* The key difference is that Frank's moment depends utterly upon his solitude and a degree of comfort with himself that he has struggled to achieve. In Eddie's case, however, his experience of timelessness takes its energy completely from Lois's movements and her presence, both of which make up her gift to him. As her audience, Eddie recognizes that her performance is only for him, just as the words that she has spoken minutes before were meant to promise. She has told him that she loved him and that that is the reason that she is with him and not her former husband Lou Reiner. At least momentarily, Eddie accepts Lois's love as a gift that she offers freely; his own independence day, then, at least from the nagging fears of unemployment, missed connections with the mysterious Jeff, and potential ruptures caused by Reiner's return, ironically is contingent upon dependence upon someone he trusts.

Through its unflinching portraits of lives that hinge on momentary decisions and mistakes, *Rock Springs* illustrates the traits of realism that critics have been quick to label in Ford's fiction. Ford renders these very ordinary lives to the page without judgment or moral censure. His characterizations are emotionally and psychologically consistent. Faithful to small details, each story recreates a specific time and place for the reader, and Ford does not shy away from dire consequences here. At the same time, whatever happens is not quite as random as the characters themselves would imagine. Ford provides enough information about his creations to suggest that their misfortunes find root in their own pasts or personal failings. Although many of these narrators and protagonists believe that luck and design often govern their lives, their stories subtly protest otherwise. More than anything, the stories in *Rock Springs* profess human fallibility; whatever connections that one human being can sustain with another here are tenuous. Though Ford of course provides no morals for these tales, one can be gleaned, and that is that life requires a kind of diligence from its participants. When these characters fail even for a minute to keep watch over their own territories, everything familiar is apt to slip away, literally or figuratively lost to the dark emptinesses all around them. Ford often cites " 'the infinite remoteness' that underlies us all," borrowing a phrase from Ralph Waldo Emerson to describe the human condition (Walker, 141). Spare and grim on the surface, the stories that make up *Rock Springs* share images of loneliness and wide open spaces illumined only briefly by the flare of meaningful connection between one character and another.

Chapter Seven

Locution, Location, and Existence: From Seeming to Being in *Independence Day*

Nothing we can say can change anything now
. . . So say goodbye it's Independence Day
Papa now I know the things you wanted that you could not say
But won't you just say goodbye it's Independence Day.
——Bruce Springsteen, "Independence Day"

Richard Ford says that his 1995 novel's title "comes as much from [Bruce Springsteen's] song as all the other sources that that name could come from," and he also claims that the "great song 'Independence Day,' this great anthem to leaving home, was probably the first thing that moved me along the path to writing a novel" of the same title (Walker, 128). The stanza above, only one part of the complete song, also suggests another of Ford's concerns in his fiction, what he has called the "provisional" nature of language. The son in Springsteen's song acknowledges his father's inability to put into words his strongest desires; not incidentally, in this novel Ford again subtly probes the inherent power *and* imprecision of the words that people use to connect with each other, or to disconnect, as the case may be. Sometimes, as Springsteen's lyrics suggest, the moments when words fail, when they cannot be uttered for one reason or another, are the very moments when integral connections between one person and another are sundered. To complicate matters, even the same words might mean different things to different people; to speak is not always to heal a rift. Meaning is up for grabs. Words may invite intimacy and rupture, bridge a distance or further a breach. Furthermore, Ford's choice of the book's title pivots on multiple meanings and differing connotations. "Independence" usually entails the act of breaking away, letting go the props that might hold one up, striking out on one's own. Certainly all of those meanings congregate in Ford's book, and Ford recognizes that primarily the word "independence" suggests putting distance between one's self and others. However, Ford also admits that his interest in "independence" sprang in part from a desire to make the word mean something else as well, to "redefine independence to aid you in making these connections" (Walker, 136). To this end, Ford's novel moves its narrator Frank Bascombe away from the "glistening one moment" that he experienced at *The Sportswriter*'s conclusion toward something more communal in nature; in the process Frank adopts a new kind of language, letting go of certain terms that describe his existence in favor of other, now more accurate, words.

Independence Day (1995) won both the Pulitzer Prize and the PEN/Faulkner Award, the first time a novel had ever garnered such dual recognition. The "sequel" to *The Sportswriter* (1986), *Independence Day* continues the chronicle of Frank Bascombe's life. Like the earlier novel, it is narrated in the first person by Frank himself and told in the present tense; such stylistic choices at times make Frank's voice problematic, as I have already assessed in chapter 4. At once truthful and oblique, Frank's narrative signature can require deliberate deciphering. Here he continues to coin terms that explain his mental whereabouts; the governing mode of thought and action in this novel is the "Existence Period," a time of relative solitude that makes keeping affection for others at some remove quite possible. Still searching here, Frank embarks on more literal and figurative journeys, relating his thoughts as he travels with his son Paul on the Fourth of July weekend to the basketball and baseball halls of fame. The novel in part is the story of Frank's attempts to connect with 15-year-old Paul, who suffers emotionally from past memories from which he cannot shake loose and the present reality of his mother's remarriage to Charley O'Dell and their move away from Haddam, New Jersey, and up to Deep River, Connecticut. In this novel, Frank's ex-wife, known as X in *The Sportswriter,* has a name, Ann Dykstra, and she continues to be a force in Frank's life even as he tries, albeit fitfully, to create a meaningful relationship with his present girlfriend, Sally Caldwell. Because his Hoving Road home has been turned into the Chaim Yankowicz Ecumenical Center, Frank now occupies Ann's old house on Cleveland Street, in the "Presidents Streets" neighborhood of Haddam. These places are not insignificant, since Frank has abandoned his occupation as sportswriter and has now become a "Residential Specialist," or, simply put, a real estate agent. Some portion of the novel concerns Frank's professional relationship with clients Phyllis and Joe Markham, who have come from Vermont to find a suitable home in Haddam in which to raise their daughter, give her access to the city's excellent school system, and still be close enough to New York City to take advantage of its art scene, since both Joe and Phyllis are artisans. Parallel to the Markhams' attempt to find a house are Frank's efforts to rent out one of two properties on Clio Street, residences in a respectable black neighborhood where Frank finds himself from time to time to collect rent from his tenants, a chore that makes him uncomfortable but that he cannot avoid; his present tenants refuse to mail him the check. Indeed the search for a home becomes one metaphorical crux of this novel: the quest for the delicate balance between dependence on and independence from place, people, and self.

The novel's other metaphorical crux finds its origins in Frank's philosophical quandary, perpetuated by what he has called the Existence Period. That Richard Ford is preoccupied by an existential question should come as no surprise by now. In *Independence Day,* the question is not "how do I know I exist?" or even "how can I know others?" Instead, its protagonist and narrator Frank struggles with the *degree* to which he should exist. That is to say, he rejects as emotionally perilous the possibility of living a life connected to others and to his past and instead embraces an existence devoid of such complexities. He banishes from his mind any kind of attachment that might make him vulnerable to other people. He consigns to the past what is past, and he refuses to allow old mistakes, regrets, or even joys to impinge upon the present. As a result, however, he is apt to feel somehow diminished, at times referring to the possibility of "disappearing," being unnoticed, unseen. It is as if by severing himself of these ties he also loses, bit by bit, metaphorical pieces of himself, risking if not literal invisibility, then certainly some kind of figurative vanishing. He is himself but not completely. He occupies the present moment but not completely. The Existence Period requires of its supplicant a willingness to seem to be. *Independence Day* recounts how Frank finally rejects seeming for being, opening himself again to unforeseen contingencies, and *in dependence,* discovering something of what it means to be *independent.*

The Existence Period: Time for Independence

Paced in a slow, meandering cadence that keeps time with Frank's ruminations, *Independence Day* finds Frank apparently recovered from what he calls a "psychic detachment" (25) that he suffered and that propelled him first to Florida (as *The Sportswriter* reveals) and then to France with

Catherine Flaherty, a trip that has occurred in the interim between the two novels. Frank refers to these trips as "fugues," a term he borrows from psychology; in psychological jargon, a fugue is a period during which a patient flees his or her old life for a new one, not in and of itself a bad thing. The complication is that usually this flight is accompanied by varying degrees of amnesia, so that the patient, upon returning to the old life, has no recollection of the flight from it. Frank, of course, has not really experienced amnesia, but he does describe his detachment, what seems to be a kind of vagueness about his desires that has permitted him to while away his time with someone with whom presumably he knew he did not share a future. When he "awakens," he knows suddenly that he must return to Haddam, be a better father to his two remaining children, Clarissa and Paul, and possibly even win back the affection of his former wife, Ann Dykstra. Typically, however, he manages only tentative reconciliations, remaining passive enough that Ann marries Charley O'Dell. Before Frank knows it, his family has moved up to Connecticut, leaving him in Haddam to refashion his existence all by himself. These several events all conspire to send Frank into a new phase, what he terms the "Existence Period," a condition to which he refers several times before explaining it.

The occasions that invite Frank's references to this period include his outings with Joe and Phyllis Markham, his clients for whom no house is the right one, in whose moments of indecision Frank sees something of his past self. He cites a failure to trust one's own judgment as a hallmark of the Existence Period: "Not trusting your own judgment—and, worse, *knowing* you shouldn't trust it for some damn substantial reasons—can be one of the major causes and also one of the least tolerable ongoing features of the Existence Period" (65–66), Frank muses. He sees in the Markhams the kind of regret he experienced earlier in his life, a regret he believes he has moved beyond in favor of a more viable approach to past, present, and future. Despite these points of recognition and identification with Joe and Phyllis, Frank acknowledges that, finally, they remain unknown to him (a lesson he has learned in the previous novel), no matter how often he hears their stories or how much time he spends with them. "And yet," he admits, "it is one of the themes of the Existence Period that interest can mingle successfully with uninterest in this way, intimacy with transience, caring with the obdurate uncaring. Until very recently . . . I believed this was the *only* way of the world; maturity's balance. Only more things seem to need sorting out now: either in favor of complete uninterest (ending things with Sally might be an example) or else going whole hog (not ending things with Sally might be another example)" (76). This passage typifies Frank's thought patterns; even as he professes a kind of maturity and understanding, he exposes the arbitrariness of his decision-making processes. Furthermore, as he builds his definition of the Existence Period, layer by layer, he reveals one of its most basic tenets, and that is a kind of imposed self-sufficiency, a way of keeping others at arm's length, a stance one might even term a kind of independence. He suggests that he can turn on and off, really at a moment's notice, caring or uncaring, depending upon what might loosely be called his philosophical bent at the time. The novel's events will chip away at this resolve, forcing Frank's emergence from the Existence Period into something possibly more permanent.

When Frank does offer a more detailed definition of this phase in his life, he does so thoughtfully and completely but in such a way that the term remains perplexingly and frustratingly imprecise. He speaks of two forces that he could identify as working in his life: a "bright synchronicity" that made anything possible coupled with another, more earthbound one:

> The other feeling, the one that balanced the first, was a sensation that everything I then contemplated was limited or at least underwritten by the "plain fact of my existence": that I was after all only a human being, as untranscendent as a tree trunk, and that everything I might do had to be calculated against the weight of the practical and according to the standard considerations of: Would it work? and, What good would it do for me or anybody?
>
> I now think of this balancing of urgent forces as having begun the Existence Period, the high-wire act of normalcy, the part that comes *after* the big struggle which led to the big blow-up, the time in life when whatever was going to affect us "later" actually affects us, a period when we go along more or less self-directed and happy, though we might not choose to mention or even remember it later were we to tell the story of our lives, so steeped is such a time in the small dramas and minor adjustments of spending quality time simply with ourselves. (*ID*, 94–95)

The Existence Period, then, seems to have as its two major components a hopeful, anything-is-possible kind of attitude ("bright synchronicity") kept in check by a utilitarian impulse ("would it work? and what good would it do for me or anybody?"). The latter seems tied to Frank's understanding of his own humanity and "the plain fact of his existence," those qualities that render him more than capable of committing errors,

making mistakes. Furthermore, this time turns out to be infinitely for-
gettable, insignificant in terms of the big picture, and governed mostly
by a self-concern that supersedes concern for others, possibly the result
of too many past disappointments, failures in love or friendships.

Underlying all of these traits, though, is simply the need to be happy,
or relatively content, with the day-to-day rhythm of one's life. For
Frank, this choice to be happy entails letting go of worries and what he
calls other "contingencies," by which he means anything or anyone that
might influence him unduly and thereby distract him from his protective and self-preserving "code of conduct" (111). Frank finds real estate
to be an "ideal occupation" (111) for one in his straits, for it allows him
to "do for others while looking after Number One, which seemed a good
aspiration as I entered a part of life when I'd decided to expect less, hope
for modest improvements and be willing to split the difference" (112).
To ensure safe passage into this deliberately adopted attitude, Frank
finds that he must concentrate less on some things and more on others.
He describes the first part of this process as a kind of "jettisoning" that
necessarily occurs as one tries to be content. In fact, he claims that "certain crucial jettisonings" (95) are required in the Existence Period. He
uses a nautical metaphor here, jettisoning being the act of throwing
overboard that which threatens to weigh down a vessel, items that then
might be called "jetsam," the discarded. Certainly among those things
to be tossed overboard were "employment, marriage, nostalgia and
swampy regret" (95), leaving Frank "now a man aquiver with possibility
and purpose" (95). In other words, Frank resolves to let go of the past,
its indiscretions, mistakes, and finer moments alike, since after all the
good may not even be as good as one remembers it being. Significantly,
Frank does not discount the possibility that people may need to be jetti-
soned as well, if only to safeguard the stability of his "vessel."

In fact, Frank claims that "intimacy had begun to matter less to
[him]" (96). He explains that since his marriage ended and other attrac-
tions waned, he had consciously avoided what he names "real" intimacy.
He makes a distinction between this kind of closeness and what he calls
sharing "private" issues that masquerade as intimate ones: talk about
laxative choices, menstrual cycles, and other subjects that too often
make their way into casual conversation. What Frank concerns himself
with is the kind of intimacy sustained with very few people over a life-
time, maybe three at the most, and which transcends even the usual
ways of communicating. He refers to *"silent intimacies*—when spoken
words, divulgences, promises, oaths are almost insignificant: the inti-

macy of the fervently understood and sympathized with, having nothing to do with being a 'straight shooter' or a truth teller, or with being able to be 'open' with strangers (these don't mean anything anyway). To *none* of these, though, was I in debt, and in fact I felt I could head right into my new frame of reference—whatever was beginning—pretty well prepared and buttoned up" (96). Having encountered his own problems with being a "straight shooter" or a truth teller, Frank wisely leaves these elements out of the equation. What he makes clear is that right now he desires no strong connection with another person, excluding those to whom he's already bound (Ann, the children), but even with them he resolves to be careful, respectful of the distances that have overtaken past intimacies. He is concerned, then, with his own independence from that which endangers him emotionally. Frank explains, "the Existence Period helps create or at least partly stimulates the condition of honest independence: inasmuch as when you're in it you're visible as you are, though not necessarily very noticeable to yourself or others, and yet you maintain reason enough and courage in a time of waning urgency to go toward where your interests lie as though it mattered that you get there" (117–18). For Frank, then, this kind of independence necessitates making one's self dispensable, or at least "not very noticeable." In the face of that expendability, though, one finds something within one's self that allows for, and even encourages, the act of pushing forward toward personal goals without the need of external affirmation, or even recognition—hence the probability of being unnoticed. Independence for the sake of existence, or vice versa, permits Frank's disappearance off of the radar screens of those to whom he was formerly important so that he can start over, unencumbered by excess needs, worries, regrets, or longings.

To become too unencumbered, though, is to risk losing parts of the self. The Existence Period exacts a price, in other words, and that loss includes a richness or roundness to life only supplied by yoking the self with another person. As I suggest in previous chapters, Ford repeatedly raises the issue of knowing the self and others, betraying epistemological and existential concerns that lurk behind the more basic elements of character and plot in his fiction. With all of his thoughts about the Existence Period, Frank continues to be a good spokesman for an existential quandary, except that he does not need convincing of his own existence (having accepted that everything is underwritten by the "plain fact of his existence"). More accurately, he engages in ontology, or the study of the nature of being. He notes a difference between existing—or seem-

ing—and living—or being, the latter presumably being a more complete and satisfying undertaking. He has chosen, however, at this novel's
inception, to strip his life down to its barest essentials, the minimum
required to feel some degree of happiness. He quickly discovers that this
enterprise entails lowering his expectations of just about everything,
including himself. Even as he remains convinced of the rightness of his
operating mode, he admits that some perils ensue:

> I try, in other words, to keep something finite and acceptably doable on
> my mind and not disappear. Though it's true that sometimes in the
> glide, when worries and contingencies are floating off, I sense I myself
> am afloat and cannot always feel the sides of where I am, nor know what
> to expect. So that to the musical question "What's it all about, Alfie?"
> I'm not sure I'd know the answer. Although to the old taunt that says,
> "Get a life," I can say, "I already have an existence, thanks." (*ID,* 117)

Frank continues his nautical metaphor here, he himself being the vessel
afloat and possibly adrift, all landmarks having slipped away. Without
others by whom to navigate, Frank risks the loss of his otherwise sea-
worthy craft. So here, too, he refers to his tangible essence and its growing insubstantiality.

Ford's reader may recall Frank's previous preoccupation with what he
called "invisibility" in *The Sportswriter,* a mostly figurative state that
descends because one seeks to know others via false means: by being
other than who one is because one thinks one's audience desires such a
pretense (compare Frank's act as stoic and mentor when he first meets
Catherine Flaherty); by assuming that one can completely know another
person, which oversimplifies the act of knowing and may even risk the
loss of the other person entirely (as Frank does with X and, arguably,
Walter Luckett in the previous novel); or by trying in vain to know
another person before one has come to terms with one's own self (what
Frank seems to realize at *The Sportswriter*'s end). These misprisions result
in becoming "invisible," also unknown, and with no bearing on another
person's existence.

Significantly, in the quotation above from *Independence Day,* Frank
uses another word, "contingency," which continues to accrue meaning as
the novel progresses. Any kind of contingency is that which presupposes
something else. For example, a person might say, "our sailing plans are
contingent upon the weather." In other words, to be contingent upon
something is to *depend* upon something that is uncertain and to some
degree unpredictable. A contingency, then, would seem incompatible

with independence; it would certainly be incompatible with the Existence Period, which requires the jettisoning of all that might make the voyage longer, rockier, or otherwise less efficient. Frank uses the word contingency to refer not to things such as the weather but to all possible forces that seem to cause trouble for him. These forces might include people and places and indeed any arena wherein he has met with failure before. As he strips himself of these influences, however, he once again risks disappearance, not utterly, but in part; he is less himself because he is less contingent upon others.

Somehow all of these terms tie in to Frank's notion of independence. The Existence Period is the phrase he uses to describe this phase of his life, but it also characterizes an approach to life that might get Frank that much closer to the independence that he believes he desires. He ascribes certain tenets to the Existence Period, which I will continue to point out and explicate in this chapter; so far these include a purposeful jettisoning of all nonessentials, including people; a less purposeful but equally desirable release of worries and contingencies; and an accompanying throwing-off of old mistakes, past regrets, and otherwise nonconstructive memories of failure. Its dangers thus far include mainly a risk of disappearance, or loss of visibility, but for Frank these risks are outweighed by the benefits of possible independence. He is free of others; they are free of him. All parties may go about their business without excessive concern for anyone else. Frank explains,

> (It's not exactly as if I didn't exist, but that I don't exist *as much*.) So, if I didn't appear tomorrow to get my son, . . . or if I showed up with the fat lady from the circus or a box of spitting cobras, as little as possible would be made of it by all concerned, partly in order that everybody retain as much of their own personal freedom and flexibility as possible, and partly because I just wouldn't be noticed that much *per se*. (This reflects my own wishes, of course—the unhurried nature of my single life in the grip of the Existence Period—though it may also imply that laissez-faire is not precisely the same as independence.) (*ID*, 176–77)

Letting things be, or leaving things well enough alone, as the notion of laissez-faire implies, is not completely synonymous with independence, as Frank must acknowledge here. But it is freedom from attachments that he is after and what he imagines that others need as well. He is willing to be a ghostlier self whose comings and goings are unremarkable, if that's what's required for freedom's sake.

The Trip's First Lesson: Existence is Uncertain

Besides invoking the thematically relevant notions of freedom and independence, Ford's decision to set the novel—and Frank's trip with Paul
to the basketball and baseball halls of fame—over the Fourth of July
weekend also serves the book well in other ways. First, any kind of
travel over the Fourth is bound to be complicated by traffic, delays, or
any number of unforeseen events: "What on a good summer night
should take thirty minutes . . . takes me an hour and fifteen" (195),
Frank admits from his car late at night on the interstate. Second, a typically hot time of year, the Fourth of July provides the perfect backdrop
for small dangers (flaring tempers, overheated crowds, long lines) and
larger ones (exploding firecrackers, acts of violence). The congestion on
the highways becomes an apt metaphor for the desperate craving for
freedom that the holiday itself commemorates: "Along with construction slow downs, entrance ramps merging, MEN WORKING, left-lane
breakdowns and a hot mechanical foreboding that the entire seaboard
might simply explode, there's now even more furious, grinding-mad-in-
the-dark traffic and general vehicular desperation, as if to be caught in
New Jersey after tonight will mean sure death" (194–95). The Fourth
of July is, in short, the quintessential American holiday, at once evocative of chaos and order, misrule and rule, anarchy and democracy. With
freedom and independence, after all, come the possibilities for circum-
vention of the law.

Ford prepares the reader for these possibilities through three events,
one past (the murder of a fellow real estate agent), one ongoing (threats
to Frank's small business-on-the-side), and one that occurs in the book's
present (a fairly anonymous murder at a motel at which Frank stops).
The first is the recent murder of real estate agent Clair Devane, accomplished during a house showing and remaining unsolved. An African
American colleague of Frank's, with whom, in fact, Frank had had an
affair, Clair continues to be a kind of presence in the novel, a reminder of
death's sudden intrusion and other forces that defy human control.
However, her life contrasted sharply with Frank's, simply because she
made herself noticeable: "When poor sweet Clair Devane met her three
o'clock at Pheasant Meadow and got pulled into a buzz saw of bad luck,
a whole network of alarms and anguished cries bespeaking love, honor,
dependency immediately sounded—north to south, coast to coast. Her
very *moment* as a lost human entity was at once seismically registered on
all she'd touched" (176). After her death, however, when that moment

passes, her desk is occupied by someone else, and conversation about the murder diminished, Frank observes that then, "it can ... seem as though Clair Devane had not fully existed in anyone's life but her very own" (145). Clair's untimely demise makes Frank's recollections of their liaison seem all the more poignant to him, but it also introduces disorder into the apparently logical world of selling real estate and the reality that the sheer fact of existence is not in and of itself a thing to be taken for granted.

Other circumstances that provide a degree of palpable uncertainty in Frank's current existence are the partial ownership and responsibility for a root beer/hot dog stand, of all things, called Franks, without an apostrophe, and pun intended. Having befriended Karl Bemish on the verge of Karl's bankruptcy and upon the very inopportune occasion of having run his car smack into the picnic table and flower beds near the roadside stand, Frank not only pays for his damages but also assumes Karl's debts and backs him as a financial partner. Frank admits, "our transaction was more or less what I had been searching for when I came back from France but didn't find: a chance to help another, do a good deed well and diversify in a way that would pay dividends (as it's begun to) without driving myself crazy. We should all be so lucky" (135). The weekend of the Fourth finds Karl busy and preoccupied by what appears to be a car full of would-be burglars who drive through the parking lot to case the place. Karl tells Frank not to worry, that Karl himself has a gun, a "sawed-off twelve-gauge pump" or "alley sweeper" (219), words that offer small consolation to Frank and the idea of which "scares [him] silly" (219) and "makes [him] goddamn nervous" (220). During Frank's road trip, Karl leaves updates on Frank's answering machine, to which Frank can respond from his various stops along his way, putting in calls from pay phones at rest areas, motel rooms and so forth. In this way, in fact, Frank maintains ongoing conversations not only with Karl but also with his clients the Markhams, his girlfriend Sally Caldwell, and his former wife Ann Dykstra. The trip itself controls the mode of communication: incomplete and halting messages on answering machines, which Frank can check via a *remote* function (evoking both the literal and figurative meanings of that word), and his own often cryptic responses to them.

Finally, another event that occurs en route keeps the possibility of death foremost in Frank's mind, and that is the homicide motivated by robbery that happens in a room at the motel where Frank finally finds a vacancy as he travels to pick up Paul. Committed by kids hardly older than Paul, the murder gives Frank an unpleasant reminder of all that can go wrong in the minds of teenage boys even as he glimpses in them the boyishness that also characterizes his son. Frank finds himself in the parking lot observing this spectacle; next to him is an African American moving van driver with whom he strikes up a conversation. Mr. Tanks is the man's name, information Frank gleans from the sewn tag on his Mayflower uniform. Frank observes, "We aren't socializing here . . . only bearing brief dual witness to the perilous character of life and our uncertain presences in it. Otherwise there's no reason to stand here together" (202). Nonetheless, circumstances provide the context for conversation, and their talk turns to real estate. Mr. Tanks wonders aloud if he should move out East and sell his home in California, uttering questions that imply to Frank that Mr. Tanks views such a prospect as more than a simple economic transaction. Frank speculates that Mr. Tanks is in fact considering the "character of eventuality" (204), or where his life might take him and what the nature of that existence will be, all the inevitable effects of Mr. Tanks's prior decisions. As Frank goes on to analyze Mr. Tanks's predicament, he rambles back into a discussion of "synchronicity," one of the dual forces that precipitates the Existence Period. Here he gives a lengthier definition:

> [Mr. Tanks's] is the sort of colloquy most of us engage in alone with only our silent selves, and that with the right answers can give rise to rich feelings of synchronicity of the kind I came back from France full of four years ago: when everything is glitteringly about *you,* and everything you do seems led by a warm, invisible astral beam issuing from a point too far away in space to posit but that's leading you to the place—if you can just follow and stay lined up—you *know* you want to be. (*ID,* 204)

Frank's definition of synchronicity, then, has as a central component a real, but Frank believes healthy, concern for the self that will eventually, if heeded, direct him toward whatever place—possibly emotional more than physical—that he should be. Ironically, it is of course the propensity to think that everything is about *him* that gets Frank into trouble with others. To some degree Frank imposes his thoughts upon Mr. Tanks, as if the two shared kindred impulses, but he nonetheless runs right up against the very issue that divides them: race. As Mr. Tanks ponders the possibility of moving East, he asks Frank, "You got any niggers down there in your part of New Jersey?" (209), a question to which Frank responds thoughtlessly: " 'Plenty of 'em,' I say. Mr. Tanks looks at me steadily, and of course, even as sleepy as I am, I'm awfully sorry to have said that, yet have no way to yank the words back" (209). The almost inevitable end to this otherwise pleasant conversation puts Frank back on the alert; he's slipped into too much ease with this stranger in his longing to find in Mr. Tanks the very same inquiries that motivate Frank's own mental journey. Instead, in this very literal journey, Frank encounters a man whose individuality Frank has forgotten to take into account, a lapse that Frank rues but cannot revoke. This moment of communion gone awry leaves Frank "bracketed, limbo'd, unable to budge, as illustrated amply by Mr. Tanks and me standing side by side in the murderous night, unable to strike a spark, utter a convincingly encouraging word to the other, be of assistance, shout halloo, dip a wing; unable at the sad passage of another human to the barren beyond to share a hope for the future" (216–17). These thoughts certainly betray, among other things, Frank's fascination for metaphor and his ability, even under duress, to summon language in abundance that might describe his predicament. Stalled in his journey, Frank runs right up against loneliness and death, an end that "seems so near now, so plentiful, so oh-so-drastic and significant, that it scares [him] witless" (217). To this grim inevitability Frank offers a rejoinder, and that is the prospect of his trip, not alone, but with Paul, in a "hopeful, life-affirming, anti-nullity" (217) direction, where Frank will find, "armed only with words," that he can "build a case" (217) for Paul's improvement. Words convey power and can be wielded for union or fracture, as Frank's untoward response to Mr. Tanks amply illustrates.

Reaching Paul and Other Destinations

Before Frank's holiday officially begins, he must fulfill other obligations, and it is in this way that Frank's trip with Paul circumscribes the plot. To sum up Frank's peregrinations before the actual car trip begins, one would note that he drives over to Clio Street to attempt to collect the rent, where he is met with more than usual suspicion by the area's black residents and where he is, once again, denied the money he has come for since his tenants refuse to answer the door; he drops by the office to get the key to what he hopes will be *the* house for the Markhams and thereupon waxes prolifically, not to the Markhams but to his own audience, about his new occupation in real estate; he shows the Markhams the house, about which they remain ambivalent; he checks on Karl at Franks; and he ends the day by having dinner with Sally at her beach house, from which he leaves to go to Connecticut to pick up Paul, stopping en route to spend the night, encountering Mr. Tanks, sleeping at the motel, and finally arriving at Ann's house the next morning, where Paul awaits him. Each of these occasions allows Frank to provide exposition, explaining how he gets along with the Clio Street residents; how he's come to own two rental properties there in the first place; what he perceives in the Markhams' marriage and in their desires for housing; how he happened to achieve part ownership in Franks; what his relationship with Sally is like; and so on. It might bear mentioning that Frank arrives at the O'Dells' on page 236, only slightly less than half-way though the novel.

Ford has of course introduced Paul earlier in the book, via the favored medium of communication, the phone call, and Frank's own thoughts about Paul's varying afflictions. Indeed, Paul suffers from myriad ills, some mysterious and others more typical of standard adolescent angst. Subject to excessive memories of the day that Mr. Toby, the Bascombes' beloved basset hound dog, was hit by a car and died in Paul's arms, Paul continues to invoke Mr. Toby often, speculating about how he'd be doing if he were still alive. He has even told Frank that "even then (at only age six) he was afraid the incident would stay in his mind, possibly even for the rest of his life, and ruin it. For weeks and weeks, he said, he lay awake in his room thinking about Mr. Toby and worrying about the fact that he was thinking about it" (14). This mild obsession also seems to connect with Paul's unusual propensity every now and then to bark himself. In addition, he makes other odd noises, "*eeeck-eeecking* sounds" (13), deep in his throat, that occur during inappropriate moments. More overt signs of his disturbance include shoplifting condoms, subsequently resisting—somewhat violently—the security officer who attempts to stop him, and, most recently, knocking out Charley O'Dell, his mother's new husband. The security officer at the site of the petty theft unfortunately has decided to press charges of assault and battery, the outcome of which remains unknown. Paul's court date falls on a Tuesday morning, the day after the Fourth of July. If one were to psychoanalyze Paul, these behaviors would seem to suggest a strong need for attention. Paul is, in fact, seeing a therapist, Dr. Stopler, whose sessions provide dubiously restorative powers. What Frank suspects is that Paul, having been exposed to death at an early age, now knows firsthand the uncertainties inherent in life, the possibility of bad things happening. In addition to Mr. Toby's unpleasant demise, Paul has also experienced the very untimely death of his brother Ralph from Reye's Syndrome (an event that preceded the action in *The Sportswriter*). He knows real and incontrovertible loss far earlier than most of his peers.

In some effort to counterbalance Paul's preoccupations, Frank stages this trip, practically a pilgrimage of sorts, to visit as many sports halls of fame as can be seen in 48 hours. It turns out that only two will fit into this window. This relatively small number does not deter Frank's enthusiasm, and the original scope of the trip becomes a kind of joke between him and Paul. He is hopeful that the trip will cheer Paul and provide him (Frank) the not-so-obvious opportunities to instruct his son in useful coping mechanisms. "Which is to say:" Frank muses, "if your son begins suddenly to fall at a headlong rate, you must through the agency of love and greater age throw him a line and haul him back" (15). Frank acknowledges, however, that such is easier said than done and that his role as father has its limitations. Nonetheless, he has tried to prepare his son for the journey, not letting it be lost on Paul that they will be traveling around the Independence Day holiday. Frank explains, "I've sent him copies of *Self-Reliance* and the Declaration, and suggested he take a browse. These are not your ordinary fatherly offerings, I admit; yet I believe his instincts are sound and he will help himself if he can, and that independence is, in fact, what he lacks—independence from whatever holds him captive: memory, history, bad events he struggles with, can't control, but feels he should" (16). Hopeful that Ralph Waldo Emerson's paean to self-sustenance and the Declaration's clear-cut, self-evident truths regarding separation and individual rights might inspire Paul to his own brand of independence, Frank wants to believe that these documents will to some degree make up for what he, as a father, cannot provide. Frank recognizes that his adulthood is in itself necessary (through the "agency of love and greater age") but also an impediment to real understanding: "Not owning the right language; not dreading the same dreads and contingencies and missed chances; the fate of knowing much yet having to stand like a lamppost with its lamp lit, hoping my child will see the glow and venture closer for the illumination and warmth it mutely offers" (17). In fact, "not owning the right language" will continue to plague Frank in relationships besides his one with Paul, but he remains hopeful that the conduits for communication might remain open.

Frank and Paul construct their own pattern of conversation, one that relies heavily on bad jokes and strange puns, as if this oblique method of talk might somehow bridge the language rift between them. For example, Clarissa has given Frank and Paul each one of her hair ribbons, a gesture that inspired Frank to make a "beau/bow" joke with his daughter. Later, Frank realizes that Paul possesses his bow's twin, another tiny shred of cloth that Paul has slowly opened a clenched fist to reveal. At that moment, Paul "puts the whole in his mouth and swallows it. 'Umm,' he says, and smiles at me evilly. 'Good ribbance' " (261). Frank observes that Paul "loves this kind of tricky punning talk" (20), such as when a sports announcer says of the high pay a boxer earns, "I'd let him sock *me* in the kisser for half that much" (20). Over the phone, in the car, and indeed most of the time, participating in verbal acrobatics takes both Frank and Paul's minds off of their troubles. If words become a refuge for Frank, then they also shelter Paul, whose affection for language's complexities rivals his father's. Apt to respond to Paul with such lines as, "I'm all leers" (343), Frank encourages his son's creative bent, and the two generate any number of variations on what have been phrases made almost meaningless through overuse: *"Take it for granite. A new leash on life. Put your monkey where your mouse is"* (343). In their newness, these substitutions practically make the phrases make sense again in what Frank has called the "fissures between the literal and the imagined" (343). It is this kind of word play that scissors through meaningless patter and opens a forum for relief through creativity. Moreover, the games provide a relatively safe arena in which father and son can to some degree compete. Their sports odyssey bears witness to another pastime they share, and that is more than a passing interest in ballgames and all-stars, but Frank and Paul play catch with words, not balls. These words often just glance off the objects they describe, requiring a kind of complicity between the speakers to be understood. In this way Frank and Paul sustain intimacy, though sometimes, of course, a direct statement would be of more use. Over the trip's course, in fact, Frank discovers that this mode of communication can be lacking in its effectiveness. "This is our oldest-timiest, most reliable, jokey way of conducting father-son business. Only today, due to technical difficulties beyond all control, it doesn't seem exactly to work. And our words get carried off in the breeze, with no one to care if we speak the intricate language of love or don't" (265–66). This breakdown can be traced to several different matters and will continue to wedge its way between Frank and Paul until the trip's climax.

First, although Frank correctly diagnoses Paul's problem, he suffers from the same malady himself, despite the Existence Period's exigencies. Paul finds himself engaging in the process of "thinking he's thinking"

(14), certainly a disconcerting activity. By this Paul means that he monitors his thoughts constantly in some attempt to pinpoint himself, understand who he is, why he thinks what he does (about Mr. Toby, for example), and determine how he might better control his life and pilot it in a positive direction. Although Frank himself almost constantly commits this same act, he is troubled by Paul's confession. He rationalizes that Paul is entirely too young to be caught in that cognitive net, and his desire is that Paul adopt more of an attitude that is consistent with the Existence Period, namely, the process of letting go of those things that he cannot control (i.e., the past) and indeed "jettisoning" much else in the bargain. Frank wants Paul to appreciate Emerson's perspective in *Self-Reliance*—and Frank quotes snippets from that work to himself ("shooting the gulf, in darting to an aim" [286])—which he never really articulates to Paul. Frank refers to this passage: "Life only avails, not the having lived. Power ceases in the instant of repose; it resides in the moment of transition from a past to a new state; in the shooting of the gulf; in the darting to an aim. This one fact the world hates, that the soul *becomes*."[1] Frank's interior world is aswarm with thoughts that never make it to the exterior world, where they might conceivably be of some use. He even recognizes what he should do: "I should, of course, seize the inert moment of arrival to introduce old Emerson, the optimistic fatalist, to the trip's agenda, haul *Self-Reliance* out of the back seat . . . try out the astute 'Discontent is the want of self-reliance; it is infirmity of will.' Or else something on the order of accepting the place providence has found for you, the society of your contemporaries, the connection of events" (264). Frank lifts the latter phrases from *Self-Reliance,* too, almost verbatim. He will quote Emerson again and again, referring finally to the phrase about the soul's becoming, but only to himself, not directly to Paul. Also in transition, Frank has as his deepest desire that Paul become a happy and well-functioning adult, but punning and word play aside, they cannot communicate when they need to. Finally, the two are so alike that Frank can only recognize Paul's problems—a difficulty in reconciling past with present, an excessive preoccupation with one's own thoughts—but he cannot fix them. Like any father, Frank wants to teach his son what he has already learned so that Paul won't have to learn the same lessons the hard way. But Frank is still learning, too.

Their shared journey does not reach the end that Frank has imagined: a zenith of father-son bonding that is so successful that it might persuade Ann to let Paul move back to New Jersey to live with Frank. On

their trip, Frank and Paul stop first at the basketball hall of fame, where
Frank and then Paul ride the "Shoot-Out," a conveyor belt from which
one can shoot basketballs at multiple hoops. Paul doesn't take a single
shot; rather he tells Frank that while he was riding the belt he finally
stopped thinking that he was thinking. This, of course, is not exactly the
vision that Frank has had of Paul at this site, where other fathers and
sons are shouting encouragement or heckling each other to dribble,
shoot, and score. But from this moment they are off toward Cooperstown, storied home of the baseball hall of fame, and where Frank
believes the trip will come together. As their journey continues, however, Frank himself cannot escape the clutches of his own mental
processes. The very problems he longs to correct in Paul's life are but
mirrors of his own.

For example, Frank suffers from mysterious ailments that have overtaken him from the start of his journey, various ticks and quirks that,
though subtler than Paul's strange utterances, may nonetheless emerge
from some of the same emotional swamps. Frank's heightened awareness of his own physical fragility has begun at Sally's beach house, where
Frank has gone to meet Sally before his trek with Paul. As he waits for
Sally to get home, Frank takes a snooze, what is intended to be a restful
and rejuvenating catnap in preparation for the long night of driving
ahead. To speed his drowsiness along, Frank is reading, appropriately
enough, French writer Alexis de Tocqueville's rather large tome entitled
Democracy in America.[2] Frank recalls from his college days that the book's
methodical analysis of American practices and political customs almost
ensures a soporific effect. Indeed it does, but before Frank can relinquish
himself to sleep, he is suddenly stricken by a strange wince. True to
form, Frank catalogs for his audience the varying kinds and degrees of
winces, concluding that this new one doesn't fall into any of his previously created categories. It does leave his vision marred by floating
spots, his ears ringing, and in its aftermath Frank questioning himself
and his surroundings, convinced that he really "ought to be somewhere
else. Though where? Where I'm wanted more than just expected?
Where I fit in better? Where I'm more purely ecstatic and not just glad?
At least someplace where meeting the terms, conditions and limitations
set on life are not so front and center. Where the rules are not the game"
(155). The repetition of "where" would seem significant; Frank disavows
the importance of place, as I will discuss later in this chapter. However,
he knows too well what human beings can never leave behind no matter
how many trips are taken: the self, and, as it were, the varying degrees

to which one occupies one's own identity. And what he fears is not so much that he fails to belong in this particular place, on this bed, waiting for this person, but that he fails, figuratively speaking, to occupy himself fully. He senses an emptiness to his life brought on by simply going through the motions of living. He recognizes "Nullity, in other words. Who the hell wouldn't wince?" (156). What is happening, of course, is that the Existence Period's influence is also faltering, though it is some time before Frank can recognize this fact. He speculates at this moment, on Sally's guest bed, that "Possibly this is one more version of 'disappearing into your life.' . . . You simply reach a point at which everything looks the same but nothing matters much. There's no evidence you're dead, but you act that way" (156). This suspicion, this encounter with his very own ghost of a self, and his glimpse of his simulated life all converge in Frank's wince. And Frank's wince joins a host of other physical afflictions: an annoying flutter in his right eye; a twitch to accompany his heart going "bim-bam" (183); a strange and unexplained limp that begins as Frank walks up the long hill to the O'Dells' house to get Paul, "as though a war had intervened since I last saw my loved ones and I had returned a changed and beaten veteran" (236–37); and the continuation of his rapidly beating heart going "bangety-bang" (217), as Frank puts it. All of these symptoms make Frank a dubious diagnostician of Paul's own well-being.

In addition to these physical ailments, as the trip progresses Frank feels himself slipping from his mental comfort zone until he lurks in a dangerously fragile limbo too close to dependence for his liking. To stave off such dangers, he flirts with the cook at Cooperstown's Deerslayer Inn, loses track of time *and* Paul, for that matter, giving Frank pause enough to reflect that "If I intend to have him home with me, I'll need to be more vigilant" (326). Flirting for diversion is behavior more reminiscent of Frank's former self, the one documented in *The Sportswriter.* Significantly, here he fails to follow through with the gesture, finally putting off the cook, coming back to himself, and realizing that he needs to locate his son and focus on the trip's presumable purpose. Frank's slip-ups—his mental flights from reality and his physical afflictions—suggest his gradual loss of control over his emotions, over Paul's emotions, and over his plan for the trip.

When Frank does find Paul, their conversation dwells still in the land of puns and indirection. To Frank's question about whether he's had dinner, Paul replies, "I got a mocktail, some mock turtle soup and a piece of mock apple pie. Don't mock me, please" (326). Again and again, Frank

will refer to these flights of fancy as carryovers from Paul's childhood, as
he does here, "These are all holdovers from childhood. . . . I might be
making progress with him and not realizing it (every parent's dearest
hope)" (326). Significantly, even as Frank advises a jettisoning of the
past, he and Paul are still stuck there, unable to move beyond old measures of language to adopt new ones. Frank seems to have an inkling of
this problem, suspecting that he and Paul aren't making progress
though hopeful that he is wrong and even blaming himself as the trip
continues to depart from his plan. When, for instance, he most needs to
summon them, Frank says, "I have just run out of important words, but
before I've said enough. . . . (My trust has always been that words can
make most things better and there's nothing that can't be improved on.
But words *are* required.)" (353). Repeatedly, Frank thinks of what he
ought to say, quotations he should bring to bear, wisdom from the
founding fathers, but he never manages to utter these thoughts. And,
so, at the batting cages when Paul seems to step dreamily and deliberately toward the ball hurtling at some breakneck speed from the pitching machine, Frank's words of " 'Too close, Paul' . . . 'That's too close,
son. You're going to brain yourself' " (361) linger unheeded in the air.
Paul's act puts an end to Frank's musings and hopes for a day "when the
past got pushed further away and neutralized, when a promising course
was charted for a future based on the postulate that independence and
isolation were not the same, when all concentric rings would've snapped
down and into place, and a true youthful (barkless, *eeeck*less) synchronicity might've flourished as only in youth it can" (369–70). Fortunately,
Paul will recover, but from this moment, "everything changes" (361).
The ball's sudden whack puts an exclamatory end to Frank's plan; reality crashes into dreaming, the literal into the imagined, and power is
knocked from Frank's words like breath from a body.

Words: The Terms of Seeming and Being

Paul's accident is the catalyst that begins to move Frank out of the Existence Period, but adumbrations of this change can be found in moments
when Frank has contemplated the differences between seeming and
being. These earlier hints of change to come lurk in conversations
between Frank and the significant women in his life, namely his former
wife, Ann, and his current girlfriend, Sally, both of whom accuse Frank
of *seeming* to be other than he is. Appropriately, the very phrase "Existence Period" evokes relative degrees of being—existing but not *as*

much, as Frank has put it earlier—and the attendant danger of disappearance, the failure to be visible, noticed, seen. These terms are indeed abstract and difficult to pin down, as Frank himself also can be. But words, abstract though they are, are the agents here that allow for such distinctions; words make seeming possible.

Ford's reader might recall Frank's preoccupation with truth in *The Sportswriter* and his propensity to withhold information from others out of his fear of "full disclosure."[3] In *The Sportswriter,* Frank found himself saying almost anything to a woman and then regretting it immediately afterward. Therefore he tries to monitor his talk so that he won't mislead others. If someone else tells him too much, he becomes intensely uncomfortable, though he himself uses words to excess. Aware of this tendency, he tries—but often fails—to say what he means but still keep something to himself. More often than not, however, he says what he *thinks* the other person wants to hear. He runs into the same problems with Sally, who says to Frank, "I don't think we mean the same things when we say the same things" (311). This remark follows one of Frank's declarations of affection that jars with their previously awkward parting on the eve of Frank's trip. Because he wants his relationship with Sally to achieve certain heights of intimacy even as he fears such things, Frank vacillates in his responses to her. On the one hand, when he is in her presence, he finds himself distancing himself from her, but on the other hand, while conversing with her by phone, he is apt to make rash invitations for her to join him and Paul or utter strange proclamations of love that he doesn't really mean. This may also remind the reader of his behavior in *The Sportswriter.* What Frank discovers is that when he is with Sally, he almost feels lonelier than he is, but the idea of her, from a distance, appeals to that same streak of loneliness.

Frank realizes that Sally differs from Ann in some significant ways, that is, she "superintends nothing, presupposes nothing and in essence promises to do nothing remotely like that" (177). He terms their relationship a kind of "Existence Period shared" (177), if only because she represents no real "*other*"; there are "me and my acts, her and hers, somehow together—which of course is much more fearsome" (177). It is this fearsomeness that Frank sometimes flees, finding Sally absent to be much more compelling than Sally present. As an intelligent woman whose life is arguably more settled than Frank's, Sally knows that Frank practices these evasive tactics. She remains suspect of him over the phone, often reminding him that what he is now saying sounds very different from what he has formerly said. Though they continue to talk, they fail to communicate. However, Frank's relationship with Sally seems but a small eddying current compared to the more undertow-like pull that Ann exerts.

If Sally presupposes nothing, then Ann presupposes everything, becoming by definition the biggest contingency in Frank's life. Perpetually the "audience," for whom, Frank says, "My life was (and to some vague extent still is) played out on a stage" (105), Ann presumes importance in Frank's life by virtue of "ineluctable history" (177). After her announcement of her remarriage, Frank admits that for a time he felt his life becoming "significantly less substantial" (105), as if by being exiled from Ann's presence he also lost something of his own being-in-the-world. Frank also confirms a change in self-perception wrought simply by the fact of his divorce, a kind of predivorce and postdivorce split of the self that can prove quite confusing to its host. As Frank explains, "You have, on the one hand, such an obsessively detailed and minute view of yourself from your prior existence, and on the other hand, an equally specific view of yourself *later on,* that it becomes almost impossible not to see yourself as a puny human oxymoron, and damn near impossible sometimes to recognize who your self is at all" (248). Once again, the word "existence" intrudes, this time in the sense of a dual life, or, at least, a dual way of *seeing* one's life: pre- and postdivorce. Frank alludes to the idea that, to some extent, then, one's own identity is bound up with the identities of others, making his prescriptions for the Existence Period even more problematic.

Frank devises the tenets of the Existence Period in response to his loss of Ann and what he has called the sensation of feeling himself "becoming significantly less substantial" (105). The Existence Period is the perfect antidote to this plight, since by Frank's definition he *requires* himself to live an insubstantial life, in which he can exist, but not as much, and through which he can come and go, but not be noticed. As Frank tries to come to terms with his own sense of his being, and the degree to which in fact he wants *to be,* he is forced to acknowledge that his relationship with Ann has changed his existence; that his divorce from her, at least for a time, has rendered him but a pale rendition of his former self; and, that even in the present, he battles what he has called this "ghostly self" (108). The quandary of the competing selves inspires Frank's reference to that specific ability that writers possess that makes their profession highly appealing: "Writers in fact survive this condition better than anyone, since they understand that almost everything— e-v-e-r-y-t-h-i-n-g—is not really made up of 'views' but words, which, should you not like them, you can change" (248). Frank has been a writer, first of fiction, then of sports, and he obviously remembers how to manipulate words; words, after all, can make things other than they are and, arguably, are the keys to seeming rather than being.[4]

Words protect Frank by allowing him to seem rather than be, make circumstances better than they are by talking about them in a certain way, and shy away from the truth. These acts repeatedly endanger Frank's relationship with Ann; in fact, she continues to remind Frank, " 'I divorced you . . . because I didn't like you. And I didn't like you because I didn't trust you. Do you think you ever told me the truth once, the whole truth?' . . . (This is the perpetual theme of her life: the search for truth, and truth's defeat by the forces of contingency, most frequently represented by yours truly.)" (252–53). Frank protests that he has always loved Ann and that he has a "true heart" (254), though he has to admit to her that, "You're probably right. I rely on how I make things seem" (255). With these words, Frank refers to Ann's earlier accusation, that he is willing to "let *seem* equal *be*" (184), what Frank describes as a "sneak frontal assault on the Existence Period" (184). Ann simply means that in his efforts to make everybody happy and gloss over problems for the sake of some equilibrium, Frank ignores real factors that over time of course make their presence known, usually when it's too late to address them constructively. Ann attributes Frank's past love of storywriting to this desire, in fact, because in that medium he could control utterly the thoughts of the characters and the words that they spoke, directing history and ending toward whatever resolution he desired. Ann believes that Frank just wants things to *seem* a certain way regardless of their reality, thereby letting himself off the hook of having to fix them. As Frank himself acknowledges above, there is some truth to her accusation. And, of course, part of the Existence Period's code of conduct is letting things go, gliding along on the surface of life freed of entangling attachments. For this reason, Frank perceives Ann's words as an attack on the Existence Period, which is a time of muted being in favor of less complicated existing, an endorsement of *seeming to be*.

Locution, Locution, Locution

"Locution, locution, locution" (182): revealing again his affinity with Paul (or Paul's with him), Frank creates this pun, an aside to his audience as he struggles to talk to Ann over the phone. He plays off of the mantra of realtors everywhere, "location, location, location." Here, of course, by making the simple substitution of the "u" for the "a," Frank refers to the act of speaking, not the relative merits of real estate determined primarily by place. To be a man who uses words so profusely, Frank often finds himself strangely at a loss for them when he is required actually to say something. This is the case in his phone conversation with Ann, when Frank longs to move their conversation beyond the superficial and toward the meaningful but cannot for the life of himself think of anything profound to say short of a shocking lie (that he's getting married, dying of an incurable disease, etc.). This conversation is the same one that approaches its end with Ann's "sneak frontal assault on the Existence Period" (184) and that finally concludes with Ann's frustration: "Everything's in quotes with you, Frank. Nothing's really solid. Every time I talk to you I feel like everything's being written by you. Even my lines. That's awful, isn't it? Or sad?" (184). Nothing's solid with Frank because he is not solid either, not literally, of course, but figuratively. But when Ann says to him that "You wore me out" (184), he finds in those words the modicum of intimacy for which he searches. "These are the most intimate words she's addressed to me in years! (I have no idea what might've inspired them.) Though sadder than what she thinks is sad is the fact that hearing them leaves me with nothing to say, no lines I even can write for her. Moving closer, even slightly, even for a heartbeat, is just another form of storytelling" (184–85). Storytelling becomes a kind of metaphor for Frank's relationship with Ann, encompassing pejorative as well as more positive meanings. On the one hand, to tell a story, colloquially speaking, is to tell a lie, or a small untruth. On the other hand, to tell a story is to create something meaningful from circumstances that in and of themselves are perhaps not. Ironically, as Frank tells his own story, the moments with Ann and Paul are those within which Frank finds himself most often with nothing to say, even when words are required, as he has admitted with Paul. And, of course, what Frank has stripped himself of in the Existence Period are relationships that revolve around silent, not spoken, intimacies. Finding oblique and indirect ways to communicate is not always sufficient, and Frank's most significant moments of contact usually occur when words are conspicuously absent from his lips.

Perhaps Frank himself uses words irresponsibly, a bit too freely, in the throes of the Existence Period. He seems to recognize that words can change the surfaces of what they describe but that at times the imagined is infinitely less satisfying than the real. He uses this sort of argument to explain why Ann was never a recognizable presence in his fiction.

"What I used to tell her was—and God smite me if I'm lying about it almost twenty years later—that if I could encapsulate her in words, it would mean I'd rendered her less complex than she was" (158). In a sense, Ann was too significant to be contained on the page, though she never believed Frank's reasons for her absence from his fiction. He goes on to confide to his audience, "I didn't want to use her up, bind her in words, set her aside, consign her to a 'place' where she would be known, but always as less than she was" (159). Words can be restrictive, then, forcing stasis from what should remain fluid, anchoring down what should remain free to push forward. Frank's voyage through the Existence Period and toward interconnectedness with others requires a kind of renegotiation with language, the spoken, written, and unuttered word alike.

Ironically, the discovery of his own book of short fiction, *Blue Autumn,* dust-covered and cast aside in the Deerslayer Inn's library at Cooperstown, gives Frank one of his jolts from the Existence Period's safety. First he feels as if he has stumbled upon some precious artifact, simply because the encounter is unexpected, and because the book is still, as he puts it, " 'out there,' in circulation, still official if somewhat compromised, still striving to the purposes I meant it to: staging raids on the inarticulate, being an ax for the frozen sea within us, providing the satisfactions of belief in the general mess of imprecision" (320). Frank's interpretation of the book's purpose reveals his creator Ford's awareness of all that literature is supposed to be able to do: in chief, combat isolation created by communication breakdowns in "real" life via the author's presumed ability to put into words emotions that lay persons, as opposed to writers, feel, but are unable to name. Through Frank, Ford also paraphrases the American poet Wallace Stevens here; Stevens believed that poetry's purpose was to provide some consolation in a world where religion has failed. Art, not religion, would foster belief in its powers to restore a barren universe and wreak order from chaos. Ford uses Frank's vocabulary to characterize him; Frank's words at once betray his degree of literacy, his educated and well-read mind, and his idealism. Frank believes that words defy loss. Ford, of course, sets Frank up to be contradicted, and humorously so.

As Frank gingerly and reverently blows the dust from the book jacket and opens the volume, he is prepared for evidence of his book's good citizenship in the world and for a whisper of what he has called "synchronicity" to brush back over him. Instead, his eyes fall upon the inscription, "For Esther, remembering that really *bleu* autumn with you.

Love ya, Dwayne. Spring, 1970" (321). Every line of this inscription has been marked through with what appears to be lipstick; below there is another inscription: "Dwayne. Rhymes with pain. Rhymes with fuck. Rhymes with the biggest mistake of my life. With contempt for you and your cheap tricks. Esther. Winter, 1972" (321–22). As Frank observes, "This is a good deal different—by virtue of being a good deal less—than what I'd expected" (322). Rather, however, than feeling some pang for the young-love-gone-wrong between Dwayne and Esther, Frank finds himself overcome by a "totally unexpected, sickening void opening right in my stomach—right where I said it wouldn't two minutes ago" (322). Since he has been armed with the Existence Period's tenets, Frank has believed himself immune to certain feelings, loss and regret being chief among them. Here, however, he succumbs to emotions about Ann for which he is totally unprepared: "Ann, and the end of Ann and me and everything associated with us, comes fuming up in my nostrils suddenly like a thick poison" (322). As he yields to these sensations of ending, he witnesses the gap between the past and present suddenly opening wide to reveal the very finality of their divorce and the relinquishing of their old selves: "she was never *that* she, me never *that* me, as though the two of us had never embarked on a life that would lead to this queer librarial moment (though we did)" (322). This revelation of all that has been consigned to the past and lost in the bargain leaves Frank reeling. Tears sting his eyes, evidence that he cannot, at that moment, gird himself with the Existence Period's creed and that reveals to him the irony of his priding himself on being "the man who counsels abandonment of those precious things you remember but can no longer make hopeful use of" (322). Suddenly caught in his own mourning of the past, Frank can't very well counsel Paul to forget, and his own book has been the culprit, the reason for his falling right out of the Existence Period and into the terrifying space of knowing exactly what he has lost.

It is through this emptiness that Frank operates for the rest of the trip; he suffers from a crippling kind of grief, though he doesn't really recognize it until later, that perhaps keeps him from realizing what Paul is thinking. When Paul steps right into the path of the baseball hurtling out of the batting machine at some unimaginable speed, Frank can only watch, in horror and disbelief. In fact, from this moment on, Frank becomes a rather passive observer, rendered incapable of making decisions or acting with any kind of confidence. He must rely upon the help of others, thereby shedding the cloak of the Existence Period and exposing himself as he is: a worried father who feels that he should have done something else, anything else, to prevent his son's accident. Ann, not surprisingly, is the one who rallies to the occasion, looking up a renowned doctor to examine Paul's eye, and for whom everyone waits while she flies in from New York, despite the delay caused by her actually bringing the doctor, a specialist from Yale, with her. She will make the decisions pertaining to Paul's health. She will be the responsible parent. And Frank feels grateful for her composure and her intervention. In consultation with the Yale doctor, all parties agree that Paul will be flown to New Haven for surgery. Frank finds himself trying to convince Ann that their son isn't crazy, that he probably didn't intend to put his eye out (almost the generic fear of any parent, which Ford makes good use of here) but that instead Paul probably just wanted to feel *something,* and a good hard blow seemed the best sensation that he could summon. Frank confesses to Ann that he has felt the same way, particularly after Ralph died and after their divorce, and so the two do end up, in fact, having what might be called an intimate conversation. Frank also confesses his own guilt, his worry that the accident was somehow his fault, to which Ann is responsive and comforting. This particular conversation ends not with accusations but with an embrace, during which Frank says in response to Ann's plea not to be mad at her, "I'm not mad at you. . . . I'm just so something else. I don't think I know the word. There's not a word for it, maybe" (397). He is "in between words" at the moment, though he would like to have one that fit the occasion, but Ann, again, pardons him. Since she has scolded him in the past for his glibness, one would think she would be relieved that he is bereft of language here; instead, she suspects that he's glad to have the opportunity to create language in this gap. However, he remains speechless. "Love" may be the word he is missing to describe the conjunction of an overwhelming sense of responsibility for Paul, relief over and respect for Ann's intervention, and an affection for both that defies language's attempt to gather the multiple feelings together and hold his thoughts still. Composed and efficient, Ann differs markedly from Frank under these circumstances, providing a glimpse into the ways that their dynamics might have failed them during other times of stress, namely Ralph's illness and death. Frank even imagines that Ann would know the word he needs, her midwestern practicality anchoring her while he feels unmoored from certainty. He signs the release for Paul and is "glad to" (397), glad to let go and aware of his own inadequacies.

Ford punctuates Frank's loss of words by introducing another character, Irv, actually Frank's stepbrother, who in effect summarizes Frank's life when Frank himself cannot. Irv has seen Frank in Cooperstown and recognized him, and he has happened to be coming over to Frank to reintroduce himself just as Paul gets smacked in the eye. Irv drives Frank to the hospital behind the ambulance, and as Irv talks about his own life, he creates an eerie account that almost exactly mirrors Frank's own concerns. When Frank is rendered speechless, Irv tells his story. In fact, Irv effectively names Frank's dilemma, candidly and without fanfare, summing up for the reader Frank's mental journey and even providing Frank with a new vocabulary.

Ford's slyly humorous bent comes into play here, too; in Irv, he has created a character who is actually in the simulator business—flight simulators, that is. Nonetheless, the word "simulator" acts in a particularly resonant way in a book so concerned with degrees of seeming and being. To simulate means to seem, to appear to be something that the object is actually not. A flight simulator, for instance, would allow one to *seem* to be flying and to practice and operate under those conditions, even though one was not really flying. Irv's occupation as a simulator, then, is surely a deliberate choice on Ford's part. It is also not incidental that Irv, a person from Frank's past, invites Frank, just by virtue of Irv's own presence, to reckon with all that Frank has tried to discard in the Existence Period. Irv is Frank's doppelgänger, his spiritual twin. For example, he "complains of feeling detached from his own personal history" (388), a state that has inspired Irv likewise to fear "(kept within boundaries by his demanding simulator work) that he is diminishing" (388). Frank likens Irv's fear of diminishing to his own fear of disappearance, making the connection obvious in case the reader is obtuse. Frank, too, has experienced what Irv puts into words as a "catch of dread" (388), a powerful feeling that something is wrong even when everything *seems* right. The only solutions that Frank can offer, as he himself admits, are "the general remedies of persistence, jettisoning, common sense, resilience, good cheer—all tenets of the Existence Period—leaving out the physical isolation and emotional disengagement parts, which cause trouble equal to or greater than the problems they ostensibly solve" (390). Finally acknowledging the Existence Period's flaws (though he has earlier remarked upon certain tenets' failures), Frank still does not feel very open to Irv's philosophizing.

Ford characterizes Irv as oblivious to his own theorizing, utterly convinced of the simulating trade's literalness, leaving the reader to note the irony and make the connections between his life and Frank's. Irv has cautioned Frank that the danger in the simulator business is taking work home. In Irv's opinion, it is crucial to keep the business of simulation and one's own life separate. Even though his work theories clarify that seeming and being are two distinct things that should not be confused with one another, Irv actually advises Frank to "simulate calm" (372), having admitted that there is much to life that exceeds a person's control. Newly afflicted with that realization, unmitigated by the Existence Period, Frank can only think to himself, "There is no *seeming* now. All is *is*" (369). Although he first rejects Irv's take on life's unpredictabilities and human responses to such things, Frank nonetheless must recognize a certain kindredness between Irv's predicament and his own.

Like Frank, Irv regards himself as a loner, but he is preoccupied with "community" and "continuity." By the latter he means any ties, including memories or personal history, that exert influence on his life. Irv tells Frank that he suspects that Frank, as a realtor, must surely have witnessed the rampant desire for both among the clients he's had. Frank disagrees with Irv, claiming that communities are not at all continuous, that is, that the past can exert no pull on the present, somehow binding one person to another. To Frank, communities are "isolated, contingent groups trying to improve on an illusion of permanence, which they fully accept as an illusion. . . . But continuity, if I understand it at all, doesn't really have much to do with it" (386). Frank admits, in an aside to his own audience, that community is actually a word, and a concept, that he "loathes." To demonstrate what he means by these terms, Irv pulls from his wallet an old photograph of him and Frank together, in 1963, when both were just boys. Frank has no recollection of the picture being taken, but neither does Irv. Irv offers the image, though, as proof of continuity, of the past's sneaking into the present, as this very timely meeting with Frank suggests. Irv has, after all, served Frank well in the present chaos after Paul's accident. Frank seems to miss Irv's point: "We have passed in daylight; we have interfaced, given each other good and earnest feedback. But ours is not life coterminous, though I like him fine" (392). Frank's use of hackneyed language here—"interfaced," "feedback"—suggests at least a trace of contempt for Irv. However, his assessment of their not being "coterminous," or having lives that share any real boundaries, is clearly mistaken. Frank recognizes that Irv is poised on the cusp of an Existence Period all his own, even as Frank emerges from this state. But Irv's words influence Frank, perhaps even transform him, verging on the very function that Frank has hoped his book of fiction would accomplish. Irv has named Frank's predicament.

In Irv's language and desire to exit the world of simulation, get out of the business, as Irv confesses to Frank, Frank finds his own condition identified. Soon after their conversation, Frank happens upon a new vocabulary with which to describe his modus operandi, including the notion of "Continuity—an earnest new commanding metaphor—[which] was applicable to all and was taking up the slack for synchronicity (which never carries you far enough)" (405). It is Irv's word that he is adopting, despite his earlier protestations, and via these new terms of "community" and "continuity," Frank can grapple with the meanings of independence, discarding what he now finds to be unviable tenets of the Existence Period and maybe even leaving the simulator business himself. After all, Frank now rejects what he deems "not a good part—to seem to want something but then not to" (413).

As Frank follows the trajectory from seeming to being, he accrues words previously lost to him. For example, when he visits Paul in the hospital, the two engage in their typical patterns of conversation, trying to conclude the old saying, "You can lead a horse to water, but you can't make him . . ." (401). Paul finally comes up with "dance" to describe what one cannot make a horse do, and at the conclusion of this pronouncement, Frank expects an untoward and self-conscious utterance from Paul, some barking, or maybe the "*eeeck*ing" sound. But Paul is silent. In this moment, Frank is suddenly inspired to say a direct statement himself, one unadulterated by puns: " 'I love you son, okay?' I said, suddenly wanting to clear out in a hurry" (402). Paul says, "Yep, me too" (402), and Frank takes his leave. These words have been missing from their other exchanges, and here Frank means them. He leaves them unadorned; he and Paul speak plain talk, unembellished words. There is no gap between the words and what they mean, as there is in punning talk, or irony, or jokes, or any of their "oldest-timiest" ways of communicating, as Frank has put it earlier. Significantly, here it seems that Frank and Paul have traversed the distance between the language typical of Paul's childhood and some more mature measure of making words signify. Also significantly, Frank's antsiness, his desire to "clear out in a hurry," suggests his discomfort with the exposure wrought by the direct statement, the words that *are* rather than seem to be. He rarely succeeds in such straight talk; he rarely means it when he says "I love you" to a woman, at least in any kind of permanent sense, and he never utters it to Ann, though certainly his allusions to her presupposing everything and being his constant if unseen audience suggest that he does love her. Clearly, in this moment with Paul, Frank feels terribly exposed and uncomfortable without the usual banter and the protective distance between the signifier and the signified, the literal and the imagined, that metaphor or figurative language provides. By saying these words to Paul, however, Frank steps more decisively toward being rather than seeming. As he continues to emerge, he concludes that the only belief sanctioned by the Existence Period that is "worth holding on to" (442) is that place finally cannot shelter us, an odd belief for a real estate agent to hold.

Making Accommodations: Place and Self

Frank often refers to his "ghostly self"—his postdivorce, less substantial presence that cannot easily be pinned down—both literally and figuratively. He implies, as other characters also do, that he has become a kind of simulation of his former identity; he seems to be the same person, perhaps newly improved, but he is not. He seems, in fact, to be many ways that he is not. His consistent occupation of his car in the novel fits nicely with this characterization. He belongs to no one and to no place. Place itself, such a loaded term in southern fiction, is a construct that seems to fascinate Richard Ford.[5] Ford's use of the term always defies the southern definitions of place, which tend toward the concrete; instead Ford suggests an almost metaphysical meaning, something more abstract. To Ford, a literal place harbors no power; whatever force a place provides is created simply by the person who brings with him or her certain expectations, certain memories, certain ideas of what that particular place means. In an interview, Ford describes how some writers, Henry David Thoreau, for example, have portrayed place almost as a living being, capable of imparting sensations to those who come into its presence. Ford refutes such notions:

> My view—not that it's original with me, God knows—is that those things are not animate, that they never speak. Okay, I know it's a figure of speech. But in talking about a sense of place, or locatedness, or the importance of place, or how we feel about it, that figure of speech gets made perplexingly literal sometimes, and in that transaction personally responsible for how one feels, and what's important about place gets shed or lost. Therefore, my view is that anything you feel about a place, anything that you think about place at all, you have authored and ascribed to some piece of geography. (Walker, 139)

Frank is Ford's fictional spokesman for this interpretation in *Independence Day*, since, as the Existence Period's advocate, he must cultivate a detachment from place.

Ford's own wanderlust, which has received much attention from his interviewers and critics, no doubt has informed his attitude about place, namely that place is *never* as important as most people think. As Ford puts it in his essay "Country Matters," "*Place* cannot be extolled, except in the abstract or most purely private sense" (84), and "Place . . . is wherever we do good work" (84). In other words, *what* one accomplishes is far more significant than the setting for that accomplishment. Certain places may require different responses, but it is the human being, not the place, who is responsible for the required act. Ford finds an analogy in Emerson's notion of duty, and he argues that most sentiments that one experiences about place could more accurately be understood as recognitions of "the duty the place confers once the necessary accommodations have been made" (84). The word "accommodation" bears dual meaning: one, it can refer to the literal site that houses one; two, it can mean whatever compromises, measures, or adjustments one makes or takes to provide for one's (or another's) comfort and well-being. Ford uses the word in the latter sense. That Ford casts Frank as a real estate agent in *Independence Day* only makes Frank's preoccupation with what place means to human beings a perfectly appropriate one. Frank ruminates time and again about the connections between place and self and how being—or seeming—is inextricably bound to one's assumptions about place.

Frank muses often about the literal and figurative definitions of place. For example, he speaks abstractly about whatever place one is pulled to by that bright thread of synchronicity, the "astral beam" (*ID*, 204) he has referred to in the context of Mr. Tanks's desire to go East. In this sense he alludes as much to a mental state as a literal locale. But he also speaks about places that he has invested with significance, as he did in *The Sportswriter*, extolling the New Jersey town of Haddam's pleasant literalness, and as he continues to do here:

> Haddam. Where I landed not only with a new feeling of great purpose and a fury to suddenly *do* something serious for my own good and possibly even for others', but also with the feeling of renewal I'd gone far to look for and that immediately translated into a homey connectedness to Haddam itself, which felt at that celestial moment like my spiritual residence more than any place I'd ever been, inasmuch as it *was* the place I instinctively and in a heat came charging back to. (Of course, having

come first to life in a true *place,* and one as monotonously, lankly *itself* as the Mississippi Gulf Coast, I couldn't be truly surprised that a simple *setting* such as Haddam—willing to be so little itself—would seem, on second look, a great relief and damned easy to cozy up to.) (*ID,* 93)

Typical of Frank's meandering meditations on any number of subjects, this passage is stylistically marked by Frank's almost constant modification of his claims, symbolized on the page by the frequent parenthetical aside and by the emphasis of some words over another, which Ford indicates here and elsewhere by the use of italics. Ford—and Frank—know that some words harbor associations that exceed their literal definitions and that "place" is such a word. Frank is from Mississippi, what he refers to as a "true *place,*" thereby revealing his own awareness of the South's sanctification of its landscape. At once a source of strength via memory, family legacies, property ownership, fecundity, and prosperity, *and* the site of human cruelty via slavery, place in the South is a complex construction. The "trueness" of a place assumes a kind of history and longevity. Haddam, then, in its relative newness and without the powerful associations—both good and bad—that characterize a southern town, is a refreshingly simple locale to occupy (or at least seems to be), allowing its denizen plenty of figurative room to respond to the desire to "*do*" something, as Frank says. Perhaps here Frank alludes to the Emersonian concept of duty. Haddam, New Jersey, for instance, might confer a very different duty than Birmingham, Alabama.

However, Frank finds that the tendency to sanctify place is not just a southern preoccupation; as a real estate agent, he gathers plentiful evidence that "you don't sell a house to someone, you sell a life" (112). Referring to an "almost authorial power" (106) that houses exert over their inhabitants, Frank speculates that a house's ability to outlast its owner contributes to the common, albeit wrongheaded, notion that where a person lives determines *how* a person lives. Human beings seek in places what may be lacking from their own lives: a sense of order, familiarity, continuity—in short, a substantiation of all those things that finally are insubstantial. Recalling the time when he lived in his grandfather's hotel as a child, Ford writes in his essay entitled, appropriately, "Accommodations": "Accommodation is what's wanted, a replenished idea of permanence and transience; familiarity overcoming the continual irregularity in things" (38). In this same essay, Ford concludes, "Home is finally a variable concept" (43), and this claim invariably makes its way into Frank's testimonials.

Frank knows, however, that most people subscribe to the notion that home, where they live, somehow ratifies their very selfhood and contributes to their identities, whereas, really, as Frank believes, it is the other way around. His clients, Joe and Phyllis Markham, are particularly afflicted by this idea. The entire process of finding the "right" home has taken so much longer than they expected that they have already sold their Vermont house, which they had built to suit themselves, quit their day jobs, and are presently living, much to their dismay, off of the money originally saved to be the down payment on the new place. The discrepancy between the costs of living in Vermont and New Jersey is so extreme that what they can actually afford falls quite short of the kind of house they imagined they would buy. To date, Frank has shown the Markhams 45 houses, not one of which has been satisfactory. Well aware that the market economy in no way guarantees that a person will find what he or she desires, Frank nonetheless has tried to discover inventive ways to shelter the Markhams from their own predicament. Frank calls these measures "stop-gap accommodations" (*ID,* 43). Although Phyllis is somewhat receptive to Frank's ideas, Joe has grown stubbornly emphatic about his own needs. Increasingly ill-tempered about the whole enterprise, Joe snaps at Frank, "What I mean, Bascombe, . . . is that the reason we haven't bought a house in four months is that I don't *want* to goddamned buy one. And the reason for that is I don't want to get trapped in some shitty life I'll never get out of except by dying" (52). Joe equates the place with the shape his life will subsequently take, not in itself a mistaken perception, since even Frank admits that owning a home is fraught with uncertainty. Frank acknowledges that at times he doesn't "understand why anybody buys a house" (43); in that purchase one accepts the accompanying responsibilities of its upkeep, determines the literal view of the world from the window, and possibly seals the location of one's own death and funeral. Nonetheless, he counsels Phyllis, "You *are* best coming as close as you can [to what you think you want] and trying to bring life to a place, not just depending on place to supply it for you" (76). Frank knows that following this advice, true though it may be, is easier said than done.

Ironically, Frank is engaged in his own endeavor of bringing life back into himself, though at the time that he speaks to Phyllis he is full of grandiose plans for cheering Paul into independence. Frank makes many assumptions that in the end fail him. He has, for example, blithely traveled to Florida, and afterward to France with then-girlfriend Catherine

Flaherty, content to conduct his relationships with Paul and Clarissa over the phone. Nonetheless, he is shocked when, in his absence, Ann sinks into a relationship with Charley O'Dell, one that eventuates in their engagement. The news strikes Frank hard, leaving him in a funk upon his return, prone to drink gin and hole up in his house for days, emerging just long enough to speak simultaneously to Clarissa and Paul over extension phones. As he puts it, Ann's news leaves him with "only faint, worn-out costumes to play myself with" (105). Having assumed that somehow he and Ann would remain crucial to each other's existence despite the fact of their divorce, he is horrified by the prospect of her becoming another "we." This is not to say that Frank's choice to stay home rather than travel would have prevented Ann's remarriage. The trouble is that Frank will never know. Somehow he still imagined himself and Ann growing old—if not together, then in some *semblance* of togetherness. In the face of grave illness, for example, he would care for Ann, or she would for him, because there would be no one else with exactly the same claim over the other's life, an imagined possibility that Charley O'Dell's presence clearly erases.

Frank counsels against expecting a house to offer its occupant anything significant, but he himself has moved as part of his own private search. In addition to his own growing insubstantiality in the wake of Ann's announcement, Frank's Hoving Road house, where he has lived since his divorce, seems likewise emptier, "barny and murky, murmurous and queer" (107). Suddenly, the solution seems obvious to Frank: he will move into Ann's place, the house on Cleveland Street she had bought after their separation. He makes a generous offer, and literally he is able to walk through the door without changing a thing, taking but a few nostalgic items with him, and finding Ann's furniture where she has left it. He admits that the move does not much change his life; he has spent nights wandering his old place—and hers—sometimes, when he has been unable to sleep. Frank says that he is "searching, I suppose, for where I fit in, or where I'd gone wrong, or how I could breathe air into my ghostly self and become a recognizable if changed-for-the-better figure in their [his children's] lives or my own. One house is as good as another for this kind of private enterprise. And the poet was right again: 'Let the wingèd Fancy roam, / Pleasure never is at home' " (108). Frank here quotes the last two lines of "Fancy," a poem by John Keats, words that seem to endorse his choice to wander or at the very least to let his imagination go where it will. Frank believes, after all, that "one house is as good as another" for the search for the self.

Despite this conclusion, he has for some reason felt compelled, at some point, to leave one place for another place, and on the basis in part of the former abode's murkiness. And he has returned from France before Ann's news, guided by that "astral beam" of synchronicity that has pulled him toward some *place* and the logical prescriptions of the Existence Period.

Forced to accept major changes in his existence, Frank adopts a self-protective stance, and that is a preparedness to move ahead, onward, forward, without the past bogging him down. Place's call to nostalgia is one more thing worth jettisoning, in Frank's opinion. Whenever one goes to a place expecting some kind of sudden epiphany, some redemption of the past, one is only confronted with loss. Frank himself gets choked up at times upon being in a certain place; he does so in front of Sally's beach house before his trip, concluding that the reason is "either the place's familiarity or its rigid reluctance to act familiar" (151). He goes on to note, "Places never cooperate by revering you back when you need it. In fact, they almost always let you down, as the Markhams found out in Vermont and now New Jersey. Best to just swallow back your tear, get accustomed to the minor sentimentals and shove off to whatever's next, not whatever was. Place means nothing" (151–52). Fittingly, it is this sense of nothingness that impels Frank to leave Sally's house rather suddenly, acknowledging that there's "nothing to hold me here another second" (174). Later, he will regret their awkward parting and try to repair it, not surprisingly, over the phone.

Frank tries to apply these lessons on place's emptiness to himself, and presumably with Phyllis and Joe, Frank is simply trying to pass along whatever wisdom he's gleaned from his own experience. He believes his objectivity about place makes him an ideal real estate agent, and his attitude certainly influences his peregrinations, the fact that he is never in the same location for very long over the novel's course. Nonetheless, he considers place when he plans his trip with Paul, believing that the sports halls of fame will be ideal settings for his instruction and the Fourth of July a most appropriate time frame for the trip. Ann's move to Deep River has complicated this plan, but it also makes Frank more determined than ever that his trip with Paul be an intensive course in independence. He wants to "strengthen the constitution of whoever he [Paul] is whenever I meet him—though that is not always the same boy" (210), and Frank imagines that there is something that only he can provide Paul, despite at times being remiss in his fathering, which he readily admits. The problem is that Frank doesn't quite know what that something is. Determined to salvage his fatherhood and save Paul from his past, Frank hopes to locate himself in the bargain.

Frank believes that locating the self has little to do with where one resides. He notes this fundamental difference between Charley O'Dell and himself. As he and Paul ride along in the car, Frank reflects upon the imposing facade of the O'Dell residence, the looming house upon a hill. Frank attributes Charley's apparent need for exterior stability to Charley's probable belief that "a good structure implies a good structure" (284), which is to suggest that Charley believes that external order goes a long way toward ensuring internal order. Of Charley's own childhood and background, Frank happens to know a few salient details gleaned from a reliable source. These details include Charley's father's philanderings and support of another family in addition to Charley's as well as the elder O'Dell's rather distant relationship with his son. Frank interprets Charley's past, concluding that "all was jake" (284) as long as some massive house presided over all, as if the very solidity of the house could make up for the less substantial relationships nurtured therein. Nonetheless, Frank opines, "This, in Charley's view, constitutes life and no doubt truth: strict physical moorings. A roof over your head to prove you have a head" (284). (Frank continues with his analogy between a human being and some ship with moorings, possible anchorage, and steering that is contingent upon the current.) As far as Charley is concerned, Frank implies that the only way a man like Charley knows that he exists is by the proof of his residence: if this house exists, then so must I exist within it. The structure provides the window, so to speak, into the inhabitant's selfhood, the person defined in part by the place.

As he muses over Charley's likely raison d'être, Frank diagnoses himself, assessing that "finding firm anchorage" (284) is a problem for him. He confesses that, "for all my insistent prating that they—the Markhams—haul themselves into clearer view, I've never seen myself all that exactly" (285). Although Frank recognizes that true responsibility for happiness and contentedness lies not with place but within the self, he admits that bringing the self into focus is a tricky act. And, if he encounters trouble bringing himself into focus, he can't very well envision others "sharing the frame" (285). What troubles Frank is that his own vagueness may be somehow transmitted to Paul: "These uncertainties . . . may even help to drive my surviving son nutty and set him barking and baying at the moon" (285). This thought makes him aspire to Charley's unquestioning security: "I dearly wish I could speak from some more established *place* . . . rather than from this constellation of stars among which I smoothly orbit, traffic and glide. Indeed, if I could see myself as occupying a fixed point rather than being in a process (the quiddity of the Existence Period), things might grow better for us both—myself and barking son" (285). The Existence Period is all about movement, the avoidance of getting stalled by old fears and regrets. Frank speculates that the occupation of a "fixed point" might enable him to provide more stability and a better example for Paul. But the truth is that, despite the appearance of Charley's solid world, within the walls of his childhood home there was no doubt a span of absence. Place, then, may only *seem* to provide a refuge; it is finally, as Ford himself believes, totally barren of meaning, totally arbitrary in essence, until a person breathes significance into it by occupation, thought, memory, and a history shared with someone else. Even before he recognizes the significance of his knowledge, Frank knows that love, not place, cements identity and that love, being rather unfixed itself—an abstraction that cannot assume physical dimensions—also allows for identity's flux and growth. Long before he is prepared to exit the Existence Period, Frank acknowledges that "the *mise-en-scène* for love was only that and not a character in the play itself" (284). In other words, the place where love occurs is superfluous to the fact of love itself.

For this reason, to go chasing after significance in certain places, no matter how meaningful they've seemed in the past, is a foolish enterprise. The places will still be there, of course, and some vestige of the former self may also linger there, but it is only a shadowy configuration of the long-gone real thing. Frank believes that this need to find evidence of one's past self, one's history, also drives the human tendency to imbue places with sentient qualities. Then, upon arriving at the place and noting the lessening of the sense, one experiences disappointment over the pale rendition of the memory and sorrow for what is gone. Even Frank, however, knows such sensations, as evidenced by his need, repeatedly, to counter his own thoughts. Even as he is emerging from the Existence Period, he finds himself lurking around sites that have been formerly significant, such as his old home on Hoving Road, now the Chaim Yankowicz Ecumenical Center. He notes stirrings in himself not unlike those he's named at Sally's beach house, only three nights before, and these expectations, that he will feel something of his own life brush up against him with familiarity but instead ends up feeling "unsanctioned" by the place, make him angry. He exclaims to himself,

Indeed, it's worth asking again: is there any cause to think a place—any place—within its plaster and joists, its trees and plantings, in its putative essence *ever* shelters some spirit ghost of us as proof of its significance and ours?

No! Not one bit! Only other human beings do that, and then only under special circumstances, which is a lesson of the Existence Period worth holding onto. We just have to be smart enough to quit asking places for what they can't provide, and begin to invent other options— the way Joe Markham has, at least temporarily, and my son, Paul, may be doing now—as gestures of our God-required but not God-assured independence. (*ID*, 442)

Here, Frank refers to the fact that the Markhams, after a torturous decision-making process, have finally agreed to rent Frank's property on Clio Street, an option that, had it been present at the beginning of their house-hunting journey, would have certainly been met with a resounding dismissal. However, after they have gone through the *process,* Joe and Phyllis realize certain facts that they were not capable of grasping before, information and experience that ready them for this choice and even make the choice a positive one. Frank, too, is pleased by the trans-action, which, though it is economic in nature, of course also impinges on the personal. He rhetorically asks, "What more can you do for way-ward strangers than to shelter them?" (424).

The Markhams, then, have made accommodations, in more than one sense of the word, and Frank, in turn, has accommodated them. The capacity to "invent other options" proves crucial to one's independence; making accommodations, then, depends on a person's abilities to create, invent, reconfigure—all acts made more successful in cooperation with others. That, to Frank, is the key: only other human beings prove one's significance. But such communion is not to be taken for granted; nor is it guaranteed to occur. Certainly to exist in concert with others is not a con-stant state. As Ford himself might say, it is most certainly provisional, which in a way makes the connection even more spectacular when it occurs. Most of the time, however, one finds one's self alone with one's problems, fears, and memories, as Paul no doubt has discovered, and it is likewise up to the individual to break free of these constraints, accepting help if it is offered but going it alone if that is required. This is a truth that Frank cannot really teach his son, but that Paul has learned anyway. Independence entails loneliness, as living also does.

Independence: Let Be Be Finale of Seem

It may come as no surprise that Frank is never able to define independence succinctly. He frees himself from the unviable tenets of the Existence Period, those that mandate distance from others. He allows Ann to help him at the hospital. He accepts a word from Irv, "continuity," which has the potential to become a "commanding new metaphor," as he has put it earlier. He takes from Sally, with whom he has a long conversation after the trip with Paul, what she has termed the idea of "permanent period" (434), which might very well constitute the next phase of his life. His experiences with the Markhams and others he's encountered, from slain real estate agent Clair Devane to Mr. Tanks, have certainly informed his own identity. He acknowledges a human desire for existence's certainty, for life itself to be fixed, but he concludes—modifying Irv's notions of community and continuity—that "We want to *feel* our community as a fixed, continuous entity . . . as being anchored into the rock of permanence; but we know it's not, that in fact beneath the surface (or rankly all over the surface) it's anything but. We and it are anchored only to contingency like a bottle on a wave, seeking a quiet eddy. The very effort at maintenance can pull you under" (439). In other words, once again evoking the sea's movement as metaphor, Frank identifies existence—and all that it comprises via society—as a fluctuating and fluid state. Anchored only to contingency or those very things that necessitate life's uncertainty, human beings are not really anchored at all, stabilized only momentarily by their own sense of themselves. Frank suggests that as a realtor he has also had to "come to grips with contingency and even sell it as a source of strength and father to true self-sufficiency" (439). This kind of self-reliance becomes an aspect of independence, of being solely responsible for ourselves in the midst of circumstances that constantly change and rearrange the recognizable keys to our identities.

The holiday devised to commemorate literal independence from another country's rule, however, seems to bear little resemblance to the moment it celebrates: the unification of many for the sake of a common cause. At least in one sense, then, independence does not necessitate isolation or exclusion. Ironically, it signifies the banding together of many in the name of freedom against others who want to deny that freedom, something inconceivable for an individual who acts alone. Frank observes that the way people celebrate the holiday, however, suggests almost that independence is "private and too crucial to celebrate with others; as though we should all just get on with *being* independent, given that it is after all the normal, commonsensical human condition, to be taken for granted unless opposed or thwarted, in which case unreserved, even absurd measures should be taken to restore or reimagine it" (425). The holiday, in other words, "confers upon us the opportunity to act as independently as we know how" (427), giving its celebrants permission to disregard other people and instead to fire off in the wee hours of the morning the loudest firecrackers available in spite of the fact that one's neighbors might be sleeping. Anarchy, not democracy, more often seems to prevail on the Fourth of July.

What Frank has learned over the weekend of the Fourth is that he is connected to other people no matter how hard he tries not to be. He also faces his failures with Paul, hopeful that he can do better in the future. Quoting Emerson again, he comforts himself with the thought that " 'The soul becomes,' as the great man said, by which he meant, I think, slowly" (430). By his story's end, he is even able to imagine himself as a person defined at least in part by all of the contingencies in his life, known to others, and even to himself by "whatever I do or say, who I marry, how my kids turn out" (450). He realizes that he does not have to abandon his notion that life is a process in order to be influenced by other people; he himself does not even have to occupy a fixed place for these associations to occur. The "fixing" happens via his relationships with others, which paradoxically, by definition, will change.

Independence Day's ending finds Frank first waking in the night's wee hours to answer the telephone, which has rung suddenly, and once the receiver has been picked up, has emitted no greeting from another person, just the sound of breaths being drawn in and out. But Frank responds as if he knows the person on the line's other end: " 'I just got here,' I said. 'Now's not a bad time at all. This is a full-time job. Let me hear you thinking. I'll try to add a part to the puzzle. It can be simpler than you think' " (451). The words seem random, befitting of a person who's suddenly awakened in the night, but what Frank says is exactly what some lost soul would want to hear: it's not a bad time to talk, so go ahead, and maybe I can help you out. Frank gets no lengthy response, at least in words, but he hears the breathing again—confirmation of another's life—and finally, the vaguest "Uh-huh" (451), some small token of acquiescence. As the connection is broken, he goes right back to bed and enters the "deepest sleep imaginable" (451). This episode acts as a fitting reminder of how much talk has occurred over the phone in this novel. In fact, for all Frank knows, Paul may have been at the other end of the line. It is in the context of this strange moment of communication that Frank's story ends, apparently in a dream that overtakes him after the phone call: "And I am in the crowd just as the drums are passing—always the last in line—their *boom-boom-booming* in my ears and all around. I see the sun above the street, breathe in the day's rich, warm smell. Someone calls out, 'Clear a path, make room, make room, make room, please!' The trumpets go again. My heartbeat quickens. I feel the push, pull, the weave and sway of others" (451). This passage is significant because it places Frank in a crowd, and, more importantly, a moving crowd. Within this communal moment, Frank feels the "push, pull, the weave and sway of others." Such motion implies that relationships with others are not static commitments; room exists for the process of the "soul becoming" in concert with others, in addition to the growth ordained by private endeavor.

Furthermore, the novel's closing passage achieves an almost poetic cadence. Gone are Frank's lengthy sentences, broken up by parenthetical asides, and in their place are shorter, even iambic phrases: "I see the sun above the street," for example. The inclusion of sounds written out as words, as in the "boom-boom-booming" of the drums, might even remind the reader of one of Ford's self-professed favorite poets, Wallace Stevens, himself prone to create phrases such as "tink and tank and tunk-a-tunk-tunk" (Stevens, 59) and whose statement Ford is fond of citing, "In an age of disbelief, it is for the poet to provide the satisfactions of belief with his measure and with his style" (Walker, 143). It might be appropriate to remark, then, that one of Stevens's more famous lines from the poem "The Emperor of Ice Cream" is "Let be be finale of seem" (Stevens, 64). The poem itself, though whimsical, indicts the human propensity to mask events of great significance, namely death, behind meaningless trappings, as if to deny or temper their reality; rather than covering up a dead woman, even with sheets upon which she has embroidered, the poem's speaker advises that "If her horny feet protrude, they come / To show how cold she is, and dumb. / Let the lamp affix its beam" (Stevens, 64). In other words, the speaker endorses seeing a thing for what it is because its reality cannot be nullified: death is death no matter now many flowers flourish at the funeral, a rather paradoxical lesson housed in the advocacy of being over seeming, since death is, obviously, existence's termination. Hence the poem's earlier imperative, "Let be be finale of seem," exhorts its audience to move past seeming and toward being. If accepting things as they seem is one stage of dealing with reality, then seeing them as they *are* should be the stage to which we all aspire. In addition to its resonance with Frank's own admission that at times he has let seem equal be, the poem's subject matter tangentially coincides with Frank's frequent seduction by his imagination.

Frank's imagination, of course, is the very faculty that permits his shared flights of fancy with Paul and his proficiency with language itself. It may take some time for Frank to become reconciled to being part of a community, but much earlier in the novel he actually sees himself exactly as he is: "My greatest human flaw and strength, not surprisingly, is that I can always imagine anything—a marriage, a conversation, a government—as being different from how it is, a trait that might make one a top-notch trial lawyer or novelist or realtor, but that also seems to produce a somewhat less than reliable and morally feasible human being" (*ID*, 226). This ability "to imagine everything . . . as being different from how it is" is certainly what allows Frank to make things seem other than they are, a propensity that both Ann and Sally find distasteful. But it is after all within the province of the poet to "Tell all the Truth but tell it slant," as Emily Dickinson has immortalized in her famous line.[6] Too much truth all at once can be blinding, her poem suggests, advising that success lies in circuitous ways of presenting the truth. Frank certainly pays homage to the circuitous in his storytelling; even the very languid nature of his trip demonstrates an indirect route to his destination. Fortunately, Frank can also imagine himself as other than he is, as he admits in the book's final pages. In describing his own transformation, he employs metaphor, one way of making something other than it is for the sake of understanding its meaning more clearly. He compares, for example, his odyssey to a boat's journey, his sense of self to the vessel, both figurative ways of opening the subjects to interpretation. Imagination, then, is not of itself a bad force, but it confers upon its host a certain responsibility, which one can accept or deny, as befitting of one's independence. Of course, Frank would do none of these things were it not for his own creator, Richard Ford, who also must be fascinated by the "fissures between the literal and the imagined," the line he assigns to Frank as Frank explains his and Paul's preoccupation with puns. It is in this gap that literature resides and from which *Independence Day* takes its thematic energy.

Frank Bascombe does not literally risk disappearance in the Existence Period's wake, but figuratively—by jettisoning—he loses parts of himself in his quest to go it alone and divest himself of contingencies. In this endeavor, he adopts a stance of seeming rather than being; he exists, but not as much, as he so often remarks. He almost disappears into his own life because he has made himself accountable to no one. No one expects him to be anywhere, so his absence goes unnoticed. He manipulates words to his advantage, but he finds himself strangely silent when words are most required. Having given up unspoken intimacies, he retreats into himself only to discover that his "self" is ghostly, insubstantial, a wavering image of someone he once was. In order to reconstitute this semblance of his personhood, he must actually get out of the simulator business, as his spokesperson and long-lost stepbrother Irv literally might do, and be rather than seem to be. And being entails living in concert with others, surrendering, at least occasionally, to the "push, pull, the weave and sway of others." Therein lies the path to independence: to know that there are others from whom one might break free, but with whom one chooses to stay.

Chapter Eight

Crossing the Divide in
Women with Men

Richard Ford's *Women with Men* (1997) is a collection of three long stories: "The Womanizer," first published in *Granta* in 1990; "Jealous," first published in the *New Yorker* in 1992; and "Occidentals." It is Ford's first collection of work since the publication of *Rock Springs* in 1987. Like those earlier stories, these works target their subjects unflinchingly, bringing into sharp focus the moments when the lived life seems most diffuse. Appropriately, the characters profiled in these stories seem poised between past and future at some pivotal time when their decisions assume great significance. These choices, however, often fail to render their lives into greater relief or make their existences and circumstances seem any clearer to them. In at least two of these works, Ford leaves the characters entrenched in some confusion even as he allows his reader to see their predicaments with clarity.

Ford assumes a distant third-person narrative voice in the two stories that act as bookends for the collection, "The Womanizer" and "Occidentals." In these stories, Ford utilizes a measure of "free indirect discourse," that is, the adoption of a third-person voice that nonetheless is identified more closely with one character whose thoughts translate fully to the page; thus the other characters are depicted through that character's consciousness of them. It is a kind of third-person limited stance, as opposed to the third person omniscient in which the narrator may access each character's actions, words, or thoughts to an equal degree. In both "The Womanizer" and "Occidentals," Ford's narrative angle permits a full glimpse into the heads of the protagonists, both men, yet fails to offer any kind of overt judgment of their personalities. Although both stories recall to some degree the same kinds of crises and attendant questions that bedevil Frank Bascombe in *The Sportswriter* and *Independence Day,* they lack the irony generated by Bascombe's first-person account, Ford's sly humor, and the gaps between what Bascombe says or thinks and what the audience knows about him. Bascombe's wry self-deprecation and his obtuseness mitigate his solipsism for the forgiving

reader who may find in Bascombe something he or she recognizes in his
or her own self. This kind of identification is much more difficult in
"The Womanizer" and "Occidentals." Ford turns a hard eye on his subjects here, mining the details of everyday life and the less salient aspects
of human sensibilities. Unlike the *Rock Springs* stories, where Ford has
been said to practice "dirty realism," "The Womanizer" and "Occidentals" focus on educated men whose intellects, like Frank Bascombe's, fail
to redeem them from themselves. Their exterior lives, far from being
barren or hard, exhibit instead the sheen of the privileged, and both
men have been successful even when success has not adopted the
expected guise. Despite such good fortune, both characters perceive
themselves as misunderstood, but their efforts at connection with others
leave them more isolated than ever.

"Jealous," the middle story, focuses on a subject that by now should
be familiar to Ford's readers: the boy on the cusp of adulthood whose
parents, either one or both, have left him in some literal or figurative
way. In many ways, this story fits the paradigm that I've already discussed at length in the sections on *Rock Springs* and *Wildlife* (chapters 5
and 6), so I won't cover the same ground here. "Jealous" may revise
some of Ford's earlier explorations of this subject in that its narrator
Larry does at least cultivate a relationship with his father based upon
their reciprocal abilities to put their feelings into words. In the context
of *Women with Men,* the story acts as an antidote to the isolation rendered
so completely in the other texts.

Ford links the three stories through a common subject that comprises
one aspect of the human predicament: the condition of loneliness and
the unwitting perpetuation of that loneliness through what might be
termed excessive self-concern. As the collection's title suggests, this
predicament befalls people without respect to gender; as Ford moves his
male characters in and out of contact with the women they encounter,
he cites the human tendency to become so consumed by the self that
others slip away gradually, first from the consciousness, and then, when
it is too late, from one's life entirely. These stories make clear that self-
awareness does not necessarily precipitate an accurate interpretation of
circumstance or "other." The characters in *Women with Men* attempt to
cross a divide that keeps them separate, displaced, or otherwise isolated,
but the language that they use in this attempt may only widen the
breach. It is only when words are uttered without guise or guile that
they shed, at least a little, their provisional natures and become measures by which one person may reach another.

Make-Believe Love in "The Womanizer"

The protagonist of "The Womanizer" is 44-year-old Martin Austin, a salesman from the Chicago suburbs who markets a special kind of paper to foreign publishers of textbooks. His job requires periodic travel, and this story finds him in Paris, where he has met and become infatuated with an editor of one of these publishing houses, Joséphine Belliard. Married but with no children, Martin gives in to the flirtation, a harmless enough exchange at its inception. But as time passes, and upon his return to Chicago, he grants their rather uneventful dinner together and subsequent awkward kiss a kind of significance that the incidents clearly do not merit. Martin concocts his own version of this encounter that acts upon him like a tonic, rendering his heretofore satisfactory existence untenable and provoking him to acts that even he knows are out of character. In the bargain, he risks his job, threatens his marriage, and embarks upon a liaison with Joséphine that ends disastrously, with the kidnapping and molestation of her four-year-old son, Léo, under Martin's watch.

The narrator provides a clear view into Martin's thought patterns as the story unfolds. However, no authorial intrusion occurs. As a result, the story's tone offers no judgment of Martin's decisions, but it also offers no mechanism, via humor or irony, by which to excuse Martin's self-absorption and his actions, which finally and simply speak for themselves. For example, on several occasions Martin yokes two thoughts together but then cannot even see the incongruities between them. The night before he is to fly back to Chicago, he muses in his hotel room about what has happened: "he'd felt happy—happy to be only hours away from leaving Paris, happy to be coming home and to have not just a wife to come home to but this wife—Barbara, whom he both loved and revered. And happy, also, to have effected his 'contact' with Joséphine Belliard (that was the word he was using: at first it had been 'rapprochement,' but that had given way)" (26). In this passage, he goes on to express relief that there have been no untoward consequences of his little dalliance, at first consigning his "contact" with Joséphine to the realm of the inconsequential. What is interesting about the way Martin's mind works is that he finds no gap between what he says about Joséphine and his admission that he not only loves but also reveres his wife. Surely reverence would entail honor, which would then, if not prevent entirely, certainly curtail some of Martin's rationalizing of his feelings for Joséphine. The scene becomes even more complicated in its con-

text, which is that Martin admits that he "had felt" happy, in the past
tense, before he called Barbara to check in before coming home. The call
changes his mood. Over the phone he can hear the familiar sounds of
her moving around in the kitchen, and her voice assumes a friendly and
enthusiastic tone, bearing no resentment for his absence. He all but nee-
dles her into anger by telling her, out of the blue, that he has had dinner
with another woman that very evening, a "good" time, in response to
her simple inquiry into what his day had held. Of course he does not
need to impart this information to her, and in fact seems to do so deliberately, as if he wants to provoke her. He does tell Barbara that the
woman is an editor, which certainly leaves room for the encounter to be
a business dinner, but he also goes on to mention the "good time." Not
surprisingly, after his admission, Barbara's voice changes suddenly, and
the conversation steadily deteriorates. But Barbara has stayed in control
the entire time, perpetuating a kind of "let's not argue about this on the
eve of your return" attitude, allowing for Martin's fatigue. In that spirit,
she recovers herself, banishes the edge from her voice and offers almost
too blithe a response: " 'Well, we're waiting for you,' Barbara said
brightly. 'Who's we?' Austin said. 'Me. And the house. And the plants
and the windows. The cars. Your life. We're all waiting with big smiles
on our faces' " (29). Their conversation becomes emotionally false in the
wake of Martin's divulgence, and Martin is angry, though it has been he
who has introduced the seed of suspicion. The reader will later learn that
Martin has had other affairs on the road, all of which he terms meaningless. But since he imagines that Barbara does not know about them, he
does not perceive them as blemishes upon his marriage's sanctity or
upon his "reverence" of her.

Martin's deliberation over which word to use to describe his time
with Joséphine, "contact," or "rapprochement," is typical. He spends a
good deal of time thinking about the appropriate vocabulary through
which to describe his existence. He also ponders the relative appropri-
ateness of language when he is with Joséphine, wanting to measure his
words carefully in order to achieve the desired response. The timing of
words assumes importance, also, so that in a given situation, Martin is
more apt to be thinking about creating a certain impression than he is
about what is actually occurring. In other words, he misses the moment
through his analysis of his part in it. When he feels that he has said the
wrong thing, he struggles to say the right thing next, as he does here
with Joséphine: "He wanted to say one more good word that would help
balance how she felt at that moment—not that he had the slightest idea

how she felt" (14). The latter failure, not having any idea about how the other person might feel, dooms Martin again and again. He may have words in his mind to say, but he has no way to measure their effects on someone else if he cannot plumb the emotional depths of the person to whom he is talking.

The words that Martin wants to say often materialize for the reader, albeit filtered by a more articulate narrator, even though in the story they remain unspoken. What Martin wants to say to Joséphine before he leaves is that he believes that under other circumstances they could have been lovers, even good for each other. He perceives this thought as hopeful, some consolation for the brevity of their time together, and sentiments that are meant to encourage some intimacy uncomplicated by sex, untainted by obligation. All through their last dinner together, he wants to say such things, but he can never pinpoint the right moment, leaving him with the words unsaid but still thronging in his mind. The narrator reveals, "The words seem to have missed their moment. They needed another context, a more substantial setting. To say them in the dark, in a crummy Opel with the motor running, at the moment of parting, would give them a sentimental weightiness they didn't mean to have, since they were, for all their built-in sorrow, an expression of optimism" (22). Joséphine may be similarly calculating, and indeed her dialogue suggests a flair for the dramatic ("I am not so strong enough" (25), she says to Martin, to be his lover), but the narrator never reveals her motive for engaging Martin or, more accurately, of permitting his affections although she seems not to return them as fully.

In fact, Joséphine's responses to Martin are at best equivocal. She remains silent in the face of his musings; she whispers "non" over and over during their first kiss even though her lips part slightly and apparently willingly; she perpetuates a physical coldness whenever Martin touches her, if not physically recoiling, then certainly withholding any kind of warm touch in return. In short, she never fully reciprocates Martin's advances, either emotionally or physically. Her response here is typical. Martin has put his arms around her and "put his mouth against her cool cheek and held her to him tightly. . . . Joséphine let herself be pulled, be gathered in. She let her head fall against his shoulder. . . . It was thrilling, even though Joséphine did not put her arms around him, did not reciprocate his touch in any way, only let him hold her as if pleasing him was easy but did not matter to her a great deal" (21). Interestingly, it is Joséphine's ambivalence that compels Martin, which allows him to cast himself completely into whatever role suits him, protector, confidant, full-blooded American male. He gives in to his roles with a kind of abandon that must be lacking in his "real" life, but he loses his real life as a consequence.

Joséphine's situation is less easily analyzed because of the narrator's distance from her psyche. She is about to sign her divorce papers; her husband Bernard is a novelist who has written a tell-all book about her infidelities. Her past indiscretions only intrigue Martin, and he is surprised upon seeing Bernard's picture that Bernard is not in fact better looking. Bernard seems less than savory himself; Martin encounters him, recognizing him from the photograph in Joséphine's flat, and observes him without Bernard knowing who Martin is. Bernard seems nonchalant about their son Léo, and Léo exhibits signs of insecurity in the face of his changing life. Joséphine points out these signs to Martin, but she herself seems caught up in her own needs. The fact that she leaves Léo with Martin while she goes to finalize her divorce might even be problematic; she knows little of Martin, possibly not enough to trust him with her child, and she leaves few directions for him, circumstances that all but pave the way for Martin's fateful lapse while baby-sitting that results in the harm that comes to the boy. If only through Martin's perception of her and the narrator's factual recording of her behavior, Joséphine comes across as a woman who possibly thinks only of herself and who lets herself be caught up in the moment perhaps to forget the realities of her life. Martin himself gives into a kind of fantasizing, creating a world around Joséphine having largely to do with her being French, and therefore less capable of being known, he imagines, than a "regular" woman would be. He imparts mystery to her, in other words, and he responds to that mystery he has imagined, ignoring the realities of her daily life and responsibilities in favor of his fantasy. He becomes infatuated, then, not with Joséphine herself, but with his *idea* of her.

Martin's love and idealization of Joséphine persist upon his return after his first trip to Paris, interfering with his work and with his relationship with Barbara. His feelings make clear that he is experiencing an infatuation, and one that, with the passage of time, would probably dissipate in its intensity. Instead, however, Martin encourages it to flourish, remaining abstracted from the more pressing forces upon his attention: his wife and his job. Barbara finally lets Martin have it with a string of evidence testifying to his taking her for granted. She also points out the distance that has grown between them, largely because of what she terms Martin's being "unreachable" (42). She accuses him of thinking himself "fixed," as a "given" (42) whose actions in a foreign country will not affect him later, or affect those whom he loves, but they do. Of course Martin has been distracted since his trip, and even though he acts totally surprised by Barbara's rather vehement indictment, the reader knows she is right. It is Barbara who labels Martin with the words that become the story's title: she calls him a womanizer (44), among other things, and then she gets up and leaves him at the restaurant where they have gone to have dinner. Stunned by her accusations, Martin assesses Barbara's reactions to himself as an "over-response" (45). He goes on to muse about the opposite sex: "Though women were sometimes a kind of problem. He enjoyed their company, enjoyed hearing their voices, knowing about their semi-intimate lives and daily dramas. But his attempts at knowing them often created a peculiar feeling, as if on the one hand he'd come into the possession of secrets he didn't want to keep, while on the other, some other vital portion of his life—his life with Barbara, for instance—was left not fully appreciated, gone some-what to waste" (45–46). Martin's context makes clear that in the first part of the passage he refers to women *other* than Barbara. He practically admits here that his affairs fall short of some more meaningful relation-ship he shares with Barbara, but he seems unable to stop himself. The extramarital dalliances leave him strangely unsatisfied and render his marriage underappreciated, not partaken of to its fullest possible extent. Yet Martin continues to have affairs, acknowledging something kindred to Frank Bascombe's distrust of what he called "full disclosure," pos-sessed of secrets Martin would rather not keep and dispossessed of his marriage at the same time.

As the story continues, Martin's actions reveal that he does not really know himself at all. For example, he characterizes himself as a "stayer" (48), a man who had sense enough to do the right thing, what he figures is his "one innate strength of character" (48). But what he does almost immediately after this internal monologue is to leave Barbara, take the next flight to Paris, and reinvest in his relationship with Joséphine, which has never been what he has imagined it to be in the first place. Ironically, while he wanders Paris, resting up from his jet lag before he calls Joséphine, thoughts about Barbara come unbidden to his mind, that she might like this gift or that one, and that "She occupied, he rec-ognized, the place of final consequence—the destination for practically everything he cared about or noticed or imagined" (58). Thus the narra-tor identifies what Martin risks losing in his pursuit of Joséphine. Martin calls her nonetheless, catching her as she is about to go out the door to finalize her divorce and in need of someone to watch Léo for the short time of her absence. It is on this occasion that Martin baby-sits Léo and during which he loses the boy in the park where he has taken him without his mother's permission. Even here the gap between what Martin knows and how he acts continues to widen: he was "a man, an American speaking little French, alone with a four-year-old French child he didn't know, in a country, in a city, in a park, where he was an absolute stranger. No one would think this was a good idea" (77). Although Martin usually perceives his decisions as having little potential to harm those tangentially affected by them, in this case his actions wreak irreversible damage to an innocent child. Appropriately, the reason that Martin loses sight of Léo is that he is lost in his own thoughts. By the time he comes to, and turns around, Léo has disappeared from the place he has been. Martin finds him pale and naked in some shrubbery, clearly having been molested during the moments of Martin's wandering thoughts. Of course Joséphine rejects Martin completely and utterly after this incident, and Martin is left with nothing at the story's end, not even a good excuse for his own behavior.

However, the experience leaves Martin capable of posing questions about the nature of contact with other human beings that perhaps would not have occurred to him before.

> How could you regulate life, do little harm and still be attached to others? And in that context, he wondered if being *fixed* could be a misunderstanding, and, as Barbara had said when he'd seen her the last time and she had been so angry at him, if he had changed slightly, somehow altered the important linkages that guaranteed his happiness and become detached, unreachable. Could you *become* that? Was it something you controlled, or a matter of your character, or a change to which you were only a victim? He wasn't sure. He wasn't sure about that at all. It was a subject he knew he would have to sleep on many, many nights. ("Womanizer," 91–92)

Here Martin attributes a soundness to Barbara's reasoning that he was incapable of recognizing before, allowing for the possibility of his becoming detached, separated from crucial links that offered a mooring for his happiness. The answer to his first question, of course, is that the way to do little harm and still be attached to others is to be accountable for one's mistakes and take responsibility for one's actions. The narrator leaves this didactic answer deliberately absent from Martin's thoughts, at once suggesting Martin's inability to formulate it and also keeping the story true to its tone. Martin seems to have gained the insight necessary to articulate these questions, but he is unable to determine the cause of his possible detachment, leaving the three options of personal responsibility, character-determined action, or fate open as the causes. By leaving him in this moment of indecision, the narrator neither condemns nor redeems Martin, who remains sentenced nonetheless to the appropriate fate of continual pondering, night after night.

Self-Reliance in "Jealous"

"Jealous" provides the answer that Martin Austin cannot summon at the end of "The Womanizer," and that is that meaningful connection with other people is predicated upon individual accountability. Larry, the story's protagonist and narrator, glimpses firsthand the ways that adults fail each other. His father has had several affairs, and his mother has left their Montana home for Seattle, Washington, after years of trouble in her marriage. Shortly after her departure, Larry's father moves them from Great Falls to the smaller and more northern city of Dutton, where he has taken a new job working on farm machinery. In his spare time, he trains bird dogs, though he's never cared for hunting himself. The story occasions a time in 1975, when Larry is 17, and he drives with his mother's sister Doris up to Shelby, Montana, where the two will take the train to Seattle to visit his mother. Like other of Ford's stories in this vein, Larry as narrator adopts a retrospectively poignant voice, telling past events with a present immediacy. Thus the outcome of Larry's trip seems uncertain: will he then choose to stay in Seattle with his mother, return to Montana to be with his father, or in an even more unlikely option, will his mother return home with him? But the story's opening line, "In the last days that I lived with my father in his house below the Teton River, he read to me,"[1] reveals the answer, which is then never again overtly mentioned. In this way, the questions that preside over the narrative stay current even though Larry tells his story in retrospect. Surrounded by adults whose behavior is in some combination immature, despairing, violent, indecisive, or otherwise misunderstood, Larry faces that same future unless he discovers some way to exert control over his life. Finally, it is a measure of tenderness that characterizes his relationship with his father, combined with Larry's own sense of responsibility, that promises redemption from other failures at intimacy.

Even the story's elegiac opening line establishes some communion between father and son. Larry explains that Donny reads to him from a variety of sources for any number of possible reasons: to be aware of the world, to cultivate a stance of waiting for news, to acknowledge some order in life even when life seems disorderly, to admit that there is more worth knowing, to encourage Larry to pay attention, or even to admit, tacitly, that Donny was at a loss over what to tell his son. Larry characterizes his father as a man who does not stand by passively, as a man who acts when circumstances call for action and who cares about what he does. Nonetheless, Larry admits, "And I know that even on the day that these events took place he was aware that a moment to act may have come. None of it is anything I blame him for" (96). These thoughts close the story's first section and remain tucked away there for the reader to remember or forget. Larry's admission implies the significance of what's to come, and as the experienced, retrospective narrator, he can hint at the meaning embedded in the following scenes. Thus the story's opening sets up an investigation into the relationship between Larry and his father, even though the story's plot, which is relatively action-filled, dances around that subject.

The story exhibits some traits that liken it to the work collected in Ford's earlier collection *Rock Springs* and that some readers label "dirty realism." The term implies the realistic telling of the story, that which makes it a close semblance of "real life." Every event will be believable and in keeping with cause and effect; each character will be drawn carefully and act in a psychologically consistent way. In other words, what happens in the story could just as easily happen in life. The adjective "dirty" simply adds another qualifier that suggests subjects that might be found on the seamier side of existence or even simply in areas of the country where nothing is easy, hard work the norm, disappointment common, and violence more apt to occur. In Ford's short fiction, the American West is a common setting, particularly the more remote areas of Montana. Characters in these kinds of stories may often be at rope's end, so to speak, out of all good options and convinced that the bad option is the only choice left. However, these choices always have consequences in Ford's stories. His authorial voice never intrudes in a judgmental way, but most of the time the story's context exerts its own kind of moral imperative, making individual action the final arbiter of a character's fate. "Jealous" fits loosely into this paradigm, and its first-person narrative told from a retrospective point of view further likens it to Ford's earlier novel *Wildlife* and several of the stories that I previously discussed in the chapter on *Rock Springs*. Like these other narrators, Larry witnesses events that change his perception of the adult world.

The plot of "Jealous" is simple enough. Larry leaves Dutton, where he and his father have lived alone, and drives with his Aunt Doris, his mother's sister, up to Shelby, where the two will catch a train to Seattle. The reader learns as the story unfolds that not only has Larry's father been involved with a local woman, Joyce Jensen, with whom he has a reasonable affair about which Larry has been well-informed, but that also Larry and Doris were involved for a time after Larry's mother's departure. Their liaison is over in the story's time frame. The reader also learns that Donny, who in the past was fond of a drink, has now given up alcohol for good. The same is not true of Doris, who begins taking swigs from a schnapps bottle relatively early in the car trip to Shelby. The sheer and literal cold that characterizes Montana during the time of year of their travel, the day before Thanksgiving, practically becomes another character in the story. Its force is continually present, so that the characters engage in actions simply to combat the bone-chilling sensation. Doris's drinking serves this function in part, but it also suggests her despair. She talks to Larry as if he were an adult, which at once makes him feel manly and disconcerts him. Once they reach Shelby, the pair split up, Larry to buy a small gift for his mother with money his father has given him, and Doris to "warm herself" in a bar called Oil City. It is there that Larry finds her after purchasing a watch for his mother. Larry makes this decision thoughtfully and carefully, imagining what his father would think of his choice and feeling proud that he has found a nice gift but not had to spend all of his money to do it: thrift of which his father would approve. When he joins Doris, he sees that she has engaged in a flirtation with the man on the stool next to hers. Barney has recently gotten out of Fort Harrison, a hospital for "crazy Indians and veterans" (119), as Larry's father has described it. To Larry, Barney looks vaguely Indian and like a hard drinker; his face is puffy and he appears unhealthy. He and Doris have a rather drunken and strange conversation, into which Doris tries to pull Larry, who remains on the periphery, rather confused about what his role should be and taking so long to answer Doris's questions that she grows impatient with him. Barney leaves to go to the bathroom, down a hall at the bar's rear. As he disappears, a sheriff, accompanied by several deputies, comes into the bar. They are clearly looking for someone, and as one of the men suggests looking in the bathroom, Doris says, "Barney's in the bathroom" (124). What follows is a standoff that ends in a shoot-out and Barney's death. During the gunfire, the bar's patrons are ordered to lie on the wet floor, and afterward, the sheriff's men question everyone in the bar.

By the time they are free to leave, both Doris and Larry are freezing, so they go to Doris's car to warm up again before catching the train. When they go to the depot to get on the train, Larry stops and calls his father. The story ends with Larry and Doris en route to Seattle. Thus Larry never reaches his literal destination over the story's course, but the beginning reveals the choice that he will make.

However, the story does prepare the reader for Larry's decision. It is not so much a desire to leave his father as it is a desire to escape from a particular place that drives Larry from the wilds of Montana to warmer Seattle. When Doris tells him that he smells like hay in the car and says, "You're a real hick" (109), Larry is angry, though he doesn't show it. At this point he slips into a retrospective voice, stepping out of the story's present as it is told and into some nebulous future moment that allows him to characterize his thoughts in this way:

> What I wanted to do, I thought then, was stay in Seattle with my mother and start in at a new school after Christmas even if it meant beginning the year over. I wanted to get out of Montana. . . . I was missing something, I thought, an important opportunity. And later, when I would try to explain to someone how it was, that I had not been a farm boy but just had led life like that for a while, nobody'd believe me. And after that it would always be impossible to explain how things really were. ("Jealous," 109)

Larry acknowledges his desperate longing to get out of Montana here, but he also alludes to the difficulty of explaining his past, particularly in the ways that concern "how things really were," a perspective made possible, no doubt, by this more mature voice intruding upon the recollection. His relationship with his father—and possibly even with both parents—seems to elude language's grasp, or, at least, defy his attempts to explain the complexities inherent in a long-distance bond with his father and maybe even the reasons for leaving him. Larry has referred earlier to the events that occurred which would bear telling, by which he presumably means the trip to Seattle, the violence he witnesses, and the realization he has. In this context, he has also implicated his father in some choice, or failure to make a choice: "on the day these events took place he [Larry's father] was aware that a moment to act may have come. None of it is anything I blame him for" (96). This "moment to act" seems to refer to another option for repairing the damage to the family, and that would be for Larry's father Donny to decide to accompany Larry to Seattle. Doris invites him to do so, and Donny will later tell

Larry on the phone that his mother has asked if Donny wished that he were coming with Larry. Donny explains to Larry, "I told her she'd need to ask me earlier if she wanted that to happen. I said I had other plans" (140). In other words, Larry is not the only one making decisions that affect lives. His mother has made the choice to leave in the first place; then she has failed to ask his father soon enough, and his father is unwilling to change his plans to accommodate his mother. This verbal dance of withholding suggests an emptiness already gaping in the parents' relationship. Too much goes unsaid or is said too late. But Larry does not attempt to psychoanalyze his parents or even understand what it is that has come between them. Even though he wonders what the future holds for his parents, he accepts their decisions, and his recollection of this time makes it clear that his primary concern in these moments was simply to better his own life. Indeed both his father and his mother have placed importance on certain goals that seem to exclude the other, desires and dreams that in many ways are simply selfish ones—but that are also self-preserving. His mother, for instance, is going to school in Seattle to learn how to fill out income tax forms; her schooling ends at Christmas, which leaves her future open. Likewise, Larry wants to preserve as many possibilities for himself as he can, a path that ironically leads him from an open landscape to a more densely populated one. Throughout his trip, in fact, he keeps thinking about what might go wrong—Doris might get too drunk to stay awake and they might have to stop; his father might make him come home after he hears what Larry has seen in the bar—all events that might conceivably prevent his getting to where he wants to go. But like many of Ford's stories written about these turning points in a young boy's life filtered later through a grown man's perspective, a tone of sorrow and perhaps regret shadows the narrator's rather terse assessments of decisions he has made, implying that every choice entails a risk of loss.

In Doris Larry may see an adult who wishes, perhaps, that she had followed a different path. In fact, Doris seems for a time to have coveted her sister's life, which she then tries to step into by becoming Donny's lover in her sister's absence. She tells Larry, "I used to think your father'd married the wrong sister, since we all met at the same time, you know? I thought he was too good for Jan. But I don't think so now. She and I have gotten a lot closer than we used to be since she's been out in Seattle" (112). Doris alludes to a time when she has not thought the best of her sister, referring also to her own jealousy over her sister Jan's winning the attention of Donny. Doris herself has married an Indian, a man from whom she is now separated. She also tells Larry that she wishes for a divorce, some closure that might permit her to "begin to pick up the pieces" (108). She tells Larry that she has known real depression, though she's not sure that he realizes fully what that means. In other words, Doris exhibits many signs of loneliness, including her attempt to communicate with Barney at the bar and her relentless drinking. Obviously dissatisfied with her existence, she is prone to comment again and again about what a nice boy Larry is, as if she herself wishes for a person like him in her life. Larry, of course, does not know exactly how to handle Doris, but he does the best he can. When they are huddled in the car after the Barney incident, trying to get warm, Doris clings to Larry, saying

> "You need to warm me up," she whispered. "Are you brave enough to do that? Or are you a coward on that subject?" She put her hands around my neck and below my collar, and I didn't know what to do with my hands, though I put them around her and began to pull her close to me and felt her weight come against my weight and her legs press on my cold legs. I felt her ribs and her back—hard, the way they'd felt when we'd been on the floor in the bar. I felt her breathing under her coat, could smell on her breath what she'd just been drinking. I closed my eyes, and she said to me almost as if she was sorry about something, "Oh, my. You've just got everything, don't you? You've just got everything."
> "What?" I said. "What is it?"
> And she said, "No, no. Oh, no, no." That was all she said. And then she didn't talk to me anymore. ("Jealous," 138)

Doris seems to realize that in the cold and her drunkenness she is making sexual overtures to her sister's son, so she pulls away from Larry. In her belief that Larry's "got everything," she suggests both his attractiveness and her own desperation. Doris's behavior resonates with the story's title, "Jealous," and indeed to some extent jealousy, or at least the vaguest desire to have something that someone else might have that one does not yet possess, drives the adults in this story toward their own resolutions. Getting there—to the new job, the new school—may be one step toward taking care of the self, but it is no guarantee against loneliness.

Significantly, it is Larry's father who provides him with the safest haven. When Larry calls him from the depot, Donny is careful to let his son know that he will always provide a home for him. At the same time, he gives Larry room to make his own decision about whether to stay or to go. Larry asks Donny if he thinks that Larry should stay with his mother. Donny replies, "Well, only if you want to. . . . I wouldn't blame you. Seattle's a nice place. But I'm happy to have you come back here. We should talk about that when you've been there" (141–42). Donny's reasoned response satisfies Larry, and the last thing that Donny says is " 'I love you, Larry. I forgot to tell you that before you left. That's important.' 'I love you,' I said. 'That's good news,' he said. 'Thank you' " (142). This passage marks one of the few places in Ford's fiction where two characters are able to say "I love you" directly and without self-consciousness. This plain talk between Larry and Donny is perhaps the very fact that enables Larry to make his choice. He does not sever his link to his father, and his father makes it clear that his love is not contingent upon Larry's making one decision or another. This moment lends the story its poignancy, especially as it is cast in memory by the narrator, who seems to realize, or at least suggest, that the factors driving him toward Seattle had little to do with his father and more to do with imagining some future for himself that may or may not have materialized.

Appropriately, then, at story's end, Larry is still in transit, in the train car, and he feels some degree of uncertainty that crescendos into a moment of near panic:

> I sat very still and felt as though I was entirely out of the world, cast off without a starting or a stopping point, just shooting through space like a boy in a rocket. Though after a while I must have begun to hold my breath, because my heart began to beat harder, and I had that feeling, the scary feeling you have that you're suffocating and your life is running out—fast, fast, second by second—and you have to do something to save yourself, but you can't. Only then you remember it's you who's causing it, and you who has to stop it. ("Jealous," 144–45)

Larry realizes here that it is he who has to take responsibility for his life, a choice he can make more freely perhaps because of the love that houses him. Although he is not literally shooting from a rocket with the speed pressing the breath from his chest, the metaphor that Larry uses allows him to conceptualize the state of near suffocation as one that he can control, simply by releasing his own breath. This epiphany offers Larry such comfort in that moment that he closes his eyes and sleeps. This image closes the story, providing a radically different scene from that of Martin Austin doomed to sleep on the subject of his detachment many, many nights. In "Jealous," the narrator leaves his younger self at this moment when the future has yet to be ordained and during which he achieves a sense of calm and control. Even the notes of sorrow in the narrative's tone do not detract from Larry's equilibrium here, the stasis achieved momentarily and ironically in the brief span of time between one part of his life and another.

What Gets Lost in Translation in "Occidentals"

The title of the final story of *Women with Men* refers to the state of being from the West or belonging to Europe and America. The term suggests a degree of foreignness to its object, as if it were what others, nonoccidentals, would call those who were unlike them. Like the first story, this one is set primarily in Paris, and a language barrier exists between the main characters—both Americans—and the native Parisians as well as between the American characters themselves. The title's irony is that these gaps occur among those who all are of the Occident; the term in no way makes its objects kindred. Furthermore, the story raises literal and figurative questions of conversion, or translation, through its plot and complementary subtext. Its protagonist, Charley Matthews, is a professor-turned-writer, whose novel, *The Predicament,* did not fare well upon its publication in America, but which for some reason or another has appealed to a French editor who arranges for Charley to have the manuscript translated and republished in France. Charley's trip to Paris with his girlfriend Helen Carmichael is in part to celebrate this occurrence and also to meet with Charley's French editor. At the last minute, the editor cancels their appointment, leaving Charley disappointed to be in Paris during the cold Christmas season. In some consolation, the editor suggests that Charley at least meet with his translator, and it is with the promise of that meeting, and the fact of Paris being open to his and Helen's exploration, that Charley attempts to convert his disappointment back into the joy he has previously felt. Charley's effort to convert his experience and, by extension, himself, fits together with the story's additional emphases on the perils of translation, the process of turning one thing into another for a different audience.

Even Charley's novel *The Predicament* deals to some extent with the ways that language fails, namely that words become meaningless through overuse, exhausted of their capacity to signify. Charley bases his novel on his own failed marriage, again *converting* the details of his life into a kind of roman à clef. Charley's was a "marriage in which meaningful language had been exhausted by routine, in which life's formalities, grievances and even shouts of pain had become so similar-sounding as to mean little but still seem beyond remedy, and in which the narrator (himself, of course) and his wife were depicted as people who'd logged faults, neglect and misprisions aplenty over twelve years but who still retained sufficient affection to allow them to recognize what they could and couldn't do" (159). The predicament, then, is how to sustain a relationship in the face of this kind of emptied-out language and shared existence, an endeavor at which Charley believes he has failed. He has even hoped that the book's publication would be interpreted as some new profession of faith toward Penny, his estranged wife. But Penny did not read the book; she even declined receipt of the proofs that Charley had sent to her. Having left Charley and taken their daughter Lelia to the Bay area, Penny becomes essentially unreachable, refusing all of Charley's efforts at communication. Her behavior inspires him to rewrite a portion of the novel, so that the character based on his wife is finally punished by the plot: the fictional character who is based on Penny thus dies in a traffic accident. But even this figurative death cannot rid Charley of his regrets. Although he takes Helen Carmichael with him to Paris in an effort to redeem some kind of joy from the act of writing the novel and its failure to reach its real audience, he recognizes once he is there that his act is not working. "Bringing her was his hopeless attempt to take an experience with him, and afterwards bring it home again, converted to something better. Only if he'd brought Penny with him could that've worked" (169). Helen even recognizes Charley's desire, as she puts it, to "translate *yourself*" (166). Charley's attempts to correct his life via his novel and then to convert his experience through sharing it with Helen fail.

Charley has set part of his novel's action in Paris simply on a whim. The decision, however, has entailed long hours of research to ensure that the Paris rendered on the page was at least on the surface an accurate rendition of the place itself. Since Charley has never been to Paris when he writes his novel, "he'd researched everything out of library books, tourist guides and subway maps, and made important events take place near famous sites like the Eiffel Tower, the Bastille, and the Luxembourg Gardens" (154). He experiences a thrill of recognition for certain places during the trip to meet with the editor, when he sees, for example, the street sign of the street where Penny's fictional counterpart has met with her demise. This kind of awareness, "but just for that brief moment," makes Paris seem suddenly "knowable" (155), though Charley acknowledges the transience of the sensation. In a way, the fact that he has spent so much time imagining Paris makes him almost disappointed in the city's reality. Most of the time, he simply feels lost.

His sense of unbelonging is furthered by the suspicion that he is missing out on the nuances of conversation because of the fact that he doesn't speak French. Even before his trip when he speaks to the New York office's publisher's representative who informs him of the French editor's interest, Charley has trouble understanding several different things. First, he remains unsure of the woman's name, referring to her as "Miss Pitkin or Miss Pittman" (162). Second, he tells her that he's quite unsure about why "anybody'd want to read my book in France" (162), to which she responds "You never can tell with the French" (162). She makes another rather ambiguous statement that Charley is not really sure how to interpret: " 'They get things that we don't. Maybe it'll turn out better in French.' She laughed a small laugh" (162). Finding her laugh and her response disconcerting, Charley becomes even more puzzled when she utters a French phrase, "*Honi soit qui mal y pense*" (163); he admits to her that he doesn't know what that means. It turns out, somewhat oddly, that neither does she. She attributes it to Prince Charles, translating, "It probably means 'Live it up.' " (163). In actuality the motto of the British Order of the Garter, the phrase means, "Shamed be he who thinks evil of it," about as far from "Live it up" as it could get. In this way their conversation is littered with misunderstandings, illustrating how easy it is even for two people who speak the same language to create linguistic barriers between them. And, of course, their exchange demonstrates how far from the original a translation can stray.

On the other hand, Charley is so accustomed to feeling misunderstood and to misunderstanding others that he finds it some relief to be in another country where the language barrier is a literal one. As the narrator reports, "Time spent in another country would probably always be spent misunderstanding a great deal, which might in the end turn out to be a blessing and the only way you could ever feel normal" (180). Charley knows that he misses something as he conducts conversations with the natives, even those who speak English but who pepper their English with French phrases that they assume that he knows. As a result, he often feels a step behind in their banter, knowing that even if he can get the more mundane aspects of the talk he often misses the joke at the end that, for all he knows, may very well be at his expense. This sensation, no doubt, informs a dream that he has in which he is still married to Penny, who seems to be the person he is talking to although he cannot see her face. The two sit at a café, and to his amazement, "he was speaking French! French words (all unfathomable) were flooding out of his mouth just the way they flooded out of every Frenchman's mouth, a mile a minute. No one—whoever he was talking to—offered anything in reply. So that it was only he, Charley Matthews, rattling on and on and on in perfect French he could miraculously speak, yet, as his own observer, in no way understand" (191). When Charley awakens, he is physically and mentally exhausted. Defying Charley's attempt at analysis, the dream nonetheless suggests something quite literal about his character, and that is that he remains so caught up in his own thinking, mesmerized by his interior voice just like Martin Austin in the collection's first story, that he becomes rather oblivious to those around him. Perhaps he cannot understand other people because he does not really give them a chance to talk and explain themselves. Furthermore, these incessant thoughts—like the torrent of French words in his dream—finally offer no measure for real self-comprehension.

In this story, like in "The Womanizer," the narrator speaks in the third person but is closely allied with Charley's perspective. In fact, the narrator seems to comply with Charley's assessment of which details need to be offered and when. Although the narrator spends a great deal of time describing Charley's regrets, his missing his daughter, and his wife's running off with an undergraduate student at the college in eastern Ohio where Charley formerly taught, it is some time before the reader learns that Charley himself had an affair with a woman named Margie. The story is practically over, in fact, before the narrative reveals this detail. Again the narrator offers neither condemnation of Charley's actions nor rationale for this decision on his part. Charley's infidelity, however, may lessen the reader's sympathy for him in the wake of Penny's departure. It turns out that Margie eventually left Ohio and her husband for Paris. As Charley is out walking while Helen rests in their room, he suddenly seizes upon the idea to call Margie, which he does, only to find out that her husband and children have moved to Paris to try to start over. Margie has accomplished what Charley has failed to do, and that is in some way to reinspire forgiveness and reconciliation so that all parts of his life could once again converge.

This contact only increases Charley's loneliness and his sense of displacement, as does the scene at his hotel upon his return. He finds the staff solicitous and cautious, Helen having overdosed deliberately on medication. Helen's suicide punctuates her long struggle with cancer, of which Charley has been aware. However, he interprets her pain incorrectly, unable to know the extent of it simply by virtue of his being

another person; he perceives her disease and her attitude toward the trip
through a kind of scrim that allows him a muted vision of her life's reality. He interprets her own being, in fact, in the context of his own,
admitting that her predicament makes his own less complicated. Her
life puts his in perspective, keeps him, at long last, from being "at the
center of things" (215), which is not where he wants to be. In fact,
Helen makes several references to the trip's significance, usually in the
context of wanting to see some monument and using a tone that suggests, to the perceptive listener, that she is mentally going through a list
of last things. Her rather fatalistic statements could be interpreted in
the light of her survival thus far, that she has not expected to be able to
see the things she's seen because she imagined that she'd be dead long
before this. Nonetheless, the fact of her suicide renders her past statements in a different light. Without her life's ending, however, the rest of
the story proves difficult to interpret correctly.

Charley's peregrinations through the streets of Paris have revealed
something to him that he is able to recall after Helen's death. Even as he
studies the street maps on his long walk, he finds himself repeatedly
somewhere that he has not planned to be. Although neither he nor the
narrator goes so far as to belabor this point, his wanderings nonetheless
suggest that such displacement may actually create opportunities that
he could not possibly have foreseen or planned. Furthermore, he realizes
that the lines between events are not clear-cut markers or "lines of
demarcation" (227), that he will not wake up one day and "be over"
Penny. He allows that "succeeding as an exile was possibly a slower,
more lingering process" (227) and that it is not at all necessary to fit
into some place completely. In short, Charley resolves to take control of
his life, at least to the extent that he can. The narrator reports what
Charley is thinking: "You recognized changes in yourself, he believed,
not by how others felt about you, but by how you felt about yourself"
(223). This realization frees Charley to act in his own best interest and
renews his hope in his meeting with his translator. Instead of trying to
convert events to suit his life, he resolves to "convert himself to whatever went on in Paris" (223). This attitude allows him to interpret the
translation of his novel as "the first move toward converting himself into
someone available to take on more of life" (223). He reaches all of these
conclusions before Helen's death, but he is able to summon them even
in the wake of her loss. He has not planned to keep seeing Helen,
because he knows in many ways that he is unable to be who she needs

him to be. He has imagined the fictional death of Penny in order to try
to cross the line toward getting over her, but he has faced instead the literal death of Helen. Not insignificantly, the event does not brake his
progress toward what he deems a possible conversion. At least at this
point he realizes that it is himself and not his circumstances that he
needs to change.

The story's end leaves Charley pondering the ways in which he might
put this experience into words, maybe in a letter to his parents, who are
furniture makers but who have supported his less conventional desires.
In Ford's fiction, the attempt to make sense of occurrence, especially
through the telling of a story, usually bespeaks some positive turn for
the character. In this sense, Charley's movement toward telling a story
other than *The Predicament* seems significant, suggestive that he has
emerged from a fiction into a new reality and that he might interpret
this reality more ably. The narrative ironically implies, in fact, that *The
Predicament* will not really translate that well into French, either, unless
the French translator feels free to make subtle changes to the text. What
she suggests in one sense disenfranchises Charley, especially in light of
the repeated failures in the story for one person to interpret another correctly. Perhaps the changes that the translator deems necessary arise
only from her own failure to "read" the book correctly. "Occidentals"
certainly leaves this matter open to the question. What the French
translator finds, as she tells Charley, is that certain problems with the
narration undercut the book's success, that really the book requires a
more humorous tone (though Charley has in no way planned for it to be
funny). She even starts to provide Charley with a French maxim to help
her explain what she means, though she catches herself, asking him if he
speaks French. When he says that he doesn't, she says "It doesn't matter" (253), and then she pauses to recover her line of thought. There is a
gap, in other words, between the way she reads the book and the way
that Charley has conceived of it, an inevitable breach that occurs, of
course, because one person does not think exactly like another. To the
French translator's mind, another problem resides with the narrator
(who is, as Charley has acknowledged, basically himself). She says, "you
cannot rely on the speaker. The *I* who is jilted. All the way throughout,
one is never certain if he can be taken seriously at all. It is not entirely
understandable in that way. . . . But in French I can make perfectly clear
that we are not to trust the speaker, though we try. That it's a satire,
meant to be amusing. The French would expect this. It is how they see

Americans" (253–54). When pressed to explain, she says to Charley that the French see Americans as silly, perpetually misunderstanding, but for that same reason, somewhat interesting. Having basically told Charley that his voice is not reliable, the translator arrives at her own solution for the narrative's perceived inconsistency, and that is to make it clearer that the speaker is not to be trusted even as the reader tries to trust him. The end result may be that Charley's book appeals to the French enough to sell well in translation, but it may also be that Charley's book may no longer be his story. Metaphorically speaking, if Charley's book requires revision, so may Charley himself need to change.

Certainly the ramifications of this passage reach beyond the pages of "Occidentals," which is written in the third-person perhaps to avoid the very conundrum that first-person narration creates and to which Charley's translator refers. Ford achieves a rather metafictional moment in having an editor and a writer discuss some narrative problem in the middle of a narrative written, obviously, by a writer. Taken in the context of "Occidentals," this moment may suggest something about Charley's character, and that is that all along he has been too close to his own story to be reliable. The narrator of "Occidentals" has told Charley's story from the third-person perspective but nonetheless from Charley's often limited point of view. Charley misinterprets others, misreads maps, or otherwise misses signs. Despite his epiphany that he can fashion himself in any way that he might like regardless of what others think, he would be an isolated person indeed if he never learned to communicate successfully with anyone else. In this sense, his desire to write his parents may be read as a hopeful ending to his story; presumably in that missive he would try to describe particular moments to a specific audience, and in that endeavor it would matter deeply to him whether he succeeded in his telling.

"Now and Then. Women and Men."

In the third story included in *Women with Men,* the character Helen says that she does not believe in eras, or specific and contained periods of time divided cleanly one from the other. Instead she says, "I believe it's all continuous. Now and then. Women and men" ("Occidentals," 206). Certainly Frank Bascombe of *The Sportswriter* and *Independence Day* has opined about continuity and community; he is another of Ford's characters who gets into trouble when he seeks to step briskly and unencumbered from the past to the present. In Ford's fictional universe, the most "successful" characters manage to preserve their own individuality without detaching themselves completely from what is significant. And what is significant is love, that most abstract of words that depends not on place or time or circumstance but on human beings for its cultivation. Because Ford writes many works from a male perspective and in fact has created plenty of male characters who perpetuate what might best be called a kind of obtuseness in the face of their relationships with women, Ford has often been called a "man's writer." Certainly his grittier fiction does not do much to contradict that notion. As this volume has already suggested, Ford does not care much for what critics call him, which is not to say that he doesn't care what his readers think. Ford loses patience with the critical propensity to label and thereby exclude a reader; he finds this likely when critics push writers into regional categories or categories determined essentially by gender. In response to an interviewer who asked Ford if he thought *Independence Day* was more of a man's book than a woman's book, Ford replied, "Hardly. The women in the novel seem to know so much more than the men." Sophie Majeski goes on to ask Ford, "So there is something essential about us that is beyond gender?" And he explains,

> Yes, I look to the end line. Do they die any differently? I watched my mother die, watched my father die, and I thought to myself, that's where life ends, and it's very much the same. There are some things that are beyond gender. I've discovered it in a long relationship with one person, which isn't to say that it's magic or that you have to have a long relationship with one person—maybe it's just taken me 32 years to get it in my brain. But there are qualities in human life that perhaps only literature can define, which are more fundamental than those other distinguishing qualities among us, like gender, age and sex. There is something else.[2]

For Ford, this something else is a need to connect with another person, "to narrow that space Emerson calls the infinite remoteness that separates people. And maybe that's as close to describing the thing as I can get. The need to be able to touch somebody. And not even physically. . . . And even closeness is just a metaphor for something else. Language would always be dealing in its metaphorical representations. It is something for which there is no language" (Majeski). Ironically, the quality that literature can define that transcends gender, age, and any number of other qualifiers to human life is the very quality that resists language.

For Ford, this discrepancy does not mean that one should stop trying to convey the human need for connectedness but rather that one should recognize that metaphorical representation only hints at the power of the real thing. Certainly there exist gaps between the literal and the imagined, between the original and the translation, but as Frank Bascombe would say, "words are required" nonetheless.

Chapter Nine
Richard Ford's Odyssey

Richard Ford's career to date has been incarnated in fiction that derives its energy from diverse traditions and stylistic traits. With the publication of *A Piece of My Heart* in 1976, Ford, a native Mississippian, met with reviews that would label him "Faulknerian" and find his writing a poor imitation of the original. It was not the only time that critics would try to link his work to a southern literary tradition defined by influential scholars such as Lewis P. Simpson, C. Hugh Holman, Louis D. Rubin Jr., and more recently, Fred Hobson, who called Frank Bascombe a literary descendent of Walker Percy. Close study of *A Piece of My Heart* suggests that Ford had other influences in mind, signatures of movements and genres as diverse as the gothic, film noir, local color, and southwest humor. In fact, Ford was already writing the stories—later to be collected in *Rock Springs* (1987)—that would inspire yet other critics to call him a "dirty realist" and compare him to his friend and mentor, Raymond Carver. Often associated with a tough-guy crowd that included fellow writers and outdoorsmen Jim Harrison and Tom McGuane, Ford has been known to scuffle with his neighbors, fire bullets at bad reviews, and enjoy minor league baseball. Gracious and articulate in person, Ford embodies these contradictions, suggesting in more than one interview that labels are distasteful and limiting. His creation of Frank Bascombe and introduction of him through *The Sportswriter* (1986), ten years after his first novel's publication, would confound his critics again, evoking those same comparisons to southern literature that Ford sought to evade in *The Ultimate Good Luck* (1981), a book whose spare prose suggested the influence not of William Faulkner but of Ernest Hemingway. *The Sportswriter* invited comparisons to Walker Percy's work, philosophical novels that became synonymous with a certain tradition of southern literature and identified accordingly: first-person narratives by musing, white males who professed their unbelonging, their stoicism, their lamentations for the past in language rich in cadence and meaning and whose stories featured varying degrees of concern for place, history, memory, religion, violence and the shadow, if not the outright presence, of race. Percy, too, departs from this tradition in significant ways, but

southern literary critics still likened his fictional creations to other characters in this vein. Thus, like Percy's Binx Bolling and Will Barrett,
Ford's Frank Bascombe became part of a fictional crowd that included
Faulkner's Quentin Compson, Thomas Wolfe's Eugene Gant, and
Robert Penn Warren's Jack Burden, among others. But Ford resists
these classifications, citing the huge repertoire of Western literature
open to the writer for inspiration and eschewing the regional title of
"southern writer." (Walker Percy's readers, in fact, are now apt to find
critical articles on his work that trace and untangle the varying threads
of influence by Søren Kierkegaard, Charles Sanders Peirce, and other
obviously nonsouthern thinkers and writers.) Believing that he had
nothing new to say about the South, Ford decided that he would take
"his show on the road," so to speak. Ford's wandering Frank Bascombe,
though a native Mississippian, as Ford also is, discounts his southernness
and lives a secular life largely unsponsored by any kind of traditional
religious force, further distinguishing him from the typical Percy way-
farer. If Ford concedes Walker Percy's influence, which he does in several
interviews, he also asserts that other present-tense, first-person narra-
tions, such as Joseph Heller's *Something Happened,* are as likely candidates
for resonance. Well aware of the first-person narrative's inherent unreli-
ability, Ford capitalizes on that very trait to keep Frank Bascombe's
voice compelling in both *The Sportswriter* and *Independence Day* (1995).
But Ford is not simply a story-writer, or a novel-writer; he is a writer
whose nonfiction fills the pages of such magazines and journals as
Esquire, Harper's, the *New Yorker, American Film Magazine, Rolling Stone,
Architectural Digest,* and *Aperture,* to list but a few. Even the names of
these publications indicate that Ford writes on many subjects and for
very different audiences. Ford writes to be read, and he writes to reach as
many people as he can.

Ford's reverence for language's ability to bridge the gulf between one
person and another appears in both his fiction and nonfiction and is also
revealed in the interviews that Ford has given. He acknowledges language's inherent imprecision as well as its almost miraculous capacity to
recover sensations otherwise lost to their hosts. To wield language precisely and sincerely is to keep disorder at bay, close the gap between self
and other, render knowable what otherwise might remain unknown. To
wield language irresponsibly is to accomplish almost the opposite effect.
It is the individual, however, not the words themselves, who holds the
power conferred by language, and in Ford's fiction, the individual
always faces the consequences of his or her actions or utterances. I do

not mean to suggest that Ford's characters get what they deserve—although many times they do; Ford's narratives are conspicuously devoid of overt moral judgments. Ford makes the reader respond to his fiction; he requires that his own language be interpreted actively by his audience. As diverse as Ford's fictional landscapes are, every one of them is circumscribed by Ford's belief that what a character says or does not say bears direct influence on that character's story and every plot's resolution.

Ford's work attests to the influence of both American literary traditions and Western philosophy. It is possible to identify ideas and thoughts espoused by other well-known American figures in Ford's fiction. Certainly Ralph Waldo Emerson and Wallace Stevens come to mind. But Ford is just as apt to quote from French philosopher Jean-Paul Sartre or from British poet John Keats. Ford's work also manifests his knowledge of literary traditions, such as modernism and realism, that in themselves can be shaky as identifiers of certain kinds of fiction. Almost all writing presses at the boundaries of whatever category has been invented to house it. Ford is a rather equal-opportunity writer, as happy to cite Bruce Springsteen as William Faulkner for inspiration. His fiction blends cultural influences from divergent traditions together. As I suggest throughout this volume, Ford casts philosophical concerns—existential, epistemological, ontological—in subtle, yet thematically prominent, roles in his work. In texts as diverse as *Wildlife,* the *Rock Springs* stories, the Frank Bascombe books, and *Women with Men,* characters ponder how to know themselves, how to know others, to what degree to exist or be. Interestingly, even works that critics would not perhaps think to label "musing" in tone—such as many of the stories in *Rock Springs* that have even been called "minimalist"—actually revolve around these questions of knowing and being. On the other hand, in his fiction Ford also provides many accessible touchstones for his audience: the American preoccupation with sports; real estate; holidays (Easter, Thanksgiving, Christmas, July 4th); careers; and economic opportunities—all things that most of his readers probably think about on a daily basis. Furthermore, Ford's characters speak the spoken language no matter how intellectual they are; for example, Frank Bascombe can talk about being "scared silly," or having the "bejesus" scared out of him. Ford relies on the American idiom for the conversations he reproduces in his fiction, but he also pays homage to the literary, sprinkling his characters' thoughts with references to famous essays, poems, or documents from both American and European traditions. In these ways, Ford achieves a singular effect: he combines a learnedness with a down-to-earth sensibility so that his fiction is accessible on a number of levels.

Ford's work contains repeated images, metaphors, or ideas that together suggest common thematic preoccupations. To use but one example, cars play a relatively significant role in Ford's fiction. Characters in *A Piece of My Heart, The Sportswriter, Rock Springs, Independence Day,* and *Women with Men* all engage in significant conversations either in cars or about cars. The reader may recall that in *A Piece of My Heart,* Robard Hewes's father dies in his car; in *The Sportswriter,* Frank's conversation with Wade Arcenault in Wade's basement centers largely around Wade's trapped and shining Chrysler; the car transports many a questioning boy and desperate man in *Rock Springs;* Frank spends much of his time in the car in *Independence Day;* and even in *Women with Men,* Martin Austin tries to make the "crummy Opel" he is driving the fitting setting for words of some import to Joséphine. Americans certainly engage in love affairs with their cars, spending far more time in their vehicles than their European counterparts, who either walk or take advantage of vastly more convenient public transportation systems. Ford plays off of this American obsession and has even written his own "car story," which was published in *Esquire* in 1998.[1] Furthermore, as I have suggested in earlier chapters, images of suffocation and entrapment are also often yoked with the car, or the train, or other means of transport from one literal or figurative destination to another. Of course, the journey also assumes an important role in Ford's fiction, and no doubt several critics have called *Independence Day* a novel in the tradition of the picaresque. Ford's peripatetic streak has given critics and interviewers plenty of fodder for discussions with him about his frequent wanderings, his multiple residences, and his situation of living mostly apart from his wife of many years, Kristina, to whom Ford dedicates every book.

But for Ford, place and what he has called "locatedness" are human constructions. Of course, literal places exist, but what Ford finds far more interesting is the human being's propensity to endow place with the authority to bestow upon its inhabitant meaning that only the inhabitant can embody. Such concerns appear most obviously in *The Ultimate Good Luck* and both *The Sportswriter* and *Independence Day,* as well as in numerous nonfiction essays by Ford, such as "Accommodations"; "Heartbreak Motels"; "Place Qua Place"; "An Urge for Going: Why I Don't Live Where I Used to Live"; and "S.O.P.," which stands for "sense of place."[2] This range of publications on the subject suggests the author's fascination with human response to geography. In his novels, particularly *The Ultimate Good Luck,* Ford offers an alternative to place, and that is the more metaphysical configuration, "locatedness." Locatedness has little to do with place and everything to do with a person's awareness of self and other. The sensation may occur in solitary moments or with another person and, as Ford defines it, is an unadulterated, fleeting yet intense conviction of one's being-in-the-world, one's internal, not external, location. Such a moment also provides some measure of self-appreciation, some ability to recognize one's own identity and be content with what one sees, and some wonderment over the fact of one's existence. As Ford has written in "An Urge for Going," "I have tried to contend that locatedness is not a science of the ground but of some quality within us" ("Urge," 67). Thus to look for the self in a particular place is to be forever disappointed, as Frank finds out in *Independence Day.* Ford explains that when Frank proclaims that place means nothing, he really means "this place ain't givin' me nothin'." (Walker, 139). As human beings, we give places permission to sanction us or somehow verify our existences, but it is only we who can do that. As Frank also learns, only other people can prove our significance.

Real communication with another person is predicated upon some wholeness of self, so that while Frank Bascombe experiences some degree of locatedness in the "glistening one moment" of the conclusion of *The Sportswriter,* it is not until the ending of *Independence Day* that he accepts other people as contingent forces in his life, symbolized by his surrender to the "push, pull, the weave and sway of others." Although Ford is in no sense a sentimental writer, the subtext of even some of his grittiest stories, such as "Jealous" in *Women with Men,* depends upon the notion that only the most abstract of words for the most abstract of feelings, "love," can imbue a human being with anything approaching contentedness, safety, assurance of *being.* As Ford has written, "Home—real home—the important place that holds you, always meant that: affection, love. *There* was fixity and a different sort of inward quality that could hold sway anywhere, even on the move" ("Urge," 62). It is love, not place, that redeems a person from present confusion, lostness, or, to borrow the phrase that Ford takes from Ralph Waldo Emerson, the "infinite remoteness" that separates one human being from another. Ford's concern for this kind of redemptive affection might seem at odds with what some have called his "tough guy" persona, his fondness for fishing and hunting, his occasional fistfight, his knowledge of boxing, baseball, and other such occupations. Such a label as a "tough guy" or a "man's writer," as Ford has often claimed, can only go so far toward defining their objects before they begin to fail.

Like his character Frank Bascombe, Ford is obviously compelled by the "fissures between the literal and the imagined," the gap between word and object. Ford deploys metaphors in his work with ease, even abandon, so that a car, to use the example I've provided above, becomes more than simply a mechanical vehicle; in Ford's fiction it is the literal site of crucial turning points for the characters, but it also assumes figurative significance, representative of the state of being in transit, dislocated, even trapped. Thus the car works on two levels, the literal and the figurative, the real and the imagined. Between those two levels literature finds its point of origin, in fact, since the written is once-removed from its subject, the story but a representation of life itself. Again and again in his fiction, Ford explores the paradoxical nature of language, its ability on the one hand to fix an emotion, pin it down, give it a name, and on the other hand, its absolute and utter failure to do the very same things. Much about the human condition eludes language's tenuous hold, but for Ford, the attempt to put that condition into words is forever a hopeful one. He charts his discovery of William Faulkner's *Absalom, Absalom!* (1936) as a turning point in his own literary development: "Before, I don't believe I'd known what made literature necessary; neither what quality of life required that it be represented, nor what quality in literature made such abstractings a good idea. . . . That is, until I read *Absalom, Absalom!,* which, among other things, sets out to testify by act to the efficacy of telling, and to recommend language for its powers of consolation against whatever's ailing you" ("Three Kings," 581). Although *Absalom, Absalom!* fails to make its multiple narratives yield one coherent story, Faulkner's prose is rhetorically powerful. The telling redeems the gaps in the telling, as it were. For Ford, then, language offers consolation through its aesthetic reversal of the very subjects it addresses. The subjects may be tragic, but the language that names the tragic also mitigates its sorrow simply by virtue of giving the sorrow a name.

Although it is too soon to chart Ford's influence on younger writers, his interviews and personal essays make his ambition for his own work clear. He wants his work to do for others what Faulkner's work did for him when Ford was 19. In *Absalom, Absalom!,* Ford witnessed "language . . . put to the service of some great human conundrum it meant to console me about if not completely resolve. When I was old enough to think about myself as trying to be a writer, I always thought I would like to write a book and have it do that for someone else."[3] Always cognizant of his audience, Ford writes more for others than he does for himself, as he tells Bonnie Lyons in her interview with him. It is for this reason that he resists being categorized and classified; he does not want to exclude any corner of his readership. He can, therefore, state that Mississippi is his home, "unqualifiedly" (Lyons, 72), even as he disavows being a "southern writer." Here again, it is not the literal term he objects to, for he is a southerner; what Ford chafes against are the connotations of the label, the meanings ascribed to the term by critics seeking to define the work too narrowly. It is human nature to name in order to know, but Ford believes the names themselves should be understood as provisional measures and that criticism becomes spurious when it rigidly contains its subject. Ford's commitment to his readers drives him to work; in interviews he speaks often of wanting to be of some use to other people through his writing. He says that "it's fiction's business to try to enlarge our understanding of and sympathy for people" (Lyons, 61). As his work to date confirms, Richard Ford takes his calling seriously.

Notes and References

Chapter One

1. C. Hugh Holman, Louis D. Rubin Jr., and Lewis P. Simpson distinguished southern literature from American literature by naming characteristics by which southern literature could be identified. Their predecessors, who included the Agrarians and New Critics (Allen Tate, Donald Davidson, Robert Penn Warren, and Andrew Lytle, to name a few) also influenced southern literary scholarship.

2. William Faulkner, "Address upon Receiving the Nobel Prize for Literature," in *The Portable Faulkner,* ed. Malcolm Cowley (1967; New York: Viking Press, 1974), 724.

3. C. Vann Woodward, *The Burden of Southern History* (Baton Rouge: Louisiana State University Press, 1960).

4. Richard Ford, "My Mother, In Memory," *Harper's,* August 1977, 45; hereafter cited in text as "Mother".

5. Don Lee, "About Richard Ford," *Ploughshares* 22, nos. 2–3 (August 1996): 227–28; hereafter cited in text as Lee.

6. Leonora Smith, "Richard Ford: MSU's Pulitzer Prize Winning Writer," *Muses,* Michigan State University's Alumni Newsletter, 1995–1996.

7. Jim Yardley, "The Eternal Optimist." *Y'all.* (1998). January 14, 1998 <www.accessatlanta.com/global/local/yall/culture/quill/ford.htm>.

8. Richard Ford, "First Things First: One More Writer's Beginnings," *Harper's,* August 1988, 72–76.

9. Larry McMurtry, review of *A Piece of My Heart,* by Richard Ford, *New York Times Book Review,* October 24, 1976, 16; hereafter cited in text as McMurtry.

10. Richard Ford, "An Interview with Richard Ford," interview by Elinor Ann Walker, *South Carolina Review* 31, no. 2 (Spring 1999): 130; hereafter cited in text as Walker.

11. Richard Ford, "Walker Percy: Not Just Whistling Dixie," *National Review,* May 13, 1977, 558–64.

12. Richard Ford, "The Three Kings: Hemingway, Faulkner, and Fitzgerald," *Esquire,* December 1983,: 577–84; hereafter cited in text as "Three Kings."

13. Fred Hobson, *The Southern Writer in the Postmodern World* (Athens: University of Georgia Press, 1991); hereafter cited in text as Hobson 1991.

14. Richard Ford, "An Interview with Richard Ford," interview by Kay Bonetti, *Missouri Review* 10, no. 2 (1987): 85; hereafter cited in text as Bonetti.

15. Richard Ford, *The Sportswriter* (New York: Vintage Books, 1986), 375; hereafter cited in text as *SW.*

16. Richard Ford, *The Ultimate Good Luck* (1981; New York: Vintage Books, 1986), 77; hereafter cited in text as *UGL.*

17. Richard Ford, "Accommodations," *Harper's,* June 1988, 43; hereafter cited in text as "Accommodations."

18. Richard Ford, "An Urge for Going: Why I Don't Live Where I Used to Live," *Harper's,* February 1992, 60; hereafter cited in text as "Urge."

19. Richard Ford, "Country Matters," *Harper's,* July 1981, 82; hereafter cited in text as "Country Matters."

20. William Faulkner, *Absalom, Absalom!* (1936; New York: Vintage, 1972).

21. Richard Ford, Interview, with Elizabeth Farnsworth, *The News Hour with Jim Lehrer,* PBS, April 17, 1996. Transcript, February 9, 1997 <www.pbs.org/newshour/bb/entertainment/pulitzer_novel_4–17.html>; hereafter cited in text as Farnsworth.

22. Richard Ford, "Great Falls," in *Rock Springs* (1987; New York: Vintage, 1988), 49; hereafter cited in text as "Great Falls."

23. Richard Ford, *Wildlife* (1990; New York: Vintage, 1991), 171; hereafter cited in text as *WL.*

24. Richard Ford, *Independence Day* (1995; New York: Vintage, 1996), 112; hereafter cited in text as *ID.*

25. Joan Smith, "Richard Ford: He Champions Ordinary Experiences," *San Francisco Examiner,* August 1, 1996. February 9, 1997 <nsers.ox.ac.uk/~sjoh0521/richardford.html>.

26. Richard Ford, "Occidentals," in *Women with Men* (New York: Knopf, 1997), 180; hereafter cited in text as "Occidentals."

27. Richard Ford, "The Womanizer" in *Women with Men* (New York: Knopf, 1997), 92; hereafter cited in text as "Womanizer."

28. See Richard Ford, "The Boss Observed," *Esquire,* December 1985, 326–29.

Chapter Two

1. See McMurtry.

2. Richard Ford, *A Piece of My Heart* (1976; New York: Vintage, 1985), 71; hereafter cited in text as *PMH.*

3. Richard Ford, conversation with author, Chapel Hill, N.C., March 18, 1997.

4. Newel experiences another perilous moment on the island when he steps straight into a swampy patch of ground that yields immediately to water only 36 hours after his struggle in the river. He fears drowning again in the passages on pages 184 and 185.

5. Newel's Peabody Hotel memory provides a connection with Beuna's Peabody Hotel desire and another narrative link between his and Hewes's stories.

Chapter Three

1. Nina Baym et al., eds., *The Norton Anthology of American Literature,* 4th ed. (New York: Norton, 1995), 1709–20. For more information about modernism, consult *The Columbia Literary History of the United States,* ed. Emory Elliott (New York: Columbia University Press), 1988.

2. See *The History of Southern Literature,* ed. Louis D. Rubin Jr. et al. (Baton Rouge: Louisiana State University Press), 1985.

3. T. S. Eliot's famous poem "The Waste Land" (1922) depends upon such images.

4. Wallace Stevens, "The Snow Man," in *The Collected Poems of Wallace Stevens* (New York: Vintage, 1982), 9–10.

5. For Richard Ford's own perspective on the virtues and vices associated with the well-timed punch, see his essay, "In the Face: The Metaphysics of Fisticuffs," *New Yorker,* September 16, 1997, 52–54.

Chapter Four

1. The speaker of Wallace Stevens's "Thirteen Ways of Looking at a Blackbird" says, "I was of three minds, / Like a tree / In which there are three blackbirds" (Wallace Stevens, "Thirteen Ways of Looking at a Blackbird," in *The Collected Poems of Wallace Stevens* [New York: Vintage, 1982], 92), a line that aptly describes the narrator of Richard Ford's *The Sportswriter* (1986), Frank Bascombe. As southern literary critic Fred Hobson has also observed, "Frank is indeed one of the 'thin men of Haddam,' of Stevens's poem, one of the overly cerebral men, and Ford's novel, like the poem, is about ways of seeing, ways of perceiving" (Hobson 1991, 51). Stevens's thin men of Haddam, thus addressed in his poem, imagine golden birds, a contemplative act so seductive that they are then rendered incapable of seeing the real blackbirds, who walk "around the feet / Of the women about [them]" (Stevens, 93). The "thin men" are addressed in the poem as "you"—"why do you imagine golden birds?" (Stevens, 93)—presumably by the poem's speaker, the "I." As the speaker relates his or her own state ("of three minds"), uses the third person to describe, dispassionately, images of blackbirds ("The blackbird whirled in the autumn winds"), and addresses the mysterious thin men ("Do you not see how the blackbird / Walks around the feet / Of the women about you?"), the poem subtly demonstrates the gap between subject and object, I and you, speaker and world (Stevens, 93). Even the language that Stevens uses is at odds with itself; that is, being "of three minds" (or "of a mind" about anything) is a colloquial phrase, but the rest of Stevens's diction sounds elevated, at times almost biblical in tone. Such con-

tradictions in speech and word choice appear frequently in Stevens's poetry, underscoring, perhaps, language's ability to shape human responses to that which it describes. Any devoted reader of Stevens knows the poet's fascination with opposites, such as the imagined versus the real; it is this dichotomy that also drives the narrative tension in Ford's *The Sportswriter.*

2. Fred Hobson, *Tell About the South: The Southern Rage to Explain* (Baton Rouge: Louisiana State University Press, 1983).

3. W. J. Cash, *The Mind of the South* (New York: Knopf, 1941).

4. See interview with Walker.

5. "Location" is a loaded word for Ford, as other chapters attest.

Chapter Five

1. Sartre's narrator, however, speaks only from the present moment, whereas Ford's narrators speak retrospectively about their lives.

2. A native of Mississippi, Ford and his southern background tempt readers and critics to find in his work characteristics that would ally him with a southern tradition in literature.

3. Walker Percy also read Marcel, Kierkegaard, Husserl, Heidegger, and Sartre, in addition to many linguistic and semiotic theorists. Perhaps one key difference between Percy and Ford is that Percy's philosophical apparatus is apt to be more apparent in his fiction. Ford's short fiction, particularly, is sparer in style, more likely to be compared to Ernest Hemingway's or Raymond Carver's work than to Percy's, though, again, in the longer novels, Frank Bascombe has reminded more than one reader of Will Barrett and Binx Bolling. (And fans of John Updike cite echoes of Harry Angstrom.) More to the point, often imbedded in so-called "minimalist" fiction are complex notions, and Ford is fond of quoting Sartre, Emerson, and Wallace Stevens in conversation.

4. Chapter 6 deals with these and other stories that appear in *Rock Springs.*

5. Walker Percy, "The Delta Factor," in *The Message in the Bottle: How Queer Man Is, How Queer Language Is, and What One Has to Do with the Other* (New York: Farrar, Straus & Giroux, 1984), 40. Originally published in *The Southern Review* 11 (1975): 29–64.

6. Critics often comment that Ford's musing, "bigger" books, such as *The Sportswriter* and *Independence Day,* depart from his earlier more spare style. In these texts, however, the reader may find voices that complement Frank Bascombe's philosophizing one.

7. See chapter 4 for an explication of a similar moment in *The Sportswriter.*

8. Jean-Paul Sartre, *Being and Nothingness: An Essay on Phenomenological Ontology,* trans. Hazel E. Barnes (New York: Philosophical Library, 1956), 222.

9. Jean has also uttered those words to Joe on the page preceding, illustrating her own despair and pent-up frustration.

10. Note again the syntactical separation of "my father and I, and my mother."

11. Jean-Paul Sartre, *Nausea,* trans. Lloyd Alexander (London: Purnell & Sons, 1949), 174; hereafter cited in text as Sartre.

Chapter Six

1. Richard Ford, "Children," in *Rock Springs* (1987; New York: Vintage, 1988), 69–70; hereafter cited in text.

2. Richard Ford, "Communist," in *Rock Springs,* 232; hereafter cited in text.

3. Richard Ford, "Optimists," in *Rock Springs,* 171; hereafter cited in text.

4. Richard Ford, "Rock Springs," in *Rock Springs,* 8; hereafter cited in text.

5. Richard Ford, "Sweethearts," in *Rock Springs,* 68; hereafter cited in text.

6. Richard Ford, "Empire," in *Rock Springs,* 136; hereafter cited in text.

7. Richard Ford, "Winterkill," in *Rock Springs,* 162; hereafter cited in text.

8. Richard Ford, "Going to the Dogs," in *Rock Springs,* 99; hereafter cited in text.

9. Richard Ford, "Fireworks," in *Rock Springs,* 214; hereafter cited in text.

Chapter Seven

1. Ralph Waldo Emerson, *Self-Reliance* in *The Norton Anthology of American Literature,* shorter 4th ed. Ed. Nina Baym et al. (New York: Norton, 1995), 501.

2. Alexis de Tocqueville's *Democracy in America* was first published in English in 1966. Interestingly, Ford also names a school in Haddam the De Tocqueville Academy.

3. Please see chapter 4 for a detailed discussion of this term.

4. Here, again, I would refer my reader to chapter 4, where I discuss in detail the gap between the word and the object it describes, and how language, therefore, interprets the real via the imagined.

5. See chapter 2 for a complete explanation of southern definitions of place and Ford's own substitution of "locatedness."

6. Emily Dickinson, "1129," in *The Norton Anthology of American Literature,* shorter 4th ed. Ed. Nina Baym et al. (New York: Norton, 1995), 1148.

Chapter Eight

1. Richard Ford, "Jealous," *Women with Men* (New York: Knopf, 1997), 95; hereafter cited in text.

2.   "Richard Ford," interview by Sophie Majeski in *Salon*. January 14, 1998 <www.salon.com/weekly/interview960708.html> ; hereafter cited in text as Majeski.

Chapter Nine

1.   Richard Ford, "My Car Story," *Esquire,* October 1998, 144.

2.   "Accommodations," *Harper's,* June 1988, 38–43, excerpted from a longer piece in *Trips* (Spring 1988); "Heartbreak Motels," an excerpt published in *Harper's,* August 1989, 12–15, from "So Little Time, So Many Rooms" (*Money,* May 1989); "Place Qua Place" in *American Film* 16, no. 10 (November–December 1991): 68; "An Urge for Going: Why I Don't Live Where I Used to Live" in *Harper's,* February 1992, 60–67; and "S.O.P." in *Aperture* 127 (Spring 1992): 64..

3.   "Richard Ford," interview by Bonnie Lyons, in *Paris Review* 38, no. 140 (Fall 1996): 77; hereafter cited in text as Lyons.

Selected Bibliography

This bibliography lists Richard Ford's major publications and selected secondary works. Ford's works have been translated for the following countries: France, Italy, Germany, Poland, Sweden, Norway, Denmark, Finland, Greece, Hungary, Czech Republic, Netherlands, Spain, Portugal, Israel, Brazil, Japan, Russia, China, Turkey, Egypt, and Korea; individual translations are not listed here. Ford's literary papers are on loan to the Michigan State University Library's Special Collections Division and are open to scholars for research use.

PRIMARY WORKS

Novels

A Piece of My Heart. New York: Harper & Row, 1976. Reprint, New York: Vintage, 1985. Reprint, Toronto: Random House of Canada, 1985. Reprint, London: Collins, 1987. Ford's first novel is set primarily on an island between Arkansas and Mississippi presided over by Mr. and Mrs. Lamb. The Lambs' eccentricities and physical irregularities differentiate them from the island's outsiders, namely Robard Hewes and Sam Newel, whose alternating narratives provide the novel's structure. Violent, poignant, and funny, the novel defies easy genre classification.

The Ultimate Good Luck. Boston: Houghton Mifflin, 1981. Reprint, Vintage, 1986. Reprint, Toronto: Random House of Canada, 1986. Reprint, London: Collins, 1989. The book that reminded readers of Ernest Hemingway's laconic style, Ford's second novel leaves U.S. southern territory behind as its protagonist, Vietnam veteran Harry Quinn, journeys to Mexico to free old girlfriend Rae's brother Sonny from prison. Confronted by violence and betrayal, Quinn finally surrenders himself to his "location," by which he means something that transcends literal place.

The Sportswriter. New York: Knopf, 1986. London: Collins, 1986. Reprint, New York: Vintage, 1986. Reprint, Toronto: Random House of Canada, 1986. Narrated in the first-person by Frank Bascombe, this novel depends upon Bascombe's prevarications and philosophizing for its energy. As Frank ponders his divorce from X and the death of one son from Reye's Syndrome, he also tries to determine his identity, constructing his own terminology to characterize his various states of mind.

Wildlife. New York: Atlantic Monthly Press, 1990. London: Collins, 1990. Reprint, New York: Vintage, 1991. Reprint, Toronto: Random House of Canada, 1991. Told in retrospect by Joe Brinson, Ford's fourth novel recreates a time in Joe's life when, at 16, he comes to terms with the unknowableness of his parents and reckons with language's paradoxical strengths and failings.

Independence Day. New York: Knopf, 1995. London: Harvill Press, 1995. Reprint, New York: Vintage, 1996. The "sequel" to *The Sportswriter,* this novel continues Frank Bascombe's first-person account as he seeks to connect with his son, his ex-wife, his girlfriend and himself; here the "Existence Period" and the multiple meanings of independence preoccupy Frank during his literal and figurative journey over the Fourth of July weekend. The novel won the Pulitzer Prize and the PEN/Faulkner Award, the first time a single work has received such dual recognition.

Collected Stories

Rock Springs. New York: Atlantic Monthly Press, 1987. Reprint, London: Collins, 1988. Reprint, New York: Vintage, 1988. Many stories in this collection were published first in such magazines and journals as *Esquire,* the *New Yorker, Granta, Antaeus,* and *Tri-Quarterly.* Montana provides the fictional landscape for many of these works.

Women with Men. New York: Knopf, 1997. London: Harvill Press, 1997. Reprint, New York: Vintage, 1998. This collection includes three long stories: "The Womanizer," published first in *Granta* (Summer 1990); "Jealous," originally appearing in the *New Yorker* (November 30, 1992); and "Occidentals."

Recent Uncollected Short Fiction

"Privacy." *New Yorker* (July 22, 1996): 58–59. Set during winter in the Northeast, this very short story recounts its narrator's frequent acts of voyeurism as he watches a woman in an apartment on an adjacent street.

"Crèche." *New Yorker* (December 28, 1998, and January 4, 1999): 72–85. Recounts the trip of five family members over Christmas to northern Michigan, where they have gone to ski.

Play

American Tropical. Actors Theatre of Louisville. Produced November 1983. Published in *Antaeus* 66 (Spring 1991): 75–80. Set near a mobile home in central Florida, this play concerns two characters, Evelyn and Sid, and a little girl, Suzie, Sid's daughter. While Sid and Suzie play Scrabble, Evelyn directs many lines to the audience, describing how she killed a woman in Michigan out of jealousy and passion. She concludes that each individual bears the responsibility for his or her happiness.

Screenplay

Bright Angel. Hemdale Productions, 1990. This screenplay was based on two of Ford's short stories, "Children" and "Great Falls," and was made into a film that was shot near Billings, Montana. Roger Ebert's review of the film appears in the *Chicago Sun Times,* June 28, 1991.

Selected Nonfiction

"Walker Percy: Not Just Whistling Dixie." *National Review* 29 (May 13, 1977): 558–64. Ford's praise of Percy's control of the sentence and Ford's own disappointment over several aspects of Percy's novel *Lancelot,* published in 1977.

"Country Matters." *Harper's,* July 1981, 81–84. Ford's rejoinder to other writers' convictions that to live in the country is to find literary edification. Ford believes that place is significant only insofar as how one works within its boundaries, and he cites Ralph Waldo Emerson's notion that the "lived life" is "its own evidence."

"The Three Kings: Hemingway, Faulkner, and Fitzgerald." *Esquire* 100 (December 1983): 577–86. Ford's recollections of his first encounters with these literary giants and the power their works confer.

"The Boss Observed." *Esquire,* December 1985, 326–29. Ford explains why he finds Bruce Springsteen's music and lyrics to be rock and roll of a higher order.

"My Mother, In Memory." *Harper's,* August 1987, 44–57. Ford's poignant account of his mother's influence on his life, citing her love as an ongoing presence.

"Accommodations." *Harper's,* June 1988, 38–43. Ford's memoir of the time he lived in his grandfather's hotel in Little Rock, Arkansas.

"First Things First: One More Writer's Beginnings." *Harper's,* August 1988, 72–76. Ford's look back from age 44 to his career's halting progression, charting his decision to stop writing stories and focus instead on honing his craft through novel-writing. He concludes that writing is lonely work but is also an "existential errand."

"Heartbreak Motels." *Harper's,* August 1989, 12–15. Ford's musings about the cheap room at the singular motel, fast losing its place to more generic accommodations. Ford calls these rooms "places of reference" and justifies their existence relative to their high-brow counterparts and middle-brow replacements.

"Kristina Ford." *Esquire,* June 1990, 145. Ford's tribute to his wife Kristina Hensley Ford for this special issue of "The Secret Life of the American Wife."

"Place qua Place." *American Film* 16, no. 10 (November–December 1991): 68. Ford's discussion of film's failure to convey landscapes realistically or recreate regional accents even as he explains that places don't have "essences" that can be easily captured.

"An Urge for Going: Why I Don't Live Where I Used to Live." *Harper's,* February 1992, 60–67. Ford's analysis of why he had moved, to date, "twenty times in twenty years." In this essay, he also defines "locatedness."

"S. O. P." *Aperture* 127 (Spring 1992): 64. Places are "mute," Ford claims here, despite language's attempt to imbue them with sensate attributes. Sense of place is unique to each individual's construction of that location via the imagination.

"What We Write, Why We Write It, and Who Cares." *Michigan Quarterly Review* 31 (Summer 1992): 373–89. Ford assesses the role of artistic freedom in writing, urging that young writers turn to humanity, in all of its contradictions and complexities, for their source of inspiration, rather than trying to conform to guidelines set by someone else.

"A Minors Affair." *Harper's,* September 1992, 32–34. Ford praises the minor leagues as the site of the truest enjoyment that baseball has to offer.

"I Must Be Going: In Praise of Moving and Moving and Moving . . ." *Utne Reader* 55 (January–February 1993): 102–4. Another essay in which Ford discounts place's significance—in and of itself—to a writer as he explains his own penchant for moving.

"What Happened Next." *New Yorker,* June 26, 1995, 121–22. Selected excerpts from Ford's journals during the years 1989, 1991, 1994, and 1995.

"Bonhomie for a Southern Belletrist." *New Yorker,* February 19, 1996, 36. Ford's tribute to Mississippi writer and good friend Eudora Welty after she won the coveted French Legion of Honor Award.

"In the Face: A Metaphysics of Fisticuffs." *New Yorker,* September 16, 1996, 52–53. Ford discusses fighting's allure—and its consequences—as he assesses the implications of the well-timed punch.

"Where Does Writing Come From?" *Granta* 62 (Summer 1998): 249–55. Written for a special issue entitled "What Young Men Do," this essay extols writing as invention rather than something that can be traced minutely back to some specific occasion or source.

"Good Raymond." *New Yorker,* October 5, 1998, 70–79. Ford's memoir of and tribute to fiction writer Raymond Carver.

SECONDARY WORKS

Interviews

Bonetti, Kay. "An Interview with Richard Ford." *Missouri Review* 10, no. 2 (1987): 71–96. Discusses Ford's working habits, the origins of his writing, literature's role in society, and Frank Bascombe.

Farnsworth, Elizabeth. Interview with Richard Ford. *The News Hour with Jim Lehrer,* PBS. April 17, 1996. February 9, 1997. Available on the World Wide Web at <www.pbs.org/newshour/bb/entertainment/pulitzer_

novel_4–17.html>. Discusses Ford's surprise upon winning the Pulitzer Prize for *Independence Day,* various meanings of independence, why Ford wrote a sequel to *The Sportswriter,* and the southern tradition in writing.

Gilbert, Matthew. "Interview with Richard Ford." *Writer* 109, no. 12 (December 1996): 9–11. Ford fields questions about his periodic threats to quit writing, his response to winning the Pulitzer, and other topics relevant to his writing process.

Guagliardo, Huey. "A Conversation with Richard Ford." *Southern Review* 34, no. 3 (Summer 1998): 609–20. Guagliardo and Ford talk about *Women with Men,* Walker Percy, Frank Bascombe's reliability as narrator, Ford's relationship with wife Kristina, and Ford's work habits.

Lyons, Bonnie. "Richard Ford." *Paris Review* 38 (Fall 1996): 44–77. A thorough and informative interview about many aspects of Ford's work, including Ford's interest in language and sound, his method of constructing characters, his career, whether or not he is a "male" writer, autobiographical elements in his fiction, his relationship with his mother, among others.

Majeski, Sophie. "Richard Ford," *Salon* (1998) <www.salon.com/weekly/interview960708.html>. An interview for this online magazine that covers the origins of *Independence Day,* whether it is more of a "man's" book than a "woman's" book, and Ford's conceptions of independence and preoccupation with impermanence.

Walker, Elinor Ann. "An Interview with Richard Ford." *South Carolina Review* 31, no. 2 (Spring 1999): 128–43. Discusses "locatedness," place, Ralph Waldo Emerson, southern writing and other topics related to Ford's participation on a panel as the Morgan Family Writer-in-Residence at the University of North Carolina–Chapel Hill.

Other Secondary Sources

Crouse, David. "Resisting Reduction: Closure in Richard Ford's *Rock Springs* and Alice Munro's *Friend of My Youth.*" *Canadian Literature* 146 (Autumn 1995): 51–64. Analyzes realism and characterization in Munro and Ford's work, arguing that both writers continue to operate within the Joycean aesthetic even as their works place more responsibility upon the reader than other more psychological narratives might do.

Dupuy, Edward. "The Confessions of an Ex-Suicide: Relenting and Recovering in Richard Ford's *The Sportswriter.*" *Southern Literary Journal* 23 (Fall 1990): 93–103. Situates Ford's work in the context of Walker Percy's; claims that Frank Bascombe's told tale is a confession that offers consolation to its teller; Frank himself relents to the world, thus preserving himself.

Folks, Jeffrey. "The Risks of Membership: Richard Ford's *The Sportswriter.*" *Mississippi Quarterly* 52 (Winter 1998): 73–88. Assesses Ford's artistic relationship to Walker Percy, finding that Ford offers secular consolation as opposed to Percy's religious redemption. Claims that Bascombe's source of discontent is not existential or religious in nature but rather is social and cultural.

Hobson, Fred. "Richard Ford and Josephine Humphreys: Walker Percy in New Jersey and Charleston." In *The Southern Writer in the Postmodern World,* 41–72. Athens: University of Georgia Press, 1991. Situates Ford and Humphreys's characters in a tradition of the overly cerebral, southern white male who is compelled to tell his story, finding Ford's Frank Bascombe to be the "unburdened southerner," a revised version of his southern literary predecessors.

Lee, Don. "About Richard Ford." *Ploughshares* 22, nos. 2–3 (Fall 1996): 226–35. Lee's profile of Ford appears in the same issue that Ford edited and offers a solid overview of Ford's life and career to date.

McMurtry, Larry. Review of *A Piece of My Heart. New York Times Book Review,* October 24, 1976, 16. Coins "neo-Faulknerian" to describe the vices of Ford's book.

"Richard Ford." *Current Biography Yearbook 1995* 56, no. 9 (September 1995): 174–77. Offers a concise biography of Ford and brief assessment of his works.

Schroth, Raymond A. "America's Moral Landscape in the Fiction of Richard Ford." *Christian Century* 106 (March 1, 1989): 227–30. Recounts Schroth's discovery of Ford's fiction during a search for travel narratives that addressed the moral consciousness of America during the 1980s. Geared toward the intelligent reader more so than the academic, the article argues that Ford's fiction exposes a wide swath of middle-class American life in a post-Christian era.

Shelton, Frank. "Richard Ford." *Contemporary Fiction Writers of the South: A Bio-Bibliographical Sourcebook.* Ed. Joseph M. Flora and Robert Bain. Westport, Conn.: Greenwood, 1993. 147–55. Offers biographical and bibliographical information on Ford's life and works.

Smith, Joan. "Richard Ford: He Champions Ordinary Experiences." *San Francisco Examiner,* August 1, 1996. February 9, 1997 <nsers.ox.ac.uk/~sjoh0521/richardford.html>. Ford discusses *Independence Day,* his fascination with the word "independence," and his habit of moving around.

Smith, Leonora. "Richard Ford: MSU's Pulitzer Prize Winning Writer." *Muses,* Michigan State University's Alumni Newsletter, 1995–1996. Profiles Ford in honor of his being awarded the Pulitzer Prize for *Independence Day* and upon his receipt of Michigan State University's Distinguished Alumni Award, recounting Ford's experiences at Michigan State as well as his ideas about writing.

Trussler, Michael. " 'Famous Times': Historicity in the Short Fiction of Richard Ford and Raymond Carver." *Wascana Review of Contemporary Poetry and Short Fiction* 28, no. 2 (Fall 1994): 35–53. Discusses the "neorealistic" work of Ford and Carver, finding there an investigation of the tension between history and its re-creation in short fiction. Analyzes how these writers manipulate time in their fiction: in Ford's case, the "then and now" story and the ways that events extend in influence long past their momentary occurrences. Finds that characters limit their lives by explicating what has happened to them yet face possible meaninglessness in the face of their temporality.

Yardley, Jim. "The Eternal Optimist." *Y'all.* January 14, 1998. <www.access atlanta.com/global/local/yall/culture/quill/ford.html>. Summarizes a conversation with Richard Ford upon Ford's winning of the Pulitzer Prize for *Independence Day,* including Ford's political leanings, his itinerancy, his relationship with wife Kristina, and his reputation as an opinionated man.

Index

Agrarians, 49
Anderson, Sherwood, 1
Araby. See Joyce, James

Bonetti, Kay: "An Interview with Richard Ford," 9n. 14, 85, 94
Byrd, William. *See* southwest humor

Carver, Raymond, 18, 21, 101n. 3, 201
Cash, W. J., 64
Charon, 30
Coleridge, Samuel Taylor, 12

Davidson, Donald. *See* Agrarians
Democracy in America. See Tocqueville, Alexis de
Dickinson, Emily, 175
dirty realism, 21, 118, 178, 186, 201
Doctorow, E. L., 5
Dostoyevsky, Fyodor, 4, 22, 23
drowning, imagery of. *See* entrapment and suffocation, imagery of

Einstein, Albert, 48
Eliot, T. S., 64; "The Waste Land," 51n. 3
Emerson, Ralph Waldo, 12, 23, 98, 101n. 3, 132, 147, 149, 164, 165, 173, 203, 205; *Self-Reliance*, 147, 149
entrapment and suffocation, imagery of, 25, 32, 33, 35, 36–39, 40, 85, 204

"Fall of the House of Usher, The." *See* gothic, the; Poe, Edgar Allan
Faulkner, William, 1, 1n. 2, 6, 7, 8, 12, 14, 16, 18, 21, 25, 47, 49, 50, 64, 100, 101, 131, 201, 202, 203, 205; *Absalom, Absalom!*, 205. *See also* Faulknerian; neo-Faulknerian
Faulknerian, 62, 201
Fitzgerald, F. Scott, 8
Flaubert, Gustave, 22
Ford, Edna Akin (mother), 2, 3, 4, 5, 8 (*see also* Ford, Richard)

Ford, Kristina Hensley (wife), 4, 5, 7, 15, 18, 204
Ford, Parker Carrol (father), 2, 3 (*see also* Ford, Richard)
Ford, Richard: childhood of, 3; on deciding to become a writer, 5, 206–7; disavowal of "southern" tradition, 1, 2, 13, 14, 47, 65, 66, 163, 201–2, 207; education of, 4, 5; on Ralph Waldo Emerson, 98, 113–14, 132, 199; and father's death, 3, 102; first novel: critical reception and publication of, 5, 6, 7, 201 (*see also* Faulknerian; neo-Faulknerian); first story, 4; on home, 10–13, 165; on influence of other writers, 22; on "locatedness," 12, 163, 204–5; a "man's" writer, on being, 199, 206; marriage of, 5; on moving, 12, 13, 18–19, 204; peripatetic nature of, 1, 2, 3, 4, 12, 164, 204; place, importance of, 1, 2, 4, 11, 12; on place, 7, 13, 62, 163, 164, 204–5; place in works of, 6, 7, 9, 10, 13, 17, 25 (*see also under individual titles*); on popular culture, 22–23; on "provisional" nature of language, 68, 69, 89, 98, 133, 199, 202, 206–7; and search for career, 4, 5; on the "southern" tradition, 7, 9, 14, 22, 65, 101, 207; as sportswriter, 5, 7, 8; teaching experience of, 7, 18

COLLECTIONS
Rock Springs (short fiction), 3, 11, 15–16, 21, 100, 118–32, 177, 178, 186, 203, 204
Women with Men (long stories), 3, 11, 19, 21, 177–200, 203, 204, 205

ESSAYS
"Accommodations," 10n. 17, 11, 17, 165, 204

ESSAYS (*continued*)
"The Boss Observed," 22
"Country Matters," 12n. 19, 13, 17, 164
"First Things First: One More Writer's Beginnings," 5
"Heartbreak Motels," 17, 204
"In the Face: A Metaphysics of Fisticuffs," 55n. 5
"My Car Story," 204n. 1
"My Mother, In Memory," 2, 2n. 4, 3, 8, 102
"Place Qua Place," 204
"S. O. P.," 204
"The Three Kings: Hemingway, Faulkner, and Fitzgerald," 8n. 12, 206
"An Urge for Going: Why I Don't Live Where I Used to Live," 12n. 18, 62, 204, 205
"Walker Percy: Not Just Whistling Dixie," 8n. 11

NOVELS
Independence Day, 8, 16, 17, 22, 47, 68, 70, 133–76, 177, 198, 199, 202, 204, 205
Piece of My Heart, A, 1, 5, 6, 7, 21, 25–46, 47, 201, 204
Sportswriter, The, 8, 14–15, 17, 22–23, 47, 63–99, 118, 127, 131, 134, 135, 140, 151, 153, 164, 177, 198, 201, 202, 204, 205
Ultimate Good Luck, The, 7, 10, 47–62, 67, 201, 204, 205
Wildlife, 3, 11, 15–16, 100–117, 118, 119, 124, 178, 186, 203

STORIES
"Children," 102, 119–22, 124, 129
"Communist," 102, 122–23, 124
"Empire," 128–29
"Fireworks," 129, 130–31
"Going to the Dogs," 129, 130
"Great Falls," 15, 16, 100–117, 118, 119, 124
"Jealous," 3, 19, 20, 102, 177, 178, 185–92, 205

"Occidentals," 19, 20–21, 177, 178, 192–98
"Optimists," 102, 123–24
"Rock Springs," 125–27
"Sweethearts," 118, 127–28
"Winterkill," 129–30
"The Womanizer," 19–20, 177, 178, 179–85, 195

Freud, Sigmund, 48

"glistening one moment," 9, 10, 131, 134, 205 (*see also The Sportswriter*)
gothic, the, 25, 28–31, 50, 201

Hall, Oakley, 5
Hardy, Thomas, 22
Harrison, Jim, 201
Heidegger, Martin, 101n. 3, 106, 116
Heller, Joseph, 9, 202
Hemingway, Ernest, 6, 7, 8, 21, 47, 48, 51, 101n. 3, 201; Jake Barnes, 47, 48, 49, 55, 56; *The Sun Also Rises,* 48. *See also The Ultimate Good Luck;* modernism
Hobson, Fred, 9, 13–14, 64, 65, 101, 201
Holman, C. Hugh, 1n. 1, 201
Howells, William Dean. *See* realism

I'll Take My Stand. See Agrarians
Independence Day, 8, 16, 17, 22, 47, 68, 70, 133–76, 177, 198, 199, 202, 204, 205

Joyce, James, 74, 98, 100

Keats, John, 167, 203
Kierkegaard, Søren, 78, 101n. 3, 116, 202

language, 63, 64, 65, 67, 69, 73, 76, 83, 89, 92, 95, 99, 114–16, 128, 178, 180, 188, 192, 199, 201, 203, 206–7; and dirty talk, 34; failure, frailty, imprecision, instability and limitations of, 42, 48, 68, 74, 95, 100,

104–7, 108, 109, 111–13, 192, 202; figurative, 77; and Frank Bascombe, narrative style of, 70–73; and interpretation, 40, 194, 196, 197, 198; and misunderstanding, 19–20, 194, 198; and narrative reliability, 63, 66–67, 89, 202; nonverbal, 55; paradoxical nature of, 206; and plain talk, 191; and story as cure, 113–14, 117; and subject and object, gap between, 63n. 1; and "talk was risky," 55–56; and translation, 1, 192, 193, 196, 197, 198, 200; unspoken, 87, 181; and word play, 17–18. *See also Independence Day*

Lee, Don: "About Richard Ford," 4n. 5, 5, 7, 15, 16

local color, 25, 40–44, 201

"locatedness," 10, 12, 24, 59–62, 163, 204, 205 (*see also Independence Day; The Ultimate Good Luck*)

Lyons, Bonnie: "Richard Ford" (interview), 207n. 3, 207

Lytle, Andrew. *See* Agrarians

Marx, Karl, 48

Mason, Bobbie Ann, 22

McGuane, Tom, 201

"Meditations of an Old Woman." *See* Roethke, Theodore

Mencken, H. L., 49

Mind of the South, The. See Cash, W. J.

minimalism, 21–22, 203

modernism, 10, 47–49, 203 (*see also The Ultimate Good Luck*)

modern predicament. *See* modernism; *The Ultimate Good Luck*

neo-Faulknerian, 6, 25

O'Connor, Flannery, 6

Peirce, Charles, 107, 202

Percy, Walker, 8, 9, 64, 101, 101n. 3, 107, 201, 202

Piece of My Heart, A, 1, 5, 6, 7, 21, 25–46, 47, 201, 204

Poe, Edgar Allan, 30

Pound, Ezra, 48, 116 (*see also* modernism)

Prospero, 30

Ransom, John Crowe. *See* Agrarians

realism, 21–22, 43, 131–32, 186, 203

Roethke, Theodore, 94

Rubin, Louis D., Jr., 1n. 1, 201

Sartre, Jean-Paul, 100, 101, 101n. 3, 105, 108, 114–17, 203; *Being and Nothingness,* 111, 114; *Nausea,* 101, 114

Shakespeare, William, 64

Shelley, Ben (maternal stepgrandfather), 2, 11 (*see also* Ford, Richard)

Simpson, Lewis P., 1n. 1, 201

southern literature, tradition of, 1, 9, 12–14, 21, 24, 25, 47, 49–50, 51, 64–68, 201–2

Southern Renascence, 49–50

Southern Writer in the Postmodern World, The. See Hobson, Fred

southwest humor, 25, 40–44, 201

Sportswriter, The, 8, 14–15, 17, 22–23, 47, 63–99, 118, 127, 131, 134, 135, 140, 151, 153, 164, 177, 198, 201, 202, 204, 205

Springsteen, Bruce, 22, 133, 203

Stevens, Wallace, 18, 48, 53, 63n. 1, 68, 101n. 3, 116, 157, 174, 203; "The Emperor of Ice Cream," 174; *Harmonium,* 53; "A High-Toned Old Christian Woman," 18; "The Snow Man," 53; "Thirteen Ways of Looking at a Blackbird," 18, 63n. 1, 68. *See also* modernism

Styron, William, 64

Tate, Allen. *See* Agrarians

Taylor, Peter, 64

Tell About the South: The Southern Rage to Explain. See Hobson, Fred

Thoreau, Henry David, 12, 163

Tocqueville, Alexis de, 150

Tolstoy, Leo, 22

Ultimate Good Luck, The, 7, 10, 47–62, 67, 201, 204, 205

Updike, John, 9, 64, 101n. 3

Walden. See Thoreau, Henry David

Walker, Elinor Ann: "An Interview with Richard Ford," 7n. 10, 9, 12, 14, 15, 22, 23, 68, 69, 98, 101, 113–14, 117, 132, 133, 134, 163, 174, 205

Warren, Robert Penn, 64, 101, 202 (*see also* Agrarians)

Welty, Eudora, 1, 18

Wildlife, 3, 11, 15–16, 100–117, 118, 119, 124, 178, 186, 203

Williams, William Carlos, 48 (*see also* modernism)

Wolfe, Thomas, 49, 101, 202

Woodward, C. Vann, 1

Wordsworth, William, 12, 98

The Author

Elinor Ann Walker received her Ph.D. from the University of North Carolina–Chapel Hill. She has published numerous essays on southern literature and contemporary culture in books and journals. An independent scholar, she writes from her home in Florence, Alabama.

The Editor

Frank Day is a professor of English and head of the English Department at Clemson University. He is the author of *Sir William Empson: An Annotated Bibliography* (1984) and *Arthur Koestler: A Guide to Research* (1985). He was a Fulbright lecturer in American literature in Romania (1980–1981) and in Bangladesh (1986–1987).